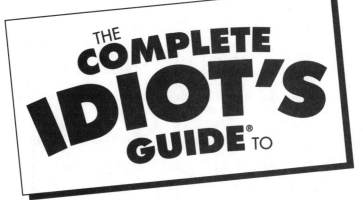

THE COMPLETE IDIOT'S GUIDE® TO

Getting Published

Third Edition

by Sheree Bykofsky and Jennifer Basye Sander

ALPHA

A member of Penguin Group (USA) Inc.

Publisher: *Marie Butler-Knight*
Product Manager: *Phil Kitchel*
Senior Managing Editor: *Jennifer Chisholm*
Senior Acquisitions Editor: *Renee Wilmeth*
Senior Production Editor: *Christy Wagner*
Copy Editor: *Drew Patty*
Illustrator: *Chris Eliopoulos*
Cover/Book Designer: *Trina Wurst*
Indexer: *Tonya Heard*
Layout/Proofreading: *Mary Hunt, Ayanna Lacey*

Contents at a Glance

Appendixes

Contents

Foreword

All your life you've had a dream. Perhaps you've told no one. Perhaps you've told *everyone*. Regardless, you know that someday you will do it.

You want to be a writer! You imagine walking into a bookstore and seeing *your* book with *your* name on the cover.

Every day we hear from dozens of people who have this same dream. Their reasons vary. Some hate their jobs. Some want to get rich. Most simply have something to say and want the world to hear it. Yet they don't have a clue where to begin. They don't know a SASE from a slush pile or a query from a cover letter. This makes us smile, because we remember when *we* were just like them!

We now have more than 50 years of publishing experience between us. We both cut our teeth on magazine articles and went on to write books. (Ann writes true crime while Leslie, Ann's daughter, writes true ghost stories.) Although we publish regularly, we will never forget the sting of the rejection slips that once filled our mailboxes.

And we'll never forget the messy job of changing the ribbons on our typewriters. When we began writing, computers were *not* household items! E-mail was unheard of, fax machines seemed like something out of a science-fiction novel, and only our most sophisticated friends owned answering machines. But if we could have reached into the future and chosen just one tool to help us with our writing, it wouldn't have been one of the previously mentioned gadgets. It would be the very book you're holding in your hands!

The Complete Idiot's Guide to Getting Published, now in its third edition, is the most valuable tool an aspiring author can own. You'll find, beneath its shiny orange and white cover, answers to questions you haven't even thought of.

Ann: I can't count the number of times would-be writers have confided to me that they plan to write a book someday "when the time is right." They need a cabin in the woods, they insist, with no distractions. Although I nod sympathetically, I hide a smile, for I suspect that the time will never be right. If *I* had waited for the perfect setting, I wouldn't have published a single word!

When I began writing, I had a house full of pets and four children under 10—the youngest in diapers. I plunked myself down in a corner of the basement rec room and pecked away on the typewriter as the children fought and the TV blared.

For five long years I sent off manuscripts and received only printed rejection slips in return. Finally, I sold my first article to a local newspaper for $35! It took another five years before I could support my family with my writing.

I don't know a single author who hasn't struggled with rejection and frustration and who hasn't asked the questions that any new writer asks. Most of us learned by making our own mistakes in the school of hard knocks. In the beginning, I checked out some library books that purported to have all the answers, but the most important thing I learned was how to format a manuscript so that it looked more professional, as if had been written by a "real" writer.

Yes, that was helpful, but there were no books like *this* one that answers scores of practical questions. I often think I could have made my first sale so much earlier if Sheree Bykofsky and Jennifer Basye Sander had only written this book 25 years sooner!

The road to publishing was a long and discouraging one for me, but it doesn't have to be that way for you! You might never have a cabin in the woods where you can do all your writing, but you do have a resource for which I would have traded my typewriter: *The Complete Idiot's Guide to Getting Published* by Sheree Bykofsky and Jennifer Basye Sander.

What are you waiting for?

Leslie: When I first attempted to get published more than two decades ago, the process seemed as mysterious as the ghost books I publish today! The fact that I was the daughter of an author did not give me an automatic "in." I bumbled along like all new writers. I misspelled editors' names, neglected to include self-addressed stamped envelopes, and wrote weak query letters. These were just a few of the faux pas that resulted in a pitiful pile of rejection letters! But the most important lesson I learned from my mother was that rejection was inevitable, and I accepted mine stoically, crying only in private.

By the time I met Sheree Bykofsky at a writers' conference, I had been publishing regularly for more than a decade. I was not exactly a novice, but when Sheree handed me a copy of *The Complete Idiot's Guide to Getting Published*, one glance told me it was a treasure! My favorite chapter is the one that addresses sample book proposals. I followed the guidelines to the letter and wrote the proposal for *Coast to Coast Ghosts: True Stories of Hauntings Across America* (Andrews McMeel, 2001). Sheree became my new agent, and within weeks of submitting the proposal for *Ghosts*, we had two offers!

Do you want to be a published author? You need just four things:

- The desire to write

- An ounce of creativity

- The ability to write coherent sentences

- *The Complete Idiot's Guide to Getting Published*

Sheree Bykofsky's and Jennifer Basye Sander's brilliantly written book will show you how to be a pro from the get-go! *The Complete Idiot's Guide to Getting Published,* now in its third edition, is *the* definitive tool for aspiring writers and published writers alike.

Ann Rule has published 21 books, 20 of them New York Times *best-sellers. She has more than 20 million books in print in 8 languages. Four of her books have been adapted for television miniseries, and she has sold more than 1,000 articles. Her latest books are* Every Breath You Take, Last Dance, Last Chance, *and* A Heart Full of Lies.

Leslie Rule's books include suspense novel Whispers from the Grave *and* Coast to Coast Ghosts: True Stories of Hauntings Across America.

Introduction

Books, wonderful books. It seems like such a dream that you might someday see your very own name on the cover of a book that's sitting proudly on a bookstore shelf. Well, dream no longer. It's high time you turned that dream into reality—*your* reality!

Together, we've been in the book business for 40 years, and we've seen it all (or nearly all). We've been interns, editors, authors, agents, and packagers, and we've learned what works and what doesn't.

As interns, well … we won't tell you what we did as interns, but as editors, we've evaluated thousands of projects. As authors, we've struggled to come up with ideas for books that would catch an editor's eye. As agents, we've sorted through thousands of query letters in search of potential authors, and as packagers, we've tried to craft marketable books. Now we'd like to share all our hard-won knowledge with you. We will explain the whole book publishing process and guide you through it as smoothly as possible. You'll find yourself going from first-time writer straight through to publishing know-it-all in the time it takes to read this book.

Every writer has a reason for wanting to be published. Some of us want a forum for our ideas; some want fame, and some just flat-out want fortune. No matter what your reason, to get published you'll need to convince many other folks along the way to believe in you and your writing. There's an art to doing that, and we'll explain it to you step by step.

The book publishing business can be tough, and it can be crazy at times, but it's an exciting industry that's pretty darn fun just to be around. Although you may well experience some frustration and a disappointment or two on your way to becoming a published author, you can look forward to the satisfaction you'll feel: the pure pleasure of knowing that your ideas and your vision are being shared with the world.

How to Use This Book

The book publishing process is really a rather easy one to understand when you break it down into its five major steps:

Part 1, "Great Expectations: In Which You Begin to Write," explores the many reasons that writers write (what's yours?) and helps you determine what the market is like for the book you want to write. What are the hot and not-so-hot topics and genres today, and how you can stay in the know?

Part 2, "Gone with the Wind: Submitting to Publishers," is where you find the different, sometimes bewildering methods of submitting your proposal. Here you find everything from how to avoid looking like an amateur on the page to the reasons why so many manuscripts are rejected.

Part 3, "Romancing the Stone: How to Get a Book Contract," tackles the age-old problem that all prospective authors face: Just how do you get an editor and a publisher to fall in love with your proposal and offer you a contract? Do you need an agent, and if so, how do you get a good one? How do you find editors and win them over all by yourself, if that's the route you want to take? Here's where you find out what you need to know about how publishers decide to publish. Here's also where you find out what to ask for—and what to avoid like the plague—in book contracts.

Part 4, "War and Peace: Working with a Publisher," walks you through the actual process of being published. Now that you have a book publishing contract, a deadline, and an editor to work with, what's gonna happen? Here's where you'll see the entire production process.

Part 5, "My Brilliant Career: Continuing Your Career as an Author," helps you develop a life that extends beyond just one book. From building yourself a career as a speaker or consultant, to learning how to supercharge the number of book projects you create, this is where you'll find out about the many ways to make money from your writing skills.

And to make sure you don't get lost in publishing lingo, there's a glossary that contains all the words and terms you'll need to hold your own in conversations with agents, editors, publicists, and other book people. Want to see what a sample book contract looks like? Say no more! You'll find one near the back of the book, along with a sample author-agent agreement, a proposal for a best-selling book, a press release, and a collaboration agreement.

Extras

Look for the little asides and comments sprinkled throughout the chapters, extra bits of inside dope that we just can't resist whispering into your ear as you read:

 Hot Off the Press _____
We've got many tales to tell about the publishing world. Some will make you wiser, and some are just for chuckles.

 **Experts Say** _____
Here's where our friends and colleagues share their expertise, too. This is real advice from those involved in the book world.

Bookmarks

Publishing terms are clearly defined here. Never again will you feel out to sea when the book talk turns technical.

Slush Pile

These are dire warnings, things to be avoided at all costs. They're the worst mistakes, the biggest pitfalls, and the most dangerous missteps to which writers can fall prey.

Acknowledgments

Jennifer would like to thank the person from whom she has learned the most about the book business: Ben Dominitz, who founded Prima Publishing in 1984 and sold it to Random House almost 20 years later. He was always willing to take a chance on my ideas. And how can I write a book without thanking my family? My husband, Peter, and my sons, Julian and Jonathan, were all amazingly cheerful about the amount of time I was unavailable; thanks, guys. And to the fabulous Paula Munier—without her assistance, the chapters on fiction would be blank.

Sheree thanks the people who have been so very helpful with her agency: Janet Rosen and Megan Buckley. Thanks to all the authors whom I represent—you are the reason I love my work. I'm grateful to all my agent and editor friends and colleagues for all their guidance, support, knowledge, and all the laughs.

We'd both like to thank all the knowledgeable publishing folks who took our repeated phone calls and shared their expertise as we researched and wrote this book—and, indeed, throughout our careers. We'd also like to thank the folks at Shaw Guides for sharing their list of writers' conferences with us. Thanks also to senior production editor Christy Wagner for superhuman production editing. Finally, thanks to Renee Wilmeth and her colleagues at Alpha Books for giving us this opportunity to share our knowledge with you.

Trademarks

Part 1

Great Expectations: In Which You Begin to Write

You think you'd like to write—actually, you know you want to write. So just how do you get started? In this part of the book, we'll take a look at the major reasons why people write. The more you know about why you want to write, the greater your chances for doing it successfully.

We'll also give you an inside look at how book professionals come up with ideas for books that sell and sell. When you've mastered this end of the business, you'll get a close-up look at the markets for different types of books. From fiction to how-to, from health to travel, you'll learn what's hot and what's not.

Chapter 1

So Why Write?

In This Chapter

- The best reasons to write
- The future of books
- The big business of book business
- Getting published can be like getting on a game show
- 100,000 chances to win

Congratulations, you've taken a big, big step. You've gone out and bought yourself a book on getting published. And that is exactly what you will learn in the following pages: how to get published.

Just imagine the glory and hosannas that await you as a published author: fat royalty checks, impressive literary awards, newspaper articles, speaking engagements, applause, and public recognition. Ah, life will be grand!

Well, life might be grand—or there's a very good chance that getting published won't change your life at all. In many ways this book hopes to serve as both a cheerleader (you *can* do it!) and a reality check (that's *reality*, not *royalty* check). Take it from a couple women who know: Writing is very hard work. Getting published is very hard work. Selling books is very hard work.

But before we usher you onto the path toward a career as an author, let's step back to ask a critical question: Just why do *you* want to write a book? Writing an entire book is a whole lot of work and effort. What's in it for you?

What's Your Reason?

There are as many reasons to write as there are books on a library shelf. Is yours on the list?

- ◆ I'm compelled to write.
- ◆ I want the personal satisfaction of being published.
- ◆ I hope to advance my cause.
- ◆ I want to share my knowledge.
- ◆ I'd like to advance my career.
- ◆ I'd like to achieve fame.
- ◆ I'd like to earn a fortune.
- ◆ All of the above.

> **Bookmarks**
>
> An **author** is one who writes a book or books. The word usually implies a published writer. The **royalty** is the percentage of book sales that the publisher pays the author for each copy of a book sold.

I'm Compelled to Write

Some folks sit down and write because they are consumed with an inner need to write. These people must write—they can't not write. They wake up in the middle of the night with the urge to jot down a few lines or even write entire pages. For these folks, writing comes naturally; it just feels right.

Have you ever heard a novelist say that "the characters are writing the book, and I'm just holding the pen"? Or "I've got to get these ideas on paper!" If either sounds like you, then you're someone who's *compelled* to write. Getting published may very well be your primary goal; making money would be nice, but it could be of secondary importance.

I Want the Personal Satisfaction of Being Published

Putting pen to paper (or fingers to keyboard) can be very fulfilling. And once your writing project is finished, you will have accomplished something very real. Instead of talking endlessly about how you plan to write a book someday, you will have done it!

Not only is the process of writing satisfying, but there are also psychological rewards to be gained from being published. The pride and satisfaction that can come from writing a book are unsurpassed. Imagine the day when you can stand in a bookstore aisle and see your name on a book. Or better yet, imagine the first time someone asks for your autograph!

I'd Like to Advance My Cause

Have you got a message you want to share with the world (or at least with anyone smart enough to buy your book)? You want to share your beliefs—political, philosophical, religious, or whatever—to advance a cause. A great example of this is John Robbins, who turned his back on his family's ice cream fortune (you've heard of Baskin-Robbins, haven't you?) in order to write and lecture about the dangers of the typical American diet. His book, *The New American Diet* is now a classic, and was his way of advancing his cause.

I Want to Share My Knowledge

You might know how to build a better mousetrap, and you think the world needs to know, too. This is not quite the same thing as writing to advance a cause, but it's a mission to help people do something—or do something better. Perhaps you've spent 20 years lying underneath cars and believe you can tell car owners a better way to care for and maintain their automobiles.

The market for how-to information seems endless, and writers with useful knowledge to share can sometimes hit the big time. "Find a need and fill it" is an old business axiom that still holds true in today's book market.

I Hope to Advance My Career

Publishing a book in your field can be a very powerful way to supercharge your career. Why languish in obscurity when you can gain recognition as an expert in your field? Who knows, you could build a second career as a consultant or a speaker.

David Bach was a stockbroker like thousands of others in the San Francisco Bay Area when he decided to write a book called *Smart Women Grow Rich*, inspired by his own grandmother's investment savvy. His first book became a best-seller and spawned a series. He is now a well-paid New York–based writer and speaker, no longer an ordinary stockbroker.

There are almost as many marketing consultants in the nation as there are stockbrokers, but only one of those marketing consultants has written a book about marketing to the group with the biggest purchasing power—moms. Maria Bailey wrote the book *Marketing to Moms: Getting Your Share of the Trillion Dollar Market* and used it as a handy springboard to increase her professional reputation. Maria is now regularly quoted in the pages of *The New York Times* and *The Wall Street Journal* and is the acknowledged "go to" expert in this field.

Don't get the idea that only business people can advance their careers with a book. Doctors see a huge boost in patients when the medical books they've written become popular. It worked for Drs. Andrew Weil, Pamela Peeke, and Christiane Northrup. Almost any other type of career can be built up this way, including careers as motivational speakers, beauticians, massage therapists, and childcare providers. Could writing a book be your ticket to the top?

I'd Like to Achieve Fame

Similar to writers who hope to advance their careers, some writers hope that getting published will make them famous, if only in their own neighborhoods, towns, states, or among their colleagues. The world is a celebrity-conscious place, and who wouldn't want the things that come with fame: the best table in a restaurant, a complimentary bottle of wine, your picture in *People* magazine, admiring fans, and maybe a spot on the couch with Katie Couric on the *Today* show some morning.

> **Hot Off the Press** _____
>
> Perfectly ordinary folks with perfectly ordinary lives sometimes become famous authors. Danielle Steel was a high school teacher, John Grisham was a lawyer, Ernest Hemingway was a newspaper reporter, and Wallace Stevens sold insurance. Richard Paul Evans of *The Christmas Box* fame was in the advertising business until he hit it big with his self-published book. He later sold it to Simon & Schuster for $4.2 million. So why not you?

Do you long to be recognized as you walk down the street? A published book might get you that. Fame is not always linked directly to fortune, however. And getting your book published may make its title, but not your face (and sometimes not even your name) familiar to many. Quick, who wrote *Robert's Rules of Order?**

I'd Like to Earn a Fortune

It's by no means guaranteed, but writing a book (or writing several books) is a possible route to fortune. Just ask Mark Victor Hansen and Jack Canfield, the creators of

---

**Major Henry M. Robert compiled the Rules in 1876.*

the best-selling *Chicken Soup for the Soul* series. When giving inspirational talks to writers, these two authors delight in showing overhead slides of their seven-figure royalty checks. "And we get these a couple of times a year!" they chuckle.

Making big bucks by writing books is a big goal that, quite frankly, isn't achieved by many. But if this is what drives you, then give it all you've got. Begin by making sure that your book idea has mass appeal. The smaller and more specialized the potential audience for your book, the dimmer the chances that you will make lots of money from it.

Bookmarks

The term **best-seller** is used loosely in the publishing business. Strictly speaking, it refers to a book that has appeared on a best-seller list somewhere. In reality, publishers and their publicity staffs attach the word to almost any book that they haven't lost their shirts on!

Just as fame does not always follow fortune, fortune is not always linked to fame. You might have recognized Mark Hansen and Jack Canfield's names, but there are many authors whose names you'd never recognize who have nevertheless earned lots of money writing books. The unsung authors of popular textbooks and other homely books that sell year after year without ever showing up on *best-seller* lists might be unrecognized on the street, but they are very well known at the bank.

All of the Above

Few writers have one single reason for writing. Most of us combine an emotional need to write with a secret desire for fame and a not-so-secret desire for fortune.

Why should you stop to examine the reasons that you write? Because if you understand why you want to write, you can do a much better job of planning how to get published.

Is a need for inner satisfaction the only thing driving you? Then you might be happy seeing your work published in a small literary journal. Do you have grand plans to advance your career and raise your professional profile? That calls for a specific plan of attack. Is making a fortune your primary goal? Then you'd better skip ahead to Chapter 3. To avoid disappointment, make sure that your ultimate goal and your book's sales potential match.

Experts Say

According to a survey by the Jenkins Group, fully 81 percent of Americans "feel they have a book in them." Many of those same folks have acted on that feeling, as the Jenkins folks went on to estimate that six million Americans have written actual manuscripts.

Do People Still Buy Books?

"Writing a book will take me the next few years. By the time I finish all bookstores might have disappeared!" It seems like every newspaper and magazine has carried a story with dire predictions: Americans don't read anymore; the book publishing industry is dead; books as we know them will soon cease to exist. So why bother writing a book?

Our well-informed and professionally stated response to those naysayers: "Not!"

Mergers and Chains

Ever since Gutenberg invented his printing press, the publishing industry has been evolving. Many working in publishing today like to reminisce about the bygone days of yore in which literary editors and their beloved authors could while away the afternoon with a pitcher of martinis and a discussion of the finer points of writing. Large publishing companies are seldom run by men with martini pitchers in their offices these days but rather are headed by business folks with a strong sense of the bottom line. Even the number of large publishing houses is shrinking—these companies are being bought up and combined into "super houses" with 10 or 20 different imprints. One editor at a major New York house likes to joke that although she's had only two different jobs, as a result of mergers she's actually worked for seven different companies. But small and medium-size publishers all over the country are willing to take risks with topics and authors that other houses might avoid. They might also have the time to linger over a glass in the afternoon, too …

And while publishing companies are merging, more bookstores are opening across the country. The decision-making power has quickly become concentrated in the hands of two or three large retail chains, and this, too, has affected the publishing business—as has the rise in book sales in nontraditional nonbook outlets such as Target and Wal-Mart. The brunt of this change has been borne by locally owned bookstores; sadly, many small, *independent booksellers* are disappearing. But the good news for writers is, no matter where they buy, Americans are still buying books, and that is what keeps the industry going.

Hot Off the Press

Publishing businesses are still anachronistically known as "publishing houses" after the days when most companies operated out of brownstones or townhouses that were formerly single-family dwellings.

Online Book Sales

As further proof of the health and vibrancy of the ancient art of publishing, we need only point to the newest development of all: the Internet and the arrival of e-commerce. One of the most remarkable things about the last few years is that one of the most frequently purchased items online is also one of the most old-fashioned—books. Amazon.com continues to be far and above one of the highest-profile e-commerce companies. And beyond book sales, there is a continuing interest (at least on the part of the media) in electronic publishing, or as e-books. Despite the flurry of investment in this idea and the enormous publicity that Stephen King's foray into e-book publishing garnered, actual sales for e-books are estimated at just $\frac{1}{10}$ of 1 percent of the total book market, but right now let's just add it to the plus column for the future of books.

Bookmarks

An **independent book-seller** is a locally owned bookstore. Before the rise of national chains such as Borders and Barnes & Noble, most towns were served by independents. Sadly, many of these stores have been unable to compete and have closed their doors. Fans of independent booksellers believe the staffs there were more knowledgeable and better able to promote little-known and local authors.

Hot Off the Press

Unlike other retail businesses, books are 100 percent returnable in the bookselling business. If a dress shop has trouble selling a dress, it marks the price down until the dress gets bought. But if a bookseller can't sell a book, she puts it in a box and returns it to the publisher for full credit. According to industry figures from Open Book Publishing, the average bookstore sends back to the publisher 20 percent of its books. Publishers have tried unsuccessfully in the past to wean bookstores off the returnable model, with no success. (After all, they've got a good thing going; why change it?)

Leaner and Meaner

The days when publishing was a genteel pursuit for the wealthy are gone. The book business is catching up to the rest of the world and is streamlining its processes. After a few rocky years of high book returns, book publishing as an industry has emerged stronger and healthier, and is ready to compete in the fast-paced entertainment-driven world we now occupy. So should you put a part of your life on hold and devote yourself to writing that book you dream of? We say, "Go for it!"

Open for Business

Now that we have convinced you that the book business is a healthy one, here's your first insider's tip for success. If you learn only one thing from this book, let it be the following: *The book business is a business.* Seems simple, doesn't it? But so few authors who want to be published approach it as a business.

Product Is King

Let's forget about writing books for a moment and pretend that you have an idea for a coffee company that you've long dreamed of opening. What would your first step be? You'd plunge headfirst into learning everything you could about how the coffee world operates, wouldn't you? You'd spend hours sitting in Starbucks trying to figure out where their success comes from, sipping cup after cup in order to develop a better sense of what kind of roasted bean seems to be the most popular. You might even do a bit of travel and visit coffee plantations to see how the front part of the business operates. And when you've learned everything possible, then and only then you would start to draw up the plans for your own coffee company. Now, if you decide to write a book, do you take all those same steps to achieve success? Sadly, far too few authors do. But they should!

The book publishing industry is a business just like the coffee industry, the breakfast cereal business, or the auto industry. Product is king, and you need to learn how to approach the industry with your product. The more businesslike you are, the greater your chances for success.

Experts Say

"I stay in touch with the publishing world by reading *Publishers Weekly* (*PW*). At around $150 a year, it is expensive but worth every darn penny," says Lynne Rominger, a full-time teacher and part-time author. To subscribe to *PW*, call 1-800-278-2991. You might also find *PW* in your local public library or on the magazine rack at a big bookstore.

Research, Research, Research!

Start right now to learn everything you can about the book business. Become a permanent fixture in your local bookstore. Take the manager out to lunch and ask about the business. Read the trade magazine *Publishers Weekly*. Find out what the proper etiquette is when trying to get published. Learn the lingo. (Far from an admission of idiocy, buying this book was a master stroke of genius; you're on your way to learning the ropes!) Your goal is getting published, so be serious about it.

Once again the Internet can be a tremendous help here. Websites geared toward writers abound. One of the best is run by the *Writer's Digest* folks—check out www.writersdigest.com. To keep abreast of publishing news, take a look at www.thewritenews.com, or visit www.publishersmarketplace.com to read about what kinds of books are being sold and who is buying them.

But I Don't Live in New York!

Although it sometimes seems that way, not all writers live in New York City. One of the great things about becoming a writer is that you can live anywhere in the country—anywhere in the world, even—and still pursue a career writing books. As long as the UPS driver can find your house (or you've got a phone, fax, and modem), you can deal with agents, editors, and publishers.

Co-author Sheree does live in New York City and wouldn't dream of living anywhere else, but co-author Jennifer has managed to build a book publishing career without ever having moved away from her hometown of Sacramento, California—not exactly a well-known publishing metropolis. If you are determined and professional, and if you keep at it, you can get published no matter where you live.

Think of Yourself as a Contestant

Sheree likes to encourage unpublished writers by telling them the story of how she got on the television game show *Wheel of Fortune*. She believes that for many types of books, both publishing and game shows require similar paths to success.

"I decided that I wanted to be on *Wheel of Fortune*, and so I studied everything about the show," explains Sheree. "I learned how to dress like the contestants I'd seen every night on the show, how to talk the way the contestants talked ('Hi, my name is Sheree and I'm a literary agent'), and in general, how to act like a contestant. So when I walked into the room filled with hundreds of other folks who wanted to be on the show, I stood out as someone who looked, sounded, and acted like a contestant. And it worked! The producers chose me." And as Jennifer was recently a successful contestant on *The Weakest Link*, there might be something to this theory!

Literary agents, publishers, and editors (especially those involved in popular trade books) are like the producers of a game show. They know just what they are looking for to suit their needs. And it's up to you to show them that you are a contestant.

So you want to be a published author? Then learn how to walk, talk, and think like a published author. Go out of your way to meet other writers and learn what you can from them. Join writer's groups, go on writer's retreats, and buy books on writing and writers. Keep track of what authors are coming to your town to give bookstore talks and sit front and center in the audience, soaking up what they have to say. Seek out other writers online. Ask published writers to tell you how they made it. And don't be surprised when they tell you! Everyone likes to talk about his or her own success (and maybe even about some of the disappointments). You just have to ask.

100,000 Chances to Win!

When newspapers and magazines aren't trumpeting the approaching downfall of the book publishing industry, they are warning readers against the avalanche of the 100,000 or so books published each year. As writers, it is all too easy to look at that figure and be discouraged. But we say, what a great business this is! With 100,000 books published every year, that's 100,000 chances to win! Why shouldn't yours be among the chosen? Although many (if not most) manuscripts meet with rejection, the odds that one of those books will be yours are much better than the likelihood of Ed McMahon and the Publishers Clearing House team showing up on your doorstep.

Writers Wanted!

Don't ever lose sight of the fact that the book business needs writers so that it can keep publishing books. Agents need authors, publishers need authors, and editors need authors—no matter what they tell you. Don't be intimidated or discouraged by your encounters with these folks because they need you to stay in business. As best-selling author Robert G. Allen of *The One Minute Millionaire* likes to say, "It's a tough business if you don't know what you're doing. But it can be extremely lucrative and very rewarding when you learn the ropes."

If your first efforts meet with rejection, use that as an opportunity to rework and refine your ideas. Perhaps a different approach might work. In our next few chapters, you'll learn more about how to successfully develop an idea for a book and put together a proposal that will help catch an agent (or editor's) eye.

So *why* write? Because you could get published!

The Least You Need to Know

- Writing can be a very rewarding experience emotionally or financially—or both!
- Perfectly ordinary folks have become published writers; there's no reason to be intimidated by the idea.
- Book publishing is a business, and you need to approach it in a businesslike manner.
- Americans are reading more and buying more books, and the market for books is strong and healthy.

Chapter 2

Write What?

In This Chapter

- ◆ The importance of identifying your category
- ◆ Books the world doesn't need
- ◆ Major book categories defined
- ◆ Good-selling categories identified

So there you are at your big family Thanksgiving dinner, seated next to your brother-in-law. "What's new with you," he asks. "I'm writing a book," you answer proudly, anxious to trump the announcement he just made about his big promotion. "Oh yeah, what kind of book are you writing?" Silence descends as you search for a way to describe your book. All eyes turn toward you as you sit there at the festive holiday table, dumbstruck by such a basic question.

What kind of a book are you writing? It is a simple question but one that too few first-time authors can answer with ease. What is your book about? If you can't clearly define it, you're headed for trouble every step of the way.

Start at the beginning. What book category does it fall into? Envision yourself for a moment in your local bookstore. Notice how carefully the categories are divided. There are shelves dedicated to cookbooks, health books, Westerns, new fiction, romance, and inspiration—there's row after row of books on all different topics. Where do you picture your book?

"What kind of a book am I writing?" you answer. "Well, it's kind of difficult to say, sort of a cross between a health book and an inspirational book, with a tiny bit of romance thrown in."

Sorry, but that won't cut it. If you can't clearly define your book, neither can an agent or a publisher—or, worse yet, a bookseller. So pick a category, the closest category that fits your book. Then stick with it.

What the World Doesn't Need

Books of all kinds exist, but some topics are overpublished, and some categories have too many books in them. We checked with booksellers to find out what topics they felt are currently overpublished. Here are their top picks:

- ◆ Surviving terrorism
- ◆ Sweet story collections
- ◆ Retire rich
- ◆ Low-carb diet books

Experts Say

A grim statistic in a recent *Times* of London article states that a million copies of books are destroyed each week in the United States because they don't sell. The more you research your category and make sure your book is needed, the less likely your work will end up in the shredder.

So are these the areas that we think you should steer clear of? Not necessarily. Stay clear of most of these topics unless you have some really new way of looking at them. But there just might be another collection of sweet stories that could hit it big like the *Chicken Soup* books did. Co-author Jennifer's long-time publishing mentor, Ben Dominitz, believes there are two good reasons to publish a book: "One, because no one has published a book on that topic, and two, because everyone has published a book on that topic."

But Enough About You

What the world hardly ever needs, however, is a book about your life story. This is harsh news to deliver so early in a book on getting published, but we want you to have an honest idea of how personal *memoirs* are viewed in the world of book publishing. Somebody's got to tell you, and it might as well be us.

Personal memoirs are a tough sell. If the story of your life is rejected, don't take it personally. This is hardly a sign that your life's worthless. It only means that there aren't 10,000 or more people interested in buying a book about it! From a strict business standpoint, there is no market for the story. Remember your first big lesson in Chapter 1—the book business is a business.

When is there a market for your life story or personal memoir? When it is compelling and well written. When there is a core message or theme that will appeal to large numbers of people. Frank McCourt won the Pulitzer Prize for his book *Angela's Ashes*, the gritty story of his youth in Ireland. Are large numbers of readers interested in McCourt's childhood? With hardcover book sales of more than a million copies and the release of the movie, it sure looks like it.

Bookmarks

A **memoir** is an account of the events in one's own life.

Hot Off the Press

Playwright Mark Dunn shopped his novel *Ella Minnow Pea* everywhere, finally landing a contract. The hardcover edition became a cult hit, and the auction for the paperback rights became frenzied. To his amusement, many of the same publishers waving checks for the paperback rights were the very same folks who'd passed on it the first time. What happened? The theme of Dunn's book—a fictional island which bans the use of certain letters—suddenly seemed timely when the Bush administration started to discuss restrictions due to "homeland security."

And the Categories Are ...

Before we tell you which are the biggies, we've got to ask you one question: Are you writing *fiction* or *nonfiction?*

Fiction

Long works of fiction are called novels. Short stories are just that—shorter pieces of fiction. If your writing is fiction, you're creating your own situations and characters. Or you're taking real people, places, and/or events and weaving them into your own story—or substantially embellishing them with your own creations.

Bookmarks

Works of **fiction** are the products of imagination, creativity, and invention. Fiction does not claim to be true. A **nonfiction** work is one that relates actual events, facts, and information. It includes books of all types other than fiction.

There are two major fiction classifications: literary fiction and commercial fiction. Literary fiction has a smaller, more intellectually inclined audience. This is the kind of book you had to read in English class—Virginia Woolf, William Faulkner—you know the type. Commercial fiction can be broken down into more classifications, such as hardcover mainstream, and then many subcategories, or genres. These include mystery, romance, science fiction, Western, and fantasy.

Nonfiction

Nonfiction is a very broad category that runs the gamut from personal finance to travel books to car manuals and everything in between.

Fiction Categories

Let's take a stroll through an imaginary bookstore and see what's on the shelf. First we'll take a look at the major categories, or *genres*, of fiction:

◆ Mainstream fiction

◆ Westerns

◆ Romances

◆ Mysteries

◆ Science fiction

◆ Fantasies

◆ Thrillers

◆ Religious fiction

◆ Horror books

◆ Erotica/adult books

◆ Young adult books

◆ Children's

Bookmarks

Genre fiction, usually published in paperback, refers to a particular type of fiction. This could be a Western, a romance, a sci-fi book, a horror book, a fantasy, or the like.

Mainstream Fiction

Mainstream fiction is pretty much everything that isn't defined in another category! Usually published first in hardcover, mainstream fiction is suited for a large, general audience. John Updike, Michael Chabon, Toni Morrison, and Philip Roth all write in this category.

Westerns

Usually published in paperback, Westerns range from classics like Zane Grey's novels to the works of Larry McMurty or Pete Dexter's witty book *Deadwood*. Westerns are set in the old West and are filled with tough guys on horses, bumbling sheriffs, and saloon girls with hearts of gold.

Romances

Girl meets guy, girl hates guy, guy slowly wins girl over. The romance category is a large one, ranging from historical romances to very contemporary stories that deal with modern themes. Fully 55.9 percent of all popular paperback fiction sales are due to this evergreen category.

Mysteries

Who dunnit, and how? Mystery novels center around a murder (or murders) and sift slowly through all the possible suspects and motives. The kings include Elmore Leonard and Tony Hillerman, and among the queens you'll find Sue Grafton. Mysteries can be published in either hardcover or paperback. Paperback mysteries are often published as a series, with at least one recurring character with unusual sleuthing ability.

Science Fiction

Sci-fi novels take place far in the future, in imaginary worlds and on imaginary planets. Alan Dean Foster's *Commonwealth* and the *Star Trek* and *Star Wars* series dominate the best-seller lists here, but many obscure sci-fi authors have devoted fans. Once again, this is primarily a paperback category.

Fantasies

Also set in imaginary realms, fantasy novels are populated with elves, maidens, and animals that talk. The original fantasy novel was J.R.R. Tolkien's *The Hobbit*. It's usually published in paperback (unless it's a gift edition of *The Hobbit*). The success of the movies based on this series has given rise to a new generation of fantasy fans. Many of the young readers now devouring the *Harry Potter* books will migrate to this category when they mature.

Thrillers

Thrillers are several steps above mystery novels in terms of gore and violence. There might be serial killers with twisted motives and determined FBI specialists on their tail. James Patterson has built a franchise around his Alex Cross character. The first printing of *Four Blind Mice* had a whopping 1.5 million books. Many thriller writers publish first in hardcover.

Religious Fiction

Although there have long been novels written and published to appeal to a Christian audience, this category has exploded into the mainstream in the last few years due to the *Left Behind* series of books by LeHaye and Jenkins. Co-author Jerry Jenkins has gone out on his own, striking a reported $45 million deal with Bantam.

Horror Books

Stephen King. Dean Koontz. Anne Rice. Any more questions? Horror books are an extremely popular genre. The pages drip with blood, ghouls, vampires, and other unworldly creatures that will keep you lying awake at night.

Young Adult Books

Novels that are written for young teens are called young adult novels, or YA, for short. For those of you dreaming of emulating J. K. Rowling's success, this is what you want to write. YA novels can fit into almost every category, including horror, romance, mystery, and others.

Erotica/Adult Books

Yes, someone has to write those books, and we'll bet you even know where this part of the bookstore is, don't you? Off in a hidden, yet well-visited corner. There is a definite formula to this kind of writing, and our shyness prevents us from describing it to you here. Suffice it to say that these paperback books are, uh, action-oriented.

Children's Fiction

Much of what we think of as children's books is fiction, although that seems like such an adult word to use. Winnie the Pooh wasn't real now, was he? Although we will touch on the topic of children's books throughout the book, we do recommend reading our sister book, *The Complete Idiot's Guide to Publishing Children's Books.*

Nonfiction Categories

That's it in a nutshell for fiction. Just about everything else in the bookstore is a further breakdown of the huge nonfiction category. Now, nonfiction means you didn't make it up, so don't. There have been a few famous examples of best-seller sold as nonfiction that later have to be reshelved. *The Education of Littletree* was one example in the 1980s. The major types of nonfiction books fall into these categories:

- Biographies
- Travel books
- Self-help books
- Computer books
- Cookbooks
- Health books
- Business books
- Humor books
- Children's books
- Political controversy/current events
- History
- New Age and inspirational books
- True crime books
- Poetry and belles-lettres
- History

Biographies

A biography is a nonfiction study of a real person, living or dead. The most successful biographies are well-researched and lively accounts of someone with a bonafide place in history. When a real person writes his own story, it's an autobiography. *Whittaker Chambers*, by Sam Tanenhaus, is a biography. *Witness*, by Whittaker Chambers himself, is an autobiography.

Travel Books

Travel books can be broken down into destination guides, travel accounts, and travel guides. Destination guides are meant to provide information about traveling in a specific geographic location. They offer details on hotels, restaurants, and interesting sights in a particular place. Destination guides have lots of phone numbers, addresses, and maps. The Frommer's and Fodor's lines are destination guides.

Travel accounts, on the other hand, are more lyrical descriptions of a place. A travel account may contain hotels, restaurants, and interesting sights, as does a travel guide, but instead of providing short descriptive listings of such places, a travel account might devote an entire chapter to describing a good meal the author ate and the breathtaking ramble she took in the nearby countryside afterward. *A Thousand Days in Venice* is a romantic travel account that has appeared on many best-seller lists.

Travel guides are nondestination travel books about how to travel. A good example is *All Aboard*, a book about how to travel by train in North America. All types of travel books slumped dramatically after September 11 and have recovered slowly, but the industry is nowhere near as healthy as it was just a few short years ago.

Self-Help Books

The self-help category is another extremely large nonfiction category. Self-help includes books about improving relationships, being a good parent, managing stress, and almost anything in what's called the field of pop psychology. Self-help books are designed to help readers try to solve problems in their personal lives. Some self-help books come and go quickly, others, like *How to Survive the Loss of a Love*, stay evergreen.

Computer Books

This how-to category came into prominence in the early days of the computer age when none of us could turn on the computer without checking the manual first. The sales have faded somewhat, but high-end programming manuals and other specialized books still have an audience.

Cookbooks

Everybody knows what these are—books filled with recipes. Bookstore shelves abound with cookbooks, from those that contain regional foods (such as *The Regional Foods of Northern Italy*) to those devoted to a particular type of ingredient (such as

Lemons! Lemons! Lemons!) to cookbooks about only one type of cooking (such as *Cooking Under Pressure*). The *Fix It and Forget It* cookbooks for slow cookers have become million-copy best-sellers tied to a specific type of equipment. Like travel guides and travel accounts, some cookbooks contain stories about food in addition to recipes.

Health Books

Health books provide helpful information about our bodies. From books by medical doctors about specific ailments (such as *What Your Doctor May Not Tell You About Premenopause*) to alternative health titles (such as the *Encyclopedia of Natural Medicine*), the health book category has grown significantly in the past 15 years. To learn why, check out the "Life in the Fast Lane" section later in this chapter, and read Chapter 5 for information on the hot markets.

Business Books

The category of business books lumps together everything from books on management techniques to books on selling real estate, from exposés of high finance shenanigans to personal finance. Two very different best-selling books, *Good to Great* and *The One-Minute Millionaire*, are both—strictly speaking—business books.

Humor Books

Cartoon books, joke books, parodies, and books with humorous observations are all classified as humor. This category ranges from *Dilbert* and *Garfield* to Dave Barry.

Children's Books

Nonfiction books for children abound. Some books explain science, some are biographies of important figures, and some are activity books for rainy days. An extremely popular area is that of bodily functions. A book called *Grossology* started the trend. You can imagine how delighted young children are to read all about snot!

Political Controversy/Current Events

Could be a liberal like Michael Moore and his *Stupid White Men*, or it could be a conservative like Ann Coulter and her book *Slander*. No matter which way you vote, a loud voice and an attitude sell these politically provocative books.

History

History books for the general audience (as opposed to text books) have always existed but were brought into new popularity by the works of the late Stephen Ambrose and television programs like Ken Burns's *Civil War* on PBS, which sent readers to the bookstore.

New Age and Inspirational Books

These books first appeared in the 1960s. New Age and inspirational books run the gamut from books on near-death experiences (such as *Embraced by the Light*) to books about astrology, feng shui, meditation, and other spiritual pursuits. "Feel-good" books (such as the *Handbook for the Soul* and co-author Jennifer's own book, *Christmas Miracles*) also fall into this category.

True Crime

Ever heard of Ann Rule? This author of the Ted Bundy book *The Stranger Beside Me* and the recent best-seller *Every Breath You Take* is the queen of true crime books. True crime books deliver the heart-pounding story behind the dry newspaper head-lines. Murders, terrorists, gangs of bank robbers—all real-life events are fodder for a true crime book.

Poetry and Belles-Lettres

Poetry is getting harder and harder to define. Long gone are the days when poetry was prose that rhymed. (If you are a poet, you just know it.) And *belles-lettres?* That's a very fancy term that refers to literary studies and writing. Extremely high-end literary works fall under this category. Interest in poetry has risen recently due to the poetry slams that take place around the country, and the recent bequest of $100 million to *Poetry* magazine might also give this part of the industry a shot in the arm.

Although most would-be writers daydream about becoming wealthy novelists, in fact the book that holds the record for the longest time spent on *The New York Times* best-seller list was a nonfiction book. *Midnight in the Garden of Good and Evil* spent a

> **Hot Off the Press** _____
>
> Publishing poetry has never been a way to get rich. More often, it is a way to stay poor. Copper Canyon Press' Sam Hammill recently joked that after publishing poetry for decades he'd only recently entered the middle class. Copper Canyon is in Port Townsend, Washington, and one of their books recently won the National Book Award for poetry.

stunning 216 weeks on the hardcover list. So maybe a career in one of these afore-mentioned nonfiction categories can pay off.

So what did we leave out? Gardening books, sports books, computer books, reference books—there are far more than just 11 different nonfiction book categories in the world. But we are not writing *The Complete Idiot's Guide to Book Categories* (which, FYI, would be categorized as a reference book). Instead of writing another 20 pages on this, we've got a better idea for you.

Walk out the door of your imaginary bookstore and through the door of a real one. Spend as much time as you can there. Wander the aisles. Familiarize yourself with the ways that bookstores divide their sections and subsections.

Here's another great way to learn more: Pick a book off the shelf and turn it over. On the back cover of most paperback books—and some hardcovers, too—on the very top line, you will see a category printed. In the book trade, this is often called the shelf reference. This is how the publisher defines the book (and this is where the publisher hopes the bookseller will shelve it). Become familiar with these categories.

Choose which category best defines your book.

Life in the Fast Lane

Although book sales are strong overall right now, it is possible to identify some categories that are moving faster than others. Here's a quick look at two of them: health books and inspirational books.

Health Books

Baby Boomers and their bodies are aging, and they're reading lots of books about staying healthy and fit, particularly alternative health books that deal with such subjects as acupuncture, herbal healing, vitamin therapy, and the like. Changes in the national healthcare system, particularly the growth of HMOs, have also helped turn many Americans to health books for medical help. This is a category that is expected to sell strongly in the years to come.

> **CAUTION**
>
> **Slush Pile**
>
> Don't describe your book as "a little bit of this and a little bit of that." To succeed in today's book market, you need to be very clear about the category that best describes your book.

Inspirational Books

"I think we are returning to our storytelling roots," a radio talk show host told Jennifer recently. He was explaining his take on why books such as *Small Miracles*, the *Chicken Soup for the Soul* titles, and other inspirational storytelling books are on the rise. Modern life is a fast-paced and scary place, and to sit down with a reassuring book such as *Simple Abundance* and drink tea for an hour is a welcome respite. The market for these books will be strong in the years to come.

You can read more about the individual markets in Chapter 5.

From Category to Specific Topic

Now that you have a better understanding of where the book category lines are drawn, is there a market for what you want to write? In the next few chapters, you'll discover professional tips on how to create a best-selling book idea, if you don't already have one. We'll also give you a solid sense of the kinds of books that publishers, both big and small, are seeking—and how to find the right publishing house for your book.

The Least You Need to Know

- ◆ You are either writing fiction or nonfiction, not both.

- ◆ Countless categories and subcategories of fiction exist, from mainstream novels to mystery, from romance to science fiction, and many in between.

- ◆ Nonfiction is an even larger category, with cookbooks, travel books, self-help books, how-to books, and so on. This category covers any book that contains true information.

- ◆ The best way to learn all the different categories and distinctions is to spend time in bookstores, looking, looking, looking ….

- ◆ Do careful research to make sure you are not trying to enter an already over-published area or write a book about a trend that has already passed.

Chapter 3

If You Need an Idea, Stalk the Best-Seller List

In This Chapter

- The high-concept approach
- Find a subject need and fill it
- To write well, read
- Eavesdrop your way to the top
- Hanging out in bookstores

Chances are, you bought this book because you already have an idea, and you think it's a good one. So why do you have to wade through all the information in this chapter about how to come up with a good book idea? You've already got one of those.

That's great, but we want you to know how the professionals do it. We want you to have a solid understanding of how the book business works and how to succeed in that world, no matter what your main reason is for wanting to get published. Even if you don't expect to make lots of money from your book, you do want people to buy it and read it, don't you? To share your knowledge and to advance your cause, you need readers.

Despite the relative health of the book business today, publishers are taking fewer chances on books than before. If getting published is your goal, it is more important than ever that the book you're writing is one that will work in the marketplace. The methods you'll learn about in this chapter have been used by professional writers to develop marketable ideas that sold—and sold well.

The High-Concept Approach

Have you heard the term "high concept" before? It's a movie business expression. The screenwriter pitches his idea to the producer like this: "Baby, you'll love this one! It's a cross between *Top Gun* and *The Sting*. A group of Air Force pilots pull a fast one on some Libyan terrorists." In two sentences, the screenwriter paints a picture that the producer can quickly understand and get a sense of its market potential. That's high concept.

To the chagrin of many traditionalists, the book business has gradually become more like the movie business. That means that if you want your book to sell well, you've got to start thinking like the movie guys. Because sometimes the movie guys end up in the book business.

A Link in the Media Food Chain

The famously stodgy book business has on occasion crossed over into movie territory. When editor Tina Brown left *The New Yorker* for Talk/Miramax she hoped to develop a magazine and book company tied to Miramax Films. The idea was that she could find ideas for magazine articles, those articles could be developed into full-length books once they'd appeared in the magazine, then Miramax Films could develop the books into movies. The dreaded word is *synergy*. Well, it never really turned out the way Tina wanted it to, and the magazine dried up and disappeared. What stayed solidly behind, however, was Talk Books. They've had several best-sellers, the most famous of which was Rudy Giuliani's book *Leadership*.

> **Hot Off the Press**
>
> Who really is a creative genius, anyway? Thomas Edison has been widely quoted for his definition of genius: 99 percent perspiration and 1 percent inspiration. In a similar vein, writer Gertrude Stein believed that "genius is nothing more than energy." So go ahead—keep energetically thinking up those book ideas!

Having your book turned into a film or television project sounds glamorous, a certain way to pocket riches. The truth is a bit disappointing, though. Many projects that are *optioned* never get developed. Jennifer's *Christmas Miracles* book has been optioned twice and never made it beyond that stage. If you get the call from Hollywood once your book comes out, don't quit your day job. Film scouts are always on the lookout for projects with potential and continually reading the publishing trade press for early glimpses of projects, so the chances that someone will see a mention of your book are actually pretty good. Whether they pick up the phone and call your publisher for a review copy or make an offer beyond that really aren't.

Bookmarks

If a movie producer sees potential in your project you might be offered an **option**, a contract that gives them the right to develop your work. Options are usually for a defined period of time, say 12 or 24 months. If the project isn't developed within that time frame, the option expires.

Find a Need and Fill It

Granted, not all books and all reasons for publishing are conceived to appeal to a mass market—is it possible to sit down and consciously create a best-selling book? It has happened before, as this little publishing tale illustrates.

Back in the 1980s, an ambitious young woman wanted to start her own business and decided to fund it by writing a best-selling book. She hired a market research firm to find out who buys books. After spending a few days interviewing shoppers in a mall, the market research reported its findings to her: Women buy books. "Great," she said. "What are women the most concerned about?" The research came back: their bodies. "Hmmm … what part of their bodies?" she asked. Answer: their thighs. So this smart woman sat down and wrote a book called *Thin Thighs in Thirty Days.* Calculating? Yes. Best-seller? You betcha!

Whether that is the true story behind the thin thighs book, we don't know. But the message of the tale is true. You can set out to uncover a large potential audience and deliver a book that they will buy.

Finding the Success Factor

So many of us are attracted to the romantic idea of the life of the writer: long mornings spent with a steaming cup of tea and a blank pad of paper, setting the scene for the muse to come gliding in to inspire and guide us. That may be one way to write. But if you want to write and publish successful books, here is a better way: Sit down with your cup of tea and a copy of *The New York Times* best-seller list. Try to analyze why each book is on that list. Was it the Oprah factor? That worked in a big way for *Simple Abundance, Die Broke,* and *Men Are from Mars, Women Are from Venus.* These books took off after their authors appeared on her show. With Oprah announcing that her show will end in 2005, that factor will fade. Other television shows have stepped in and formed book clubs that have also contributed to hefty sales—is that the reason a book has appeared on the list? Could be. Is it because the author already has widespread name recognition or a huge following, like Rush Limbaugh or Dr. Laura Schlessinger? Millions of people tune in or turn on some of the people whose names are regularly found on the best-seller list.

Or is it because a huge potential audience is interested in this kind of information? Is it a novel with a theme that will appeal to large numbers of readers? Who hasn't at some time pined for a long-lost love? This formula has worked over and over for Nicholas Evans.

Hot Off the Press _____

Sometimes publishing success is as random as choosing a seat on the subway—literally. That's what happened to author/illustrator Daniel Peddle. He saw a woman reading a young adult novel on the subway and chose the seat next to her. Striking up a conversation, it turned out that—surprise!—she was a children's book editor. She gave him her card, he followed up, and the result was a two-book contract.

Wide Appeal = Good Sales

Unless you work for Oprah or already have your own radio or TV show, if you have your sights on selling in big numbers, you're most likely to score by choosing a subject with wide appeal.

Hot Off the Press _____

Best-seller Robert G. Allen shares this three-step formula for creating a hot book: (1) Identify a core human desire or need. (2) Find new technology for solving this. (3) Find a new way to market to this core desire/need. That is how he wrote his best-selling no-money-down real estate books.

Audience Appeal

A big *audience?* How big? If fame and fortune are your primary goals, you need to write a book that will sell big, which means that it will sell to everyone. Robert Kiyosaki did this when he wrote a book called *Rich Dad, Poor Dad*. Who wouldn't want to do what the subtitle promised—learn what rich people teach their children that poor people don't know! And a book called *Don't Sweat the Small Stuff* is designed for anyone stressed out by modern life. Those titles had big audiences—and very big sales.

You must be clear-eyed about how large the potential audience is for your book. Just because your mother raves about your idea doesn't guarantee it a mass audience. Even if your mother and your neighbor, too, like the idea, that still isn't enough. If you are hoping for big sales, you need to uncover big topics with big appeal.

> **Bookmarks**
>
> A book's **audience** is that portion of the population that will be interested enough in the book's topic to buy a copy.

Look Around You

How do you come up with an idea for a book with a big audience? The most important trait is observation. Always keep a keen eye trained on what is going on around you. What topics are in the news? On television? In magazine articles? What are your friends talking about? What kinds of concerns keep you awake at night?

> **Bookmarks**
>
> A **parody** is a comic imitation, usually of a well-known literary work. The business best-seller *Who Moved My Cheese?* spawned many a parody, most using the word *cut* in the title. Under most circumstances, parody is a constitutionally protected form of speech.

To get published, you've got to work on your writing skills. But you've also got to develop your ability to create book ideas. Try the following exercise to get started.

What's Making the News?

Sit down every day with a copy of *USA Today*. It might not be the most sophisticated newspaper in the country, but it gives lots of coverage to topics of interest to middle America. Read the newspaper from cover to cover, and think of one book idea based on the articles you've read.

Perhaps there is a large article in the food section about how many men are using bread machines, or a chart that shows how many parents are home-schooling their young children.

Could you use any of these articles to come up with an idea for a nonfiction book or a novel that involves themes and characters that would appeal to the special interests of large audiences?

Timing can be everything in this business, and if your proposal lands on an editor's desk the same day she just read an article on the topic, it just might do the trick.

A recent example is a front-page story in *USA Today* with the headline "Boomer Brain Meltdown: Generation Faces More Frequent Memory Lapses." Big topic, big audience. Have there been books on memory before? Yes. Will there continue to be interest in this topic in the years to come? Yes.

Try, Try Again

Let's be realistic: Most of the ideas you come up with using this method will be throwaways. But the more you do it, and the more you begin to think like this, the better the odds that you will eventually come up with a best-selling book idea.

What's That You Said?

Eavesdropping is also a critical skill for writers. Yep, we want you to listen in when other people talk. Let's call this skill "heightened observation." Not only can you get a great idea for a book, but you might also come up with a great idea for the title!

At a writers' conference Jennifer was seated in the back of a large room, so far back that she couldn't clearly hear the speakers. At one point she thought she heard an inspirational writer use the phrase "romancing the soul." Wow, she thought, if that isn't a book title it should be! It wasn't … but it is now that Jennifer packaged it. It also turns out that the writer actually said something quite different. So if you can't pay attention when others talk, at least let your mind wander around the edges of what they are saying.

Jennifer's travel guide *The Air Courier's Handbook* was also a product of eavesdropping. She overheard two guys in a restaurant talking about cheap courier travel, something she herself was interested in. She leaned over and introduced herself and got the phone number for a courier firm. She then went on to travel as a courier and later wrote a book about it. That's called listening for fun and profit.

Experts Say

"If you want to write, read," says Gary Krebs, editorial director at Adams Media. What does he mean? All serious students of writing must also be serious readers. You can't expect to flourish in a field that you do not enjoy and also aren't very familiar with. Read everything you can get your hands on. Read books, magazines, newspapers, and online articles. Study what other writers are doing. The hours you invest in reading will pay you back when you sit down to write.

Common phrases of speech sometimes spark an idea. They can also make great book titles. Remember that *USA Today* article about memory loss a few paragraphs ago?

The perfect title for a book on preventing memory loss was right there in the story. A memory expert said, "Use it or lose it!" Doesn't that give you a perfect image for a book? And you understand exactly what the book is about.

Let the Shows Show You

Another way to find ideas for books with large audiences is to attend major industry trade shows. There are trade shows of all stripes: food, gardening, health, fitness, computer, interior design, cars, gift shows, you name it. If you plan to write a nonfiction book on a particular topic, check to see if there is a trade show that's related to it. It's a great way to learn what's hot in the industry. Prowl the aisles, pick up literature, observe merchandise and trends, and, of course, eavesdrop on conversations to listen for news trends and possible titles!

Trade shows are also a prime way to find experts you can team up with to write books.

I'm Not Hanging Out, I'm Working!

Spend lots of time in bookstores. Pay very close attention to the books in the front of the store and those marked "New Releases." Get to know what's new and hot in the area you're considering writing about. Become an expert on what's available.

The more you know about what's out there, the sooner you'll be able to spot what is not. When you find a hole, you've found yourself an opportunity!

How to Work the Bookstore Shelves

Here's another exercise that'll help you to develop your skills. Go to a bookstore and choose a book category. Are there two, maybe three shelves devoted to that category? Spend as much time as you need familiarizing yourself with the books on the shelf. You might need to write down the titles. Now, go back to the store every few days and check your section. Have new titles been added? Have many books sold? Which books? Why do you think they sold?

What Isn't Selling?

When browsing bookstores, don't skip over the bargain tables. Examine those books marked $3.99 very carefully. If there is a big stack of sale books on bulb gardening, that might be an area to avoid. Have several titles on low-fat baking been marked down? Stay away. Learn from the mistakes of other writers about what doesn't sell.

> **Bookmarks** _____
>
> A **series** two or more books linked by a brand-name identity, such as *The Complete Idiot's Guides* or *Harry Potter*, or even the quaintly named children's books, *A Series of Unfortunate Events*, by Lemony Snicket. Publishers are fond of series because they build awareness and momentum in the marketplace. Writers also like them because it can mean steady work. Sometimes a series begins with a single book that sells so well that the audience and the publisher come looking for more.

I'm Not Surfing the Net, I'm Working

Just as you can legitimately spend hour after hour in a bookstore and call it work, you also can spend hour after hour online. Check out the news sites, the women's sites, the money sites. What seems to be the topic of conversation on chat boards? You can use the same eavesdropping techniques in chat rooms to try to pick up phrases or figures of speech that might make good book titles. And no one can catch you watching!

Surfing the online bookstores for information also helps you learn more about what's selling and why. And just like the remainder tables outside the door of a bookstore, you can tell what isn't selling online by the big, big sales ranking next to it. Anything ranked beyond 75,000 or so on Amazon.com just isn't selling in very big numbers. (In other words, the lower the number, the better the sales.) The website for Barnes and Noble, bn.com, will let you see what the best-selling titles are in any given category. Thinking of writing a book about hair braiding? Type hair braiding into the search function and then check "sort by best-selling" and there you have it! Instant research into how well the other titles are selling. Just like we asked you to try to analyze *The New York Times* best-seller list and try to figure out why those books are there, check out the Hot 100 books on Amazon and try to figure out what is making those books sell that very instant.

> **Hot Off the Press** _____
>
> All books in a series are not necessarily written by the same author. Many travel destination series, such as *Best Places to Kiss* romantic travel guides, use the same format and structure but have different authors for different locations. Co-author Sheree met Paula Begoun, publisher of the guides, at a writers' conference; not long afterward, Sheree sent her several sample pages of a possible travel guide set in New York. Although the book was unsolicited, Sheree was careful to use the exact same style as the rest of the series. Surprise! Sheree got herself a contract to do *Best Places to Kiss in and Around New York City*. Now that she's a romantic travel writer, she has written the *52 Most Romantic Places in and Around New York City* for Adams Media.

Sniffing Out Gaps and Niches

The more you can learn about what's available and how well it's doing, the better you'll be able to figure out what that category needs. Perhaps you'll notice that there's a need for a large reference volume, or maybe a small, inexpensive guidebook.

Not long after the phenomenal best-seller *Worst Case Scenario* appeared, Workman released a book called *The Best Case Scenario*. No, this doesn't fall into the parody category, but rather it takes the interest in one thing—how to get out of precarious situations—and transfers it to a broader, more useful category. Cookbook author and editor Fran McCullough saw something missing from the diet bookshelf. There were three best-selling books on the high-protein/low-carbohydrate diet, but none of the books offered much in the way of recipes. So *The Low-Carb Cookbook* was born!

Here's another example of how this kind of observation can pay off. As a long-time player in the business book category, Jennifer has known that quote books were steady sellers. Anyone who has ever had to write a speech goes out in search of one. And "quotable women" books seem to have worked again and again. Women are making huge strides in the business world, but where was the quote book that combined women and business? Say hello to *The Quotable Businesswoman*, a Big City Books project that Andrews McMeel purchased.

Backlist Books: Sure and Steady

If you follow all our suggestions here—if you come up with an idea for a big topic with a big audience and then sell it to a publisher—will it become a best-seller? Perhaps.

Only 1 percent of all the books published in any given year actually make it on a national best-seller list. You might not be one of them, but there are many authors out there whose books are paying the rent, and you might find yourself in their company. These authors have books with strong *backlist* sales. A book that backlists, that sells for years, can rack up impressive sales totals over its lifetime.

Keep the word *backlist* in mind when choosing a topic for a book. Look for book ideas on subjects with staying power.

The More You Know

Now, we do realize that you might already have your heart set on a topic for your book. We also realize that everything we have covered here sounds a bit crass and calculating. Please do not dismiss it out of hand, though.

Bookmarks

Frontlist books are books that have been published recently. Many of these are piled on tables and placed in bookstore windows. **Midlist** books are those acquired for modest advances, that are given modest print runs, and that have a relatively short shelf life. **Backlist** books are those that have been in stores for more than 90 days—sometimes for years. Most of the thousands of books on the shelves are classified as backlist books.

The more you know about what makes books work on a commercial level, the better you will be able to smooth and shape the book that you already have been working on. Read on to learn more about researching the market and gathering the information you'll need for your book proposal.

The Least You Need to Know

- Good book ideas can come from anywhere; keep your eyes and ears open!

- Read as many newspapers and magazines as you can, always looking for big ideas for books and titles.

- Spend as much time as you can in bookstores—they're gold mines of information. Study bookstore shelves carefully to see what is missing.

- Look for ideas with long-term staying power.

Chapter 4

Super-Stealth Market Research Techniques

In This Chapter

- ◆ The bookstore: your number-one resource
- ◆ Researching catalogs
- ◆ Cracking the codes
- ◆ Surfing the Net
- ◆ *PW*, directories, and newspapers

Okay, now you've got an idea for a book. But how do you know if you've come up with an idea that will work? Be it nonfiction or fiction, there are good ways to test your market well in advance of even writing your proposal and sample chapter. Let's start with the strategies to use for nonfiction. (Fiction writers, do not despair; your turn comes later in the chapter.)

Is It a Book?

The first thing you need to ask yourself is: Does my idea have strong book potential? What sometimes seems like a big idea for a book turns out to be only a big idea for a magazine article. Make sure that you have chosen a topic with enough scope and substance to sustain a few hundred manuscript pages.

We know this is hard, but you need to put aside your subjectivity and take a good objective look at your idea, just like the book professionals do. The more work you put into this step, the better your chances of success months from now, when your proposal is sitting on an editor's desk. It is heartbreaking to come to the conclusion that your book won't work, but think how much time and heartache you will save yourself. We've all been there, every published author can name a book idea that they had to reluctantly abandon. It is simply part of the professional process. The investment will also pay you back when it comes time to write your proposal—you will have already done much of the required homework! Bonus.

Meet Your Customer

Now that you're sure you have an idea for a book instead of a magazine article, try to picture your customer. That's right, close your eyes and try to imagine someone walking into a bookstore and asking a clerk for your book. If you can't envision that happening—if your idea is too weak, too abstract, or perhaps too specialized—then you need to reevaluate it.

Before working as an editor, co-author Jennifer spent several years as a book buyer for a small chain of bookstores. She met with sales reps and looked at publishers' catalogs by the hundreds. Her buying decisions were always based on one simple question: Who will buy this book? This is also a question that she asks herself today when evaluating book projects to develop. Memorize the question and ask yourself often: Who will buy this book? And then ask yourself honestly: How many of those folks are there? Are there enough to constitute a sizeable market?

Once your idea can pass these basic litmus tests (is it a book? who will buy it?), you are ready to move on to the next important step.

Sizing Up the Competition

Few books really are the first-ever ones published on their topic. You need to be clear-eyed about the books that have been done before in your area. Remember the technique in Chapter 3 about targeting a shelf in a bookstore and tracking the success of the books on that shelf? You now need to do this for the books that either compete with or complement your own book idea.

Just what do we mean by competition? Let's say that you're planning to write a book on arthritis. The first step is to go to the bookstore and look under "arthritis" on the health books shelf. Are there two books? Four? Twelve? Get out your pad and copy down the title, the author, the publisher, and the price of each book. Open up each book and look inside the *front matter*, the front few pages of the book, to find a copyright date; it's usually on the flip side of the title page.

> **Bookmarks** _____
>
> The **front matter** is the first few pages of the book. It typically contains (in this order) a half-title page, a title page, a copyright page, a dedication, the table of contents, sometimes a preface and/or foreword, and an acknowledgments page. Front matter pages are numbered i, ii, iii, iv, and so forth.

Now go home or have a seat in the bookstore café, and examine all this information carefully. You've got more than just some book information here—you've got clues to your own success.

Title

Do the titles and other language on the covers make the same kinds of promises that yours will? Are they clever and enticing? Or do they have a bland and general medical reference sound to them? We'll call your imaginary book *Accurate Arthritis Answers*. A browsing book buyer would see your book and think, "Hey, accurate answers. What I need are accurate answers about my arthritis problem," and reach for your book. The cleaner your proposed title is, the better.

What's missing from the shelf? Does the market need a beginner's guide, an A-to-Z reference, or a pocket guide to your topic? Maybe you could position yours to fill the gap. Could you target your book to women, or seniors, to make it different from the pack?

Author

You need to know who else is writing in your chosen field. Who is this author, anyway? What are his or her credentials? Does he have a big-name research school behind him? Does this author have a television or radio show?

Take a close look at your rival's credentials and see how yours measure up. Be honest with yourself. Are yours as strong as those of the authors whose books are on the shelf? If not, get to work now to improve them. Begin now to beef up your professional contacts, create workshops or public presentations on your topic, and write articles for industry magazines. By the time you are ready to shop your book to agents or publishers, you will be in a stronger position.

Publisher

Finding out who published these books can be very revealing. If all the books come from major New York houses, this tells you that arthritis is a hot topic and that major publishers thought it was hot. If a book sells well for its publisher, that publisher might just be looking for more!

But what if the topic is covered only by small publishers or by *self-publishers?* Both of those are fine and honorable ways to be published, but let's look strictly from a competitive point of view: Small publishers and self-publishers don't have nearly the distribution that the large houses do. If many of the books you've found on the shelves are from small publishers, then you might be able to use that information to your advantage when submitting to a larger publisher.

Speaking of small publishers, there is much good to say about them. Your book is less likely to get lost in the crowd, you may get more personal attention, and you may find your editor more accessible and open to your suggestions. Keep your eyes open to the books published by thriving companies like Beyond Words in Oregon.

> **Bookmarks**
>
> A **self-published** book is one for which the author himself has paid the bills. Many successful authors started out as self-publishers before the big houses sat up and took notice. It's a fine and honorable thing to do, as self-publisher Benjamin Franklin no doubt would have agreed.

> **Bookmarks**
>
> **Mass market** paperbacks are those small, softcover 4-by-7-inch books you find in the racks at the grocery store and in the airport bookstores (they're also called rack-size paperbacks). Any other larger paperback is called a **trade paperback**. Mass market paperbacks are generally printed in bigger quantities and are priced lower than trade paperbacks.

Price

Book publishing is a price-sensitive industry. If you see four books on the shelf that are expensive hardcover books, perhaps there is a need for a small *trade paperback* on the subject. Your publisher will determine the ultimate price of your book, of course, but you can always pitch the project in a particular way. When you write your proposal, you'll need to show that you've done your homework about the way the competing books are priced. Tell your prospective publishers where the pricing hole in the market is, and how your book could fill it.

Publication Copyright Date

This information is critical when assessing the competition. Are all the books on the shelf a few years old? That means that the information is sure to be at least a little outdated. That might not matter for some books, such as fiction and cookbooks, but for all types of books it will mean that the book category could use a few new books. Better yet, you'll have little competition when you try to promote your book to publishers.

Bear in mind that the publishing process moves slowly. A book with a brand-new copyright date may well have been written as long as two years before its publication.

Are all the books brand new? This is also useful information. It lets you know that publishers think this is a viable category, one worth pursuing (unless there are so many books that the publishers consider it a saturated market).

> **CAUTION**
>
> **Slush Pile**
>
> Never start a conversation with an agent or editor with the phrase "Never before has there been a book on this topic." Rather, say something like this: "To the best of my knowledge, this topic has never been covered quite in this way." You want to show that your idea is different and better than the competition, but not in a whole new category.

Staying in the Know

All this information on current books is very useful, but keep in mind that it has its limitations. Maybe some books have been selling so well that the store can't keep them on the shelves. At the very moment you're scrutinizing the shelves, more new books are being shipped to bookstores. When those new books arrive, some of the books on your list may be boxed up and shipped back to their publishers!

To keep current, you've got to visit bookstores regularly. And you've got to do two more things. You have to get your hands on the announcements issues published by *Publishers Weekly*. Many large bookstores carry this trade magazine, and some libraries also have it on hand. Several times a year there are large round-up issues in which all of the publishers announce what they plan to publish in the coming season. Thankfully, the kind folks at *PW* organize these issues by topic, so it is easy for authors to keep track of what is forthcoming in, say, paperback cookbooks, or hardcover biographies. It is a tremendous source of information. The second thing you've got to do is give your postal carrier more work.

Catalogs for the Asking

You've done good detective work so far. Now you need to hit the phones. To get a better sense of what publishers will be bringing out in upcoming months (particularly in your subject area), get their catalogs—no, not catalogs like *Restoration Hardware* and *Victoria's Secret*, but Simon & Schuster, Viking, Dearborn, and others. Identify the biggest publishers in your subject area. You already know at least some of them; you wrote down their names when doing your bookstore sleuthing. Call and request a catalog. You might also ask the booksellers you've befriended. Publishers' sales reps always leave catalogs behind with the bookseller after a sales call. Why not ask if you can sit in a corner of the bookstore flipping through the most recent?

The big publishers generally put out catalogs three times a year: fall, winter, and spring. Medium and small houses usually do only two: fall and spring. Publishers plan their programs according to seasons, a concept you'll read more about in Chapter 20.

How to Reach 'Em

How do you find the address and phone number for a publishing company? There are a couple good sources. *Writer's Market* is published annually by the folks at *Writer's Digest Books*. It includes an amazing array of information about publishing companies and is now available on CD-ROM. You can also access it online—just go to www.writersdigest.com.

There's also a book called *Writer's Guide to Book Editors, Publishers, and Literary Agents*. Written by Jeff Herman, this book is also filled with publishers' addresses and phone numbers. Of great help is the other information Herman provides: a lengthy description of each publishing company, including the kinds of books published recently.

Many large (and many small) publishers now maintain their own websites. Just take a stab in the dark by typing in their name after the old www prefix and see what comes up. Or check inside a book recently published by that house to see whether a web address is listed. If you come up empty there, just do a quick Google search.

Publishers' websites will highlight their most current titles and a few big upcoming books but won't list projects as far out in the future as the *PW* announcements issue or their catalog.

Go Over Them with a Fine-Toothed Comb

Once the catalogs arrive, study them carefully. They'll give you a good idea of what the publishers plan to publish in the next six months or so. If you find a book that is in your category, study it carefully. Does it get a full page in the catalog? This means that the publisher thinks it's a big deal. Two-page spreads mean they think it is a *really* big deal. Are big publicity and promotional plans announced? What about an appearance on the *Today* show? Just as you did with the books you studied on the bookstore shelves, analyze these upcoming books by title, price, and author.

Free Stuff on the Counter, Too!

Most bookstore chains, and even some of the independents, have book catalogs for the taking, often right next to the cash register. These in-store catalogs, as they're called, contain lots of information about forthcoming titles from a variety of publishers. And every year at Christmas, gift catalogs are produced by associations of independent booksellers that are filled with advertisements of hot new books. Pick up these catalogs whenever you see them—they're chock full of news about the book market.

What Are the Clubs Selling?

As if we haven't talked about catalogs enough already, here is one more suggestion: Try to get your hands on as many catalogs from book club mailings as you can—you know, the little catalogs that the Writer's Digest Book Club, Book-of-the-Month Club, the Doubleday Book Club, and others send out to members every few weeks. No, we don't expect you to sign up for and get lots of those "six books for a dollar" deals. Just ask around and see if your friends or neighbors already belong. Why take the time to look at these book club catalogs? Because these people know what they're doing. If you can't find their catalogs, check out the clubs' websites, which also list what books they are featuring.

Except for the highly specialized ones, most book clubs base their success on their ability to sell large numbers of books to a mainstream audience. The more you study the catalogs, the more you will learn about what kinds of books sell in big quantities.

There is a another kind of club you should be familiar with—the discount warehouse shopping clubs like Sam's Club and Costco. These stores are now a big part of the book business (much to the annoyance of booksellers) and any book sold there is moving *very* swiftly.

Cracking the Code

Important sales information on competing books is literally at your fingertips—but you have to know where to look.

The secret for finding out whether a book has sold well is to look at the number of printings it's gone through. When a book is first released, the number of books printed is referred to as the "first printing." Once most of those books have sold, the book goes back for a second printing, and hopefully a third and a fourth. You can tell just how many printings the book has gone through by checking the copyright page. You should see a series of numbers there that look something like this:

02 01 00   8 7 6 5 4 3 2 1

The numbers are a code that tells you when that particular copy of the book was printed. The rightmost number of the first series of numbers is the year of the book's printing; the rightmost number of the second series of numbers is the number of the book's printing. If you look at these numbers, you can see that the book's first printing came out in the year 2000. That was a few years ago, so if this book is still sitting on the shelf that means it still has not sold out its first print run. Not a swiftly moving title.

Except for hot-selling titles, most books are reprinted in steady but modest quantities. Subsequent reprintings in the 3,000- to 5,000-copy range are common. Publishers do not find it to their benefit from a business standpoint to keep large quantities of unsold books stacked in a warehouse. The spiraling cost of paper has also had an effect on the size of most reprints.

On the other hand, if you see from the code that the book is in a sixth printing, that is impressive. This is a book that is selling.

How is this printing information useful? If you find a book that has sold in big numbers, you might wonder: Could this be a hot topic that has room for another book? If you find a book that has not gone into a second printing after having been out for some time, you might ask: Is this a dead category that I should stay away from?

To find the answers to these questions, you will have to keep asking booksellers questions, reading topical newspapers and magazines, and watching this part of the marketplace closely.

Pick a Bookseller's Brain

Booksellers are tremendously helpful and knowledgeable. If you ask, they will tell. Why not approach a friendly bookseller and say, "Hey, I'm thinking of writing a book on Topic X. What do you think? Is that a category that sells well for you? Which book in this category sells the best?" Most booksellers, the unsung heroes of the book business, will be happy to help if you catch them when they're not too busy.

Find out who is responsible for the actual section in the bookstore where you would like to see your book. Get to know that person and learn from them what works and what doesn't work in your category.

Surfing for Info

The Internet holds wonderful information for writers. Not only is it a great place to do research, but you also can access lots of cool stuff to help you find out about the competition and the market for your book idea. Here are a few great sites.

The New York Times Extended Best-Seller List

Sure, you know *The New York Times* best-seller list. You check it every Sunday, don't you? But did you know that there are many more books on that list than are printed in the paper? To find the top 35 best-sellers, visit the paper's website at www.nytimes.com, and go into the "Books" section. You'll learn that, for instance, although in the newspaper you'll only see five slots for best-sellers in the "Advice, How-To" section, there are really 15 slots.

Amazon.com

Amazon.com, the granddaddy of online bookstores, is also a good place to do research. Amazon can offer long lists of titles on any particular subject, giving you a quick look at what has been published. It, too, has best-seller lists, but keep in mind that these still reflect the tastes of folks who are open to online shopping. Just a few short years ago, the number-one best-selling title of all at Amazon was a book on how to design killer websites.

A fun way to waste an hour, though, is to go through all 100 of the Hot 100 and try to figure out why each book is selling well that particular hour. The Hot 100 is particularly sensitive to media; you can tell pretty quickly who was on the morning talk shows or in the major newspapers by a sudden jump in rank.

You've noticed those reviews on Amazon.com, haven't you? Sometimes they can be useful in helping you assess the strengths and weaknesses of books that are in your chosen category, but do read them with a jaundiced eye. You'll start to notice that many of them seem to come either from the author's close friends or the author's sworn enemies!

Barnes & Noble

Barnesandnoble.com is a relatively recent online entry. It links up with *The New York Times* Book Review site and allows you to read reviews and articles in addition to researching titles.

One thing we really like about BN.com is that you can type in a subject such as "natural health" (or whatever your topic is), and the site will give you the top 25 best-sellers in that category. This is very helpful when analyzing markets and putting together book proposals.

Publishers Marketplace

A hardworking book packager named Michael Cader of Cader Books has developed an incredible resource for working professionals. Check out www.publishersmarketplace.com for great research features—you can track the sales rank of as many books as you'd like to enter, keep up with who is buying what, and even learn how to post your own available projects in the hopes of catching an agent or editor's eye. Some of the site is free, some is only available to subscribers, but we believe it is worth it. He also sends out a daily gossip column called "Publishers Lunch" that you should sign up for to keep abreast of the latest news.

More Assigned Reading

As a serious student of the book publishing business, you need to keep up with news and trends. Read *Publishers Weekly* and study the articles about what's selling. *PW* does annual round-up articles about many of the major book categories. If you plan to write a health book, it's important that you read the health book round-up. If you plan to write a novel, be sure to read the fiction round-up. Don't stumble around in the dark; the information is there for the getting.

In addition to *Publishers Weekly*, *The New York Times* and *The Wall Street Journal* run frequent articles on books and the publishing world. Again, www.nytimes.com often features articles about books and publishing in addition to its best-seller list and book reviews. The "Publishers Lunch" e-mail newsletter includes links to major publishing articles from a wide variety of sources. Start keeping a file of important articles. You never know what you'll learn there.

But I Want to Write a Novel!

Do you really have to go through all this advance work for fiction, too?

Yes. Just as a health writer should know what's already on the health books shelf, a novelist needs to know what fiction is being published and read. Be a student of the art of writing, of course, but to succeed, you must study the marketplace, too. Learn what kinds of novels are selling well (ask a bookseller) and what kinds are not (ask a bookseller). As we write this, "chick lit" is all the rage and many a publisher is looking to jump on the band wagon. By the time you read this they may have passed on to another hot trend. Make it your business to know these things. Don't bury your head in the sand (or your computer); get into that bookstore and learn everything you can.

You know that you're an absolute original and that your style is unique. But if you absolutely had to name a writer or book that is most like yours, what would you say? You're not doing it to compare yourself with another writer, but to establish the fact that books like the one that you have written have sold well.

> **Hot Off the Press** _____
>
> Jennifer Weiner is a best-selling novelist now, but back when she was first trying to find an agent for her book *Good in Bed,* which featured a large woman as the heroine, it wasn't easy being fat, so to speak. "Finding an agent was difficult. One said 'does Cannie have to be fat?'" But Jennifer's book sold and went on to big sales, opening the door wide for other books featuring women of size in the same way *Bridget Jones's Diary* created a market for chick lit.

Minimize Your Rejection Rate

Why, you might ask, are we giving you all this inside information about how to come up with a good book idea? Or about how to research the market and the competing titles? Because, as longtime agents and editors, we're tired of saying "No." It's hard to turn down proposals and manuscripts from good-intentioned, hopeful writers. It is truly heartbreaking to know how much time and effort went into a book project that, from a business standpoint, was doomed from the start.

So we figure that the more time and effort we put into teaching you how to come up with a book idea that will get a "Yes!" from an agent, an editor, and a publishing company, the easier our jobs will be.

Now that that's clear, let's move on to the next chapter and get back to that critical question: What do publishers want?

The Least You Need to Know

- Make sure that your topic is big enough for an entire book, not just a six-page magazine article.

- Never assume that your book is the first ever on the topic. There's at least one book already for every topic ever thought of, and your job is to learn from its/ their strengths and weaknesses.

- Pore over publishers' catalogs, snoop around bookstores, and find out what the book clubs are hawking.

- Get with it—get online.

- The more time and effort you spend researching the market for your novel or nonfiction book, the better your book proposal will be.

Chapter 5

What's Hot, What's Not

In This Chapter

- ◆ Trend spotting
- ◆ Literary and mainstream fiction
- ◆ Love 'em, thrill 'em, kill 'em
- ◆ Niche writing
- ◆ Cookbook niches
- ◆ Books for kids

Just what do publishers want? That's a tough question. And what do publishers want right now (for publication in 9 to 15 months)? That's an even tougher question, and possibly an irrelevant one. The awful truth is, if you sat down at this very moment and wrote a book on a topic that this chapter says is hot today, odds are that by the time you had your finished book in your hands, the topic would have cooled down—maybe to subzero.

Let's say it takes you six months to write the book. That's not a very long time for anyone to write a good how-to book, much less the Great American Novel. Let's say you know somebody who knows somebody with an experienced and well-connected agent, and that agent just happens to be particularly hungry at the moment. Maybe he's going through an expensive divorce, or his biggest client just got hit by a bus.

You express-mail him your ready-to-publish manuscript. He reads it that very night and sees your book on Hot Topic X as his ticket out of mounting legal bills. The first thing the following morning, he couriers copies to the hotshot editors at his favorite publishing houses.

> **Bookmarks**
>
> **Writers' conferences** are organized events during which beginning writers can meet industry folk like agents and editors. Famously discovered at the Squaw Valley Writers' Conference was a woman who wrote business brochures for a living, but you'd recognize her name now—Amy Tan.

Twenty-four hours later, he conducts an auction. Your book sells to the highest bidder for megabucks. (Why not? After all, this is a dream.) Smelling success (and desperate to recoup the investment), your publisher rushes the manuscript into production. Nine months later, your book hits the stores amid great fanfare—and is quickly placed on the remainder table. By the time your masterpiece is published, Hot Topic X is old news, and the public now wants to read about Hot Topic Y.

Sadly, this very scenario was played out on a large scale when all the books on September 11 came out for the one-year anniversary. Some books sold in big numbers, but most did not.

What's In, What's Out, by Category

What's a writer to do? Now there's a question worthy of Freud. Despite the transitory and, dare we say, fickle nature of the buying public, certain trends bear watching. So with a grain of salt and an eye on how quickly the reading public can shift their interest, let's take a look at the trends affecting each of the various book categories.

> **Experts Say**
>
> Are novels sometimes timely? You bet. "I wrote a relevant novel by accident," Mark Dunn of *Ella Minnow Pea* fame told a newspaper. His Orwellian-influenced book about censorship and restricted liberties came out in hardcover around the same time as the terrorist attacks in fall 2001 and seemed prescient when the U.S. government began to gear up for increased homeland security.

Fiction

The odds for a first-time novelist are never good, but all sorts of first novels are published each year, some to great acclaim and greater profit.

The market for fiction is as good—and as bad—as it ever was. Fiction is a star-driven game; the John Grishams, James Pattersons, and Danielle Steels have become virtual brand names that publishers can count on to drive sales. An increasing dependency on this star system has created a classic chicken-and-egg scenario: Which comes first, the best-selling book or the best-selling author?

Every publisher worth its bottom line wants to publish Grishams, Pattersons, and Steels. But there are only so many of these super authors to go around—and only so many publishers who can afford them. So everyone is looking for the next Grisham, the next Steel. That's where you might just come in.

In 2001, there was a bumper crop of young first-time novelists and Alice Sebold's *The Lovely Bones* outsold established fiction names like Tom Clancy, Nicholas Sparks, and Stephen King. Her book also renewed the hope that literary fiction can sell in the same large numbers that commercial fiction does.

As you know from Chapter 2, the fiction market is divided into two general types: literary fiction and mainstream (or contemporary) fiction. The latter includes hardcover novels and genre fiction. Genre fiction includes mysteries, thrillers, science fiction, fantasies, romances, horror books, Westerns, and the like. What's selling in these categories?

Hot Off the Press

The number of books that a "best-seller" can sell has been steadily increasing over the last few decades. Research fellow Gayle Feldman took a close look and discovered that the 1975 best-seller *Ragtime* sold 232,000. Compare that to the 2000 Grisham best-seller *The Brethren*, which sold nearly 2.9 million. Crunch those numbers and you'll see a staggering twelvefold increase.

Love Is a Many-Published Thing

The romance market is booming. Take a look at these numbers from *Forbes* about just how hot romance is:

- Harlequin sold 150 million books worldwide in 2001.

- Some 37.9 million women read romance fiction every year (and 3.5 million men do, too!).

But, you might say, I couldn't write those bodice-rippers. Well, if you think that bodice-rippers are the only romances, think again. Today's romance genre is a versatile one. It encompasses many series, subgenres, and hybrids, as well as mainstream titles. Consider these subcategories, to name just a few: historical romance, time-travel romance, science fiction romance, romantic suspense, romantic mystery, inspirational romance, multicultural romance, and young-adult romance. Then there are the new, super-sexy romances. And if you think that romance heroines are generously bosomed virgins looking for Mr. Right to carry them off into the sunset, think again. Today's romance heroines run the gamut from fresh-faced junior high school girls to divorced career women.

Bridget Jones's Diary spawned a new breed, too, and many younger readers have strayed away from the bodice-rippers and toward the more contemporary novels. Imprints like Red Dress Ink and Mira are much hipper than their old mothers and feature writers like Jennifer Crusie, who writes such sexy love scenes that she told us, "I get letters from husbands thanking me for getting their wives in the mood!"

Another hot imprint is Blaze, from Harlequin. Editor Birgit Davis-Todd describes these books as "plots that are sexy in premise and execution."

Get the Guidelines

If you'd like to cash in on this lucrative market, you'll have to do your homework. Don't write one single word without first consulting the guidelines from the publisher you plan to target, and without reading all the romance novels you can get your hands on.

Experts Say

Aspiring romance writer Caroline Amneus says, "I never had to send for guidelines. Major romance publishers attend the romance conferences sponsored by Romance Writers of America and bring along copies of their guidelines. It's a great place to meet editors and agents and learn what they're looking for." For more information, call RWA headquarters at 281-440-6885.

Harlequin, Silhouette, Bantam, and other romance publishers happily provide writers with guidelines for their series. These guidelines are jammed with information on the exact word counts for their books, definitions of style, and level of sensuality permitted. They include lots of "absolute no-no's" and "absolute musts" as well as submission information. By following these rules, you'll save yourself lots of rewriting, and you'll greatly increase your chances of breaking into the romance field. Many of the romance publishers like Dorchester (www.dorchesterpub.com) and Red Dress Ink (www.reddressink.com/writing.html) post their guidelines right on their websites, so check there first before trying to track down an address.

Love Writing About Love?

The one thing all romances have in common, from romantic suspense to mainstream historical, is that they are all stories about relationships. If you can write a love story that will move readers, this could be the field for you. Laurie Gold puts out an e-mail newsletter about the romance writing industry that you might find useful. Check out her All About Romance site at www.likesbooks.com and select "writers on writing."

Beyond Hot Romance

From the early days of publishing, "erotica" has always existed in some form or another, and the twenty-first century is no exception. Perhaps writing adult books will be your bag? Check out what Allure Books in Oregon has to offer and request their guidelines if you'd like to try your hand at this genre (www.allurebooks.com).

Thrill 'Em, Grill 'Em, and Kill 'Em

Mysteries, thrillers, and all their kin are more popular than ever, a fact that's readily confirmed by a quick glance at the best-seller list. At the time of this writing, four thrillers were on *The New York Times* hardcover best-seller list. Such news reflects not only the immense popularity of these genres, but the versatility of them as well. From forensic thrillers to historical mysteries, with protagonists as different as Teddy Roosevelt (in *The Alienist*) to Navaho shaman/policeman Jim Chee (in Tony Hillerman's books), the mystery and thriller genres rival the romance category in both variety and readership.

Today's market is witnessing a boom in historical mysteries, medical thrillers, techno thrillers, and legal thrillers. But whether you're writing a hard-boiled detective story or an *English cozy*, it doesn't really matter. In these genres, there's plenty of room for your novel, regardless of which category it fits.

Bookmarks _____

An **English cozy** is a type of mystery that typically takes place in England and follows a sweet old lady detective and a few of her doddering friends. They stumble onto a cold, dead body one afternoon, and the story unfolds from there. The term *cozy* comes either from the fact that you can settle in front of the fire for a cozy afternoon with one of these books, or from the tea cozy on the pot of Earl Grey you brew to drink while you read.

Nouveau Niche

The marketing types in publishing love nonfiction. Why? Because the nonfiction market is much more quantifiable—some would say more reliable—than the fiction market. Those marketers don't really know how many readers out there are going to want to read your coming-of-age novel, and they can't even begin to guess. But they can guess with slightly more accuracy how many of the nations millions of overweight people would be interested in *Dr. Atkin's New Diet Revolution* or whether the millions of fans of an HBO show will buy *The Sopranos Family Cookbook*.

The same goes for all the trends—demographic and otherwise—that are reported in the media each day. Nonfiction publishers pay attention to what's hot, and (as we've told you before) if you want to succeed at nonfiction, you need to pay attention, too.

Hot Off the Press

What's hot in fiction, according to St. Martin's Press senior editor, Ruth Cavin, are great books. "There is no formula for a good book, so write what interests you and what you think is good," says Cavin, who has worked with most of the greatest names in mystery fiction. "Write characters you can believe in, plots that make you keep reading, settings and minor characters that are interesting." Cavin, who reviews "hundreds of submissions" every year, says, "There may be more competition in terms of numbers, but not in terms of quality. I'm looking for books that stand out because of the writing, plot, setting, or characters."

The Niche Is Riche

Identifying a niche in the marketplace and then publishing to that niche is called—you guessed it—niche publishing. Three of the most successful niche markets right now are alternative health, spirituality, and computers. All these niches fill a need for readers.

As the world grows more technologically complex, all of us non-nerds need help keeping up. As people grow more disenchanted with conventional medicine, they're exploring alternative therapies.

And the baby boomer generation that once turned away from organized religion is now looking for spiritual guidance as they become more aware of their own mortality. A recent article in *The Wall Street Journal* noted that, in the same way boomers changed giving birth (and sold vast numbers of *What to Expect When You're Expecting*), they are now changing death.

"Fine," you say, "but I don't know St. John's wort from St. John the Baptist, and I don't know a thing about computers." No problem. There are myriad trends and niches to explore, from home-schooling to women's golf, from small business to eBay auctions. You don't even have to be an expert—you can always team up with one.

What's Cookin' with Cookbooks?

Long a staple of nonfiction publishing, the cookbook market has disappointed many publishers over the past couple years. "The cookbook field was overpublished," admits one long-time cookbook editor, who also reveals that many cookbook editors are looking for new jobs in new fields.

Despite this recent softening of the market, some cookbooks are finding favor with the public. "Editors say to me that superstar chefs are both overpublished and still selling," says cookbook agent Martha Casselman of Calistoga, California.

From her wine country office, Casselman is well positioned to observe the industry trends. "Anything that ties into a product has a chance, like grilling, for instance." What does Casselman mean? Cookbooks with product or equipment ties might succeed because the publisher can persuade the manufacturer to purchase the book in bulk. A recent success has been the *Fix It and Forget It Cookbook*, with 2.2 million copies sold of a book that tells you what you can fix in your Crock-Pot. Literary food writing is also still selling.

"It is hard for unknown cookbook writers to break in," Casselman admits. "But we still get excited when we see a good book."

The Publishing House at Pooh Corner

By definition, the children's market is a perennial one. Write for children, and you can build a body of work that will enchant the little ones generation after generation. But if you think that writing for children is easy, think again. To paraphrase beloved author of *A Wrinkle in Time*, Madeleine L'Engle, writing for children means writing stories too mature for adults.

L'Engle's point has been made quite clearly by the extraordinary success of the Harry Potter books. These enduring best-sellers have made frequent appearances on both the children's *and* the adults' best-seller lists, and fans waited for years for Rowling's fifth book to appear. The sophisticated wordplay in the Lemony Snicket books also appeals to both children and adults.

What kind of books are working now? We asked Lynne Rominger, who wrote *The Complete Idiot's Guide to Publishing Children's*

> **CAUTION**
>
> **Slush Pile** _____
>
> Never send illustrations for your children's picture book with your manuscript unless you're a talented artist. Most publishers like to hire their own illustrators. Never mention the following in a query letter or proposal: "My niece (nephew, son, daughter, or next-door neighbor) is a wonderful artist whose work would really complete the book."

Books, what the market was looking for: "Parents want to buy children's books that show an element of character, books that reinforce the notion that you shouldn't steal, or lie, or cheat. Basically, books that teach children the Ten Commandments in a nonreligious way."

When you write for children, be it picture books or young adult novels, you can expect somewhat smaller advances. But with the potential of a lifetime of royalties as each generation of little folks discovers your writing, it's a much-anticipated legacy.

The children's market is as varied as the market for grown-ups. You have your pick of options, from picture books to young adult mysteries to middle-grade nonfiction.

Picture This

Picture books have been and remain this category's biggest sellers. The classic picture book is as popular as ever, but there is an increased interest in other types of picture books as well, most notably these types:

- Picture books made into baby board books (those little books whose pages are cardboard to make turning easier for little fingers)
- Picture books for slightly older toddlers

No Kidding About Kids' Fiction

Middle-grade and young adult books also offer writers a wealth of opportunity. Trends indicate a comeback for fantasy and historical fiction geared to this age group, even as the horror trend wanes. This is largely due to the popularity of the *Harry Potter* series.

Just the Facts, Ma'am

Nonfiction for children, particularly in the areas of science, technology, and biography, are staples of this market. If your writing can entertain as well as educate, this may be for you.

Expert Lynne Rominger observed that, although the children's market used to be thought of as a "cousin of regular adult books, not really a money-making part of the industry," this has all long since changed. Publishers and booksellers alike recognize the fact that every five years they have a new crop of customers.

> **Experts Say** _____
>
> "I never intended to write a young adult novel," says Paula Munier Lee, author of *Emerald's Desire*. "But an editor who'd considered a mainstream novel that I wrote remembered me. When she took a new job as an editor for YA novels, she called me up and asked if I'd like to give it a try. As it turns out, I'm pretty good at it! I never did sell that other novel, but what the heck, it eventually got me a contract."

Market Savvy for Success

And how does knowing what's hot and what's not work in real life? Let's look more closely at the experience of two authors who found success by paying close attention to the marketplace.

Better Late Than Never

Nadine Crenshaw, author of 10 novels and 4 nonfiction books, wrote for more than a dozen years before she sold a book. During that period of time, she also wrote a column for her local newspaper, but she was bound and determined to become a novelist.

"I wrote eight novels before I wrote one I could sell," Crenshaw remembers. "It was a painful period." Eight novels is a lengthy apprenticeship. Looking back, Crenshaw believes that her publishing breakthrough need not have taken her so long. "I wrote those eight novels blind. As soon as I started writing with the market in mind, my apprenticeship was over."

What did she do? Exactly what we've advised in these last few chapters.

Crenshaw began to study the marketplace. She subscribed to *Publishers Weekly* and *Writer's Digest*, joined Romance Writers of America, and spent lots of time in bookstores familiarizing herself with the competition. Her efforts paid off: The next novel she wrote, *Mountain Mistress*, was published. That novel won the Romance Writers of America Golden Heart Award, and she went on to publish nine more historical romances.

The path to publishing has not always been smooth, however. After 10 years of writing historical romances, Crenshaw's market dried up. She turned back to her own market research. She wrote a few nonfiction books on trendy topics (Scully on *The X-Files* and *Xena, the Warrior Princess*) before turning back to fiction.

What has she chosen this time? A thriller. She plans to go on writing both fiction and nonfiction to ensure a steadier income. "Write what you want," says Crenshaw, "but write with the market in mind."

Homework

Author Mel Odom believes that writers make a big mistake by not paying attention to markets. "It doesn't matter whether you're writing fiction or nonfiction," says Odom, prolific author of some 70 fiction and nonfiction books in the past 12 years. "You need to do your homework. You have to study the type of book you want to write, as well as the market for that type of book. Take it apart and know it."

Odom attributes his prodigious output to his ability to analyze markets, genres, and trends—an ability that has given him the versatility to write in a number of categories, including action/adventure, science fiction, horror, young adult, children's books, computer books, how-to books, and even comic books!

Writers worried about slavishly following the market rather than their own hearts need not lose sleep at night. As Odom puts it: "Assimilate it and then do it your way."

The Early Bird ...

Keep your ear to the ground, and you can turn today's trends into tomorrow's bestsellers. But don't dawdle; when it comes to trends, the first writer to the marketplace usually wins. Keep abreast by reading *Publishers Weekly* on a regular basis and paying careful attention to the trend articles that interview editors and booksellers about what is working.

The Least You Need to Know

- Publisher's predictions can be hit-or-miss, but certain trends bear watching.
- If you're writing romance, get publishers' guidelines first.
- The romance field has changed dramatically, and many publishers have a need for sexier manuscripts.
- Children's books can mean small advances but long-term sales.
- Put (almost) as much effort into your market research as into your writing.

Part 2

Gone with the Wind: Submitting to Publishers

So you've got an idea for a book—now what? Here's where you'll learn the actual process of putting together a book proposal. We'll clue you in on the common mistakes new writers make so you can look like a pro on the page, right from the beginning!

From submitting professional query letters to compiling appealing proposals, these chapters explain what you need to get the attention of an agent or editor.

Both nonfiction and fiction proposals are covered in detail. You'll learn the ropes on how to do either (or both!).

Chapter 6

Submit What?

In This Chapter

- ◆ How the submission process works
- ◆ A day in the life of publishing
- ◆ Ten mistakes new writers make
- ◆ "Forward" and other foibles
- ◆ Looking like a pro on the page

Once you come up with an idea that you think is dynamite, what then? How do you move your book idea closer to becoming the finished thing? You must begin to submit.

Submit, you say? What's that? Simply stated, the *submission* process is the process by which you let the publishing world know that you have a great book available for publication.

Simply Submit

To get your book idea of a manuscript in front of the publishing decision-makers, you need to know how to make your way through the submissions process. This involves two important steps.

◆ **Important Step One:** The query letter

◆ **Important Step Two:** The book proposal

Why is the submission process broken down into two steps? To see why this came to be, let's peek in on a typical day in the publishing world.

A Day in the Life of Book Publishing

It is early morning in Manhattan, and unbeknownst to each other, an assistant editor and a literary agent are sitting next to each other on the subway. The doors open, and the two hoist their heavy tote bags onto their shoulders and head for the same towering black skyscraper. The elevators deposit them on two different floors. After greeting colleagues, they settle into small offices with their first cups of weak office coffee. And for the next two hours, on two different floors, these two hard-working members of the New York publishing world lead oddly parallel lives. Both eye the fresh stack of mail perched on their desks, and both sigh when beginning the task of opening and reading the mail.

What comes in the mail every day? *Query letters, book proposals,* finished manuscripts, editorial correspondence, newspaper clippings, promotional information—there seems to be no end to the pieces of paper that must be read. Interrupting the ritual of reading the mail, the phone rings continuously. And then, think of the e-mail that must be read daily!

Bookmarks

The process by which a writer submits a book proposal or manuscript to a publisher is called **submission.** If the author is not using an agent, it is called an **unagented submission.** The initial contact between a writer and an agent comes in the form of a **query letter,** which is meant to spark interest in the project and prompt its recipient to ask for more material. The packet of information about the writer's manuscript or book idea is a **book proposal.** It contains a solid description of the book's purpose, the potential market for the book, its competition, and the author's credentials. The proposal also contains a complete table of contents, an extensive book outline, and at least one sample chapter.

This scene takes place simultaneously not only in the office of our unnamed assistant editor and faceless literary agent, but also in the offices of the senior editor, the editor-in-chief, the publisher, the associate editor, and even the new college intern.

Let's face it—everybody wants to write a book, and everybody writes to people in publishing. So how do publishers, editors, and agents handle all this mail?

Query letters, that's how.

Quantum Query

A query letter is a simple, one-page letter. In the letter, the purpose of the book is described, and the author makes a short case for why the world needs this book. If the contents of the query letter pique the interest of the recipient, that recipient requests a proposal. If the proposal is good and the book-to-be is deemed marketable, a publisher offers a contract.

But why can't you send your entire book? Because in most cases, the harried folk in publishing haven't met you and don't know about your project. You need to try to get their attention in the easiest and fastest way possible. A query letter is the correspondence equivalent of politely tapping a stranger on the shoulder and saying, "Excuse me, do you have a minute to talk?"

Sound intimidating? Don't worry. We'll show you how to write a top-notch query letter that will help your project stand out. We'll also tell you how to put together a bulletproof book proposal that will knock the socks off everyone who sees it.

Hot Off the Press

"A little wooing goes a long way …," says Oakland, California–based literary agent Bridget Kinsella. Whatever does she mean by that? "Although this is a professional relationship, in many ways you are courting an agent in the early stages of trying to interest them. "Bridget was not amused by the fellow who sent her a fiction submission stuffed in a folder with a visible coffee cup stain on it, envelopes with stamps placed in a quirky pattern, or a cover letter riddled with typos. Not the way to woo her, or any agent. And make sure that you look good from that very first glance. Bridget shares a belief many agents hold, that they can tell from the outside of the envelope whether it holds any promise inside!

But Before We Begin …

We've seen it all. We've read thousands of query letters and book proposals. Don't make the mistakes others have. Here you'll learn the things that you must avoid, the no-no's that will brand you as an amateur. Read them, and believe them. Commit them to memory before moving on to the next two chapters. The publishing world has rules, and you've got to follow them to get people to look at your stuff.

Co-author Jennifer recently received a large package from someone she met at a writers' conference. Thankfully, it did not arrive postage due, but his letter began, "Although all the books I've read tell me to send just a query letter first, I've decided to take a different approach and send a complete manuscript of the book." *Arrgh!*

Not only did this fellow come off as arrogant, but he also signaled that he is not someone who follows the rules. What agent or editor wants to sign someone who clearly doesn't take direction? Not many.

And what happened to the package Jennifer received? She sent it right back, unread.

Top Ten Mistakes New Writers Make

If you take the following list to heart, you won't repeat that faux pas or others that raise red flags. Here are the few simple no-no's that can easily undermine all your hard work:

- Letters that contain a misspelled name
- Packages or letters with postage due
- Letters printed with outdated equipment
- Query letters that don't quickly come to the point
- Proposals that criticize other books
- Letters that are too flip or amusing in tone
- Queries that say, "All my friends think this is a great idea"
- Proposals that smell like cigarette smoke
- Queries that mention the minimum advance the writer will accept
- Proposals that arrive in a package filled with shredded paper or packing "peanuts"

Letters That Contain a Misspelled Name

How hard is it to call and check the spelling of someone's name? Why brand yourself a careless writer before the package is even open? A simple phone call helps you to show that you are serious about getting things right. Tell the receptionist that you'd like to double-check the spelling of an editor's name and they should be happy to help. Don't assume that what is printed in a professional directory is right. For many years Jennifer's name was misspelled in a major writers' guide.

In fact, any information you've plucked out of a publishing directory needs to be verified. Find out if the editor still works there and is still acquiring in the same areas.

Package or Letter Arrives Postage Due

You look careless and irresponsible from the moment your material arrives if your package requires postage due. Another way to annoy your recipient is to send a package laden with little slips of paper that need to be signed to prove that it arrived. Remember, you are sending something that, under most circumstances, this person did not request. So don't make it hard for them to receive it. This includes sending unrequested materials that require a signature or a return receipt.

Author Uses Outdated Equipment

Avoid using a typewriter, a dot matrix printer, or other out-dated equipment at all costs. Sounds harsh, doesn't it? But using outdated equipment signals that both you and your ideas are old-fashioned and behind the times. Can't afford the fancy stuff? Just go to one of the retail places or copy shops that rents computer time and use a better computer system—even just to print your proposal out. You need to look as good as you can on the page. (And this means checking to make sure that your printer cartridge is fresh enough to print nice and dark.) Handwritten notes are a lovely touch between family and friends, but remember that this is a piece of professional correspondence and that a casual, handwritten note would not set the right tone.

Letters That Don't Quickly Come to the Point

By "quickly," we mean in the first paragraph or two. Why is this so important? Remember our typical day in publishing? The one in which the agent and editor's desks were piled with mail? We didn't tell you about the blinking light on the phone message machines or the 73 unanswered e-mails and the 4 scheduled meetings for that day. Time and attention are short. You need to get to the point.

Proposals That Criticize Other Books

This is a major gripe of editors. You worked hard to put together a book proposal, and your agent spent a lot of time deciding which editors should be approached with it. So why annoy the very editor that you are hoping to impress?

"The author should never use the competitive analysis section to slam other books—chances are, publishers who published those books will be reading the author's proposal," says Laurie Abkemeir. As the former senior editor at Hyperion, she should know. "Also, many times the books that are being slammed are books that were huge successes. It doesn't make sense to slam something that was a big best-seller, but many authors do."

As an editor at Prima, Jennifer has also received many a proposal that pokes fun at some of the very Prima books she's proudest of. Once again, not the way to get someone to like you and your book idea … (Chapter 8 explains how to position your book in a positive light without making enemies.)

Letters That Are Too Flip or Amusing

A query letter is not a letter to a friend, your mom, or a long-lost chum. This is no time to be silly. Even if friends think you're the next Seinfeld, it is safer to write a straightforward, businesslike letter. Humor can easily work against you. So can arrogance, boasting, or conceit. How can you impress an agent if you can't boast about your accomplishments? Be confident, not arrogant. Don't worry—in the next chapter, you'll learn how to do this.

Queries That Mention Your Fan Club

Don't ever write, "All my friends and relatives think this is a good idea." Book publishing is a business. And professionals in the book business aren't interested in hearing about your friends and relatives (unless they are famous friends and relatives who will be endorsing your book). They want to know about markets and demographics and national publicity.

Proposals That Smell Like Cigarette Smoke

Hey, go ahead and smoke, it's none of our business, but you'd be amazed at how the smell attaches itself to paper! An editor notices when they open a proposal that makes their eyes swim from the tobacco fumes. If you smoke, you probably don't notice it, but take our word for it: Smokers send letters that smell like smoke. So just to be sure, take your disk over to Kinko's and print out your work in a smoke-free environment. Does this seem like petty advice to you? Yes. But remember, you want these publishing people to like you and your project. You need to use every little method you can to woo them.

Letters That Mention a Minimum Advance

Letters that mention the minimum advance the writer will accept or the phrase "resources needed to complete this project" expose you as a beginner. Like writers who are paranoid that someone might steal their ideas, this is the mark of an amateur. Never mention money in a query letter. Never mention money in a book proposal. When considering whether to pursue a book idea, agents and editors don't care what kind of "resources" are needed to complete your project. That's your problem, not theirs. Sooner or later the topic of money will come up, but let them mention it first, not you.

CAUTION

Slush Pile

A big no-no when approaching an agent or editor is to be cagey about your idea, or worse yet, not reveal it at all. More than one amateur has expressed anxiety over sharing their sure-fire book idea for fear that someone will steal it. Trust us, they won't. This attitude only makes you look naïve and foolish to a publishing pro. The same theory applies to asking an editor to sign an NDA—a nondisclosure agreement.

Proposals That Are Buried in Shredded Paper

You want these publishing folks to be in a pleasant mood when they're reading your material. But years of experience in opening packages has taught us that there is no way to open one of these types of packages without getting a lapful (or noseful) or shredded paper. Maddening! You want someone to love your project. Don't risk ticking them off before they can get to it.

Can't find a padded envelope that doesn't have that shredded paper stuff in it? If your proposal doesn't fit in a FedEx letter-size envelope, it's probably too darn long. And a query letter that doesn't slip right into a regular envelope is definitely too long.

"Forward" and Other Foibles

The world of book publishing is a peculiar place with peculiar rules, and it's frequently filled with peculiar people.

Even if you have learned all you can from the many books you've read, the courses and seminars you've attended, and the writers you know, there are still tiny mistakes that only persnickety publishing people will notice.

Here's the big one: *forward* vs. *foreword*.

Look up these two words in your dictionary. Here's what ours says:

> **forward** (adj.) directed or moving toward the front, situated in front

So if the president of the United States has agreed to write something nice for the front of your book, you think, it must be a forward. These are introductory remarks situated in front of your book, so it would seem perfectly logical.

But no! The president is writing a *foreword*, not a *forward*, for your book.

> **foreword** (n.) introductory remarks at the beginning of the book, usually by someone other than the author

Even longtime authors make this mistake sometimes, and persnickety publishing people feel very smug when they spot it.

As long as the dictionary is out, let's tackle two more confusing words.

> **which** (adj. and pronoun) what particular one or ones of a set of things or people

> **that** (adj. and pronoun) the person or thing referred to or pointed to or understood

Co-author Sheree spends a great deal of her time combing through her clients' proposals changing *which* to *that*. What's the rule? If *that* works, use it.

Look Like a Pro on the Page

If you've got a computer, no doubt it's loaded with the latest tricks. This is not the time to use them. Query letters and book proposals are not the right place to show off your fancy fonts and graphics capability. Use a basic font, such as Times New Roman or Courier. Skip the shaded boxes, the cartoons, and the artistic borders. Keep it plain.

Plain is also the order of the day for paper. Don't send off a query letter on scented paper, fancy marbled paper, or anything other than plain white, businesslike stock. And don't get fancy with the inks. Use plain black ink, please.

Now Where Should I Send It?

With all this talk of submitting, to whom shall you submit? It's a reasonable question. Sometimes writers submit their stuff to an agent, who decides to represent them. The agent then submits the writer's material to an editor. Other times a writer just goes ahead and submits to an editor. So what do we think that you should do?

If you plan to write a book with broad national appeal, we think that you should first try to get an agent. (More about agents will come in the following chapters—particularly Chapter 10.) If that doesn't work, you should try to submit directly.

In the next two chapters, we discuss query letters and book proposals. It is our aim to help you prepare these materials in such a way to interest an agent. And if you can't? We'll cross that bridge when we come to it, in Chapter 13.

The Least You Need to Know

♦ There is a well-defined process for submitting your materials: Submit a query letter and then, if requested, a book proposal.

♦ Follow the rules, or you risk looking like an amateur—or, worse, a difficult author to work with.

♦ Careless errors in query letters or book proposals can undermine your other efforts.

♦ If you are writing a book with a large potential audience, try first to get an agent to represent you.

Chapter 7

Query Letters That Sell Nonfiction

In This Chapter

- ◆ Query? What's that you say?
- ◆ But I can't say it all in one page!
- ◆ Why does this have to be perfect?
- ◆ An agent's five pet peeves
- ◆ Hook 'em early
- ◆ Can't I just phone?

Now that we've frightened you into thinking that your entire publishing career rests on a single typed query letter, how can we calm you down? By telling you this: The formula for writing successful query letters can be learned, and your lessons begin now.

This chapter tackles query letters for nonfiction books. Novelists, your turn comes up soon, in Chapter 9. We do, however, urge you to keep reading this chapter, too.

Although you learned the basic idea behind a query letter in the last chapter, it bears repeating: The query letter is your first contact with either an agent or an editor. It is your calling card, your way of introducing yourself and your book idea to the publishing world at large.

Query? What's That You Say?

A successful query letter should contain the following items:

◆ A brief description of the book

◆ A brief description of the market for the book

◆ A brief description of the author

Brief? Just how brief are we talking here?

But I Can't Say It All in One Page!

One page, that's how brief. Your query letter should never, ever be longer than one page. You need to distill your brilliance, your wisdom, and your expertise into one potent page-long brew that will leave a reader reeling from its power.

Here is a quick exercise to help you distill that brew:

◆ Sit down with one blank page of paper.

◆ Write out a two-paragraph description of the book.

◆ Write out a two-paragraph description of the market for the book.

◆ Write out a two-paragraph description of yourself, the author of the book.

Okay, now pretend you are Ernest Hemingway. No, you don't have to run in front of a herd of bulls; all we want you to do is simplify your writing. Take a hard look at what you have written, and start cutting out extra words. Make two long sentences into one sentence of medium length. Get rid of adjectives. Turn two wordy paragraphs into one punchy paragraph.

Here is an example of a Hemingway-esque transformation.

About the Author, Take One

This is the first draft of the bio.

> Jennifer Basye Sander entered publishing as a way to escape a failed career in California politics. Her first book was published in 1983, *The Sacramento Women's Yellow Pages*, a directory of woman-owned businesses. She worked for several years as a book buyer for a small, independent northern California bookstore chain before becoming an acquisitions editor for a nonfiction publisher.

> As an editor, Jennifer worked with many best-selling authors, including Mary Kay Ash of Mary Kay Cosmetics, and award-winning writers such as the James Beard and IACP Award–winning food writer Elaine Corn. As an author, Jennifer's own books range in topic from travel (*The Air Courier's Handbook*) to small business (*Niche and Grow Rich*) to inspiration (*Christmas Miracles*). Her book, *Christmas Miracles*, was a *New York Times* best-seller. A senior editor at the Prima Publishing division of Random House, Jennifer also operates her own book packaging company, Big City Books, in Granite Bay, California.

About the Author, Take Two

After a short consultation with Mr. Hemingway, we now give you the revised paragraph.

> Jennifer Basye Sander first entered publishing in 1983 with the publication of her book *The Sacramento Women's Yellow Pages*. Her early success with that book led to a career in publishing that includes both a short stint as a book buyer and many years as an acquisitions editor. She worked with several best-selling authors and has herself authored six books, including the recent best-seller *Christmas Miracles*. A Random House editor and book packager, she lives in Granite Bay, California.

Get the idea? Write as much as you want, and then go back and delete most of it. (Don't really throw it away, though; you'll need the long stuff for your proposal.) Keep the good stuff that sells you and your book.

About the Book, Take One

Let's see how that works with a description of a book. Here is a two-paragraph description of our imaginary book *Accurate Arthritis Answers*.

Accurate Arthritis Answers is a unique idea. Instead of relying on the advice of just one arthritis doctor, I plan to seek out advice from top arthritis experts around the world. Research schools, government studies, magazine and newspaper articles, and medical journals will all be scoured to cull the latest information on arthritis. Arthritis sufferers will learn about cutting-edge medical treatments, the dramatic difference that exercise can have, and the effects of nutrition upon their affliction. Special attention will be paid to recent discoveries in alternative treatments, such as herbal therapy.

The book itself is divided into four different sections: Traditional Medicine, Nutrition, Exercise, and Alternative Therapies. Each section is written by a top expert in the field. Organized in an easy-to-understand style, *Accurate Arthritis Answers* will also contain colorful charts, illustrations, and a useful medical glossary. At 175 pages, the book will be a small and handy size for the lay reader.

About the Book, Take Two

Okay, how do we say that in one short, punchy paragraph? Like this:

> *Accurate Arthritis Answers* fills a real need in the marketplace. Unlike other large medical books, it is a short, easy-to-read book for the general reader. Instead of relying on the knowledge of just one doctor, it brings together the expertise of a wide range of international experts in the field. All types of treatments are examined, from the traditional medical approach to the latest research in herbal and other nontraditional remedies. Arthritis sufferers will now be able to turn to one single source for all the latest information.

Slush Pile

Does your pitch have a professional tone? Why not read a few book pitches from the pros to find out. At Michael Cader's Publishersmarketplace.com website you can read actual book pitches being made by literary agents. Click on "rights available" to read what is being pitched and how it is being pitched.

Writer, Edit Thyself

Go ahead, give this exercise a try. Start writing long descriptions of your book, your market, and yourself. Then shrink them down to query size. You'll quickly learn to spot what needs to stay and what needs to go.

A one-page query letter does have more than three paragraphs sometimes. What is your strongest area? Your credentials, your book idea, or the potential market? Choose your strength and devote two entire paragraphs to it.

Why does your query letter have to be perfect? A well-written query letter is your best shot at seeing your book published. So work on it, over and over again, until it looks right to you. This is not the time to dash off a quick little something. This is the time to set aside a week to perfect your query letter.

Writer Candy Chand has got her queries down to a sweet science. "Every one of my queries is four paragraphs long," she told us. "In the first paragraph I introduce myself and my other published projects. I spend two paragraphs describing my new project, and then close with one paragraph thanking them for considering it." Does it work? She's sold several projects that way, including *Ashley's Garden* from Andrews McMeel.

What Not to Say

Agent Martha Casselman is not alone in her pet peeves. Here are five things she (and most other agents) don't want you to put in your query letter:

- The kind of computer program you write in (it doesn't really matter)

- That this is an exclusive submission if it really isn't (don't lie)

- Asking after her health and happiness (she wants to know more about you)

- How well you can write (show her how well you can write)

- Stating that if an editor doesn't want this particular project, you'd be happy to write anything he or she wants (you're writing to demonstrate your knowledge and your talent, not your flexibility)

Hook 'Em Early

The best query letters have a strong hook in the first two lines. What is a strong hook? Something that grabs the readers' attention and keeps them reading. Let's look at a good example, a query letter that co-author Sheree received:

Dear Sheree,

More than 2.2 million families in the United States are affected by death every year—6,027 each day.

Studies reveal that more than 90 percent of the survivors of a death in the family are unprepared to handle the heavy responsibilities that arise when a death occurs.

What do you do first? And then what? How do you cope with the hundreds of urgent decisions and details to be handled in the difficult days and weeks ahead?

People don't know what to do, and—just as unsettling—they don't know how to behave in the face of death. When death comes, the survivors must not only cope with their grief, but at the same time organize an event of great significance emotionally, socially, and financially. They urgently need help.

Saying Goodbye with Love is the only step-by-step workbook for survivors who are responsible for handling the practical, legal, and financial decisions after a death in the family. This book is not a dense, sociological treatise as are so many books on death. Instead, *Saying Goodbye with Love* is a warm and well-organized "tool kit" for use in a time of crisis.

The first question people ask me when they learn of this book is: "Did this book come from your own experiences?" The answer is "Yes." Most of all, it comes from looking after the details following the deaths of my grandmother, Jenny; my friend, Paul; my cousin, Bob; and my sister, Toni. My experience as a technical writer taught me to organize information in a way that is easily accessible and useful to the reader.

Readers have told me that *Saying Goodbye with Love* is like having a knowledgeable, organized friend at their side.

Would you like to see a proposal? I've included an SASE. I look forward to your response by phone, fax, mail, or e-mail.

Yours truly,

Sheila (Simpson) Martin

Great letter. Sheree picked up the phone and called her right away. Why? Let's take a closer look at this query letter:

♦ In her first few paragraphs, the writer established a huge market for her book (more than 2.2 million families a year, 6,027 a day), and a big need for her book ("people don't know what to do …").

♦ She describes the book itself ("the only step-by-step workbook for survivors") in one short paragraph.

♦ When describing her own credentials, she takes what could have been a drawback (no professional experience with medicine or grief counseling) and puts a very positive spin on it by first mentioning her own personal experiences with death and then tying in her background ("My experience as a technical writer taught me to …").

It all pulls together into a very effective query letter that grabbed an agent's attention. It also grabbed a publisher's attention; Sheree sold the project to The Crossroads Publishing Company.

> **Experts Say** _____
>
> "Here are the three things I look for in a query letter," says literary agent Bill Adler Jr., based in Washington, D.C. "One, that the writer can write. Two, that she understands her market. Three, that she is professional in her approach to me." Don't be overly familiar in your query letter. You are not writing to a long-lost college buddy. You are trying to interest a professional literary agent or editor in taking you on as a client. Use a businesslike tone in your writing.

Another Approach

Here is another good approach for a query letter to an agent:

Dear Bill,

Mmmm, chocolate. The bad news is it can't make you thin. The good news is it could make you rich! Investing seems like such a scary thing to do nowadays, the time is right for a reassuring book that helps investors feel at ease.

In several best-selling financial planning books, Peter Lynch has urged Americans to become better stock pickers by using what he calls "The Power of Common Knowledge" and simply paying attention to what goes on in their own neighborhood. As a longtime stockbroker and financial planner, I have taken Lynch's theory one step closer to home by advising chocolate lovers to simply walk around their kitchens, peek into their refrigerators, and look closely at vending machines for terrific investment ideas!

Chocolate Can Make You Rich: The Chocolate Lover's Guide to the Stock Market will give investors a whole new way of looking at the stock market. Forget "Blue Chip" stocks; think "Chocolate Chip" stocks instead! Chocolate cookies, cakes, candies, drinks, and more—Americans literally do eat chocolate by the ton. What stronger, more stable market can there be? When I give speeches, I like to tell my audience it's time they put their money where their mouth is!

Many investors—particularly women—are scared off by volatile high-tech stocks in industries that they don't understand, and have watched their investments plummet. With the knowledge gained in *Chocolate Can Make You Rich*, skittish investors could invest in solid megacompanies such as Procter & Gamble (who make the Duncan Hines brand of cake and brownie mixes), Hershey Foods

(Reese's Peanut Butter Cups, York Mint Patties, and their own Hershey's brand), or Archer Daniels Midland (corn syrup producers, without which candy bars would cease to exist). More adventurous investors will learn about Starbucks Coffee (now not only the kings of coffee, but leading ice cream makers as well) or Eskimo Pies (yes, a publicly traded company!).

I have been a stockbroker for the past 10 years, ever since graduating from UC Berkeley with a degree in business. I developed my theories about "comfort stocks" as a way to make women feel more comfortable with investing, and I would like to bring my message to greater numbers of readers.

A 30-page proposal is available for *Chocolate Can Make You Rich*. Chapters include "Frozen Assets," "Sugar-Coated Investments," "Eat and Grow Rich," and many more. I look forward to hearing from you soon.

Regards,

Julia Berenson

> **Experts Say**
>
> Robert Kosberg is known as Hollywood's "Mr. Pitch." He pitches 20 to 50 ideas a year to studio heads. What can you learn from him for your book pitch? "Ask yourself if your idea can be boiled down to two power-packed sentences that generate excitement." Look for more ideas on his website at www.moviepitch.com.

"Ummm, chocolate." Now there's a delicious hook! Kept you reading, didn't it?

Chocolate can make you rich? Sounds like a goofy idea, so the writer's second paragraph wisely links her idea to those of perennial best-selling author Peter Lynch—a smart way to look even smarter.

She quickly describes the book and the theory, and establishes herself as qualified (a stockbroker for 10 years and public speaker) to write on this topic. By describing the names of some of her chapters, she whets the readers' appetite for more. It's a good letter.

Write a Good One and Then Let It Be

Go ahead and write that query letter—as perfect a letter as you can make it. But once you drop it in the mail, leave it alone. Believe it or not, many authors out there can't leave it alone even after mailing it.

Agents and editors have all received them, the letters that begin, "Please disregard the query letter that I mailed to you on January 22, and replace it with this version, which I think more accurately captures the essence of my book." Or "This information should be added to the proposal that I sent to you last week. Please remove pages 4 through 8 and replace them with these new pages." Crazy, but true.

Do not under any circumstances attempt to do this! Once your query letter disappears through the slot in the mailbox, move on to something else in your life. Don't lie awake at night wondering how you might have done it differently. It will just drive you nuts.

Online Etiquette

As in other parts of the world, publishing is going online. And although online queries would have been strange just a few years ago, they are becoming more acceptable. Agent Bill Adler Jr. enjoys receiving online queries from prospective authors. It gives him a good chance to answer back quickly and not make writers wait for weeks for him to open the mail. Sheree, on the other hand, doesn't care much for lengthy online queries.

Each agent has his own policy, of course. The major guides to agents, such as Jeff Herman's *Writer's Guide to Book Editors, Publishers, and Literary Agents*, have only a few e-mail addresses listed now, but as the years go by, expect to see more of them. It is worth typing an agent's name into your search engine—some even have home pages. Sheree's website, at shereebee.com, was designed to help writers.

The nice thing about an e-mail query is that you won't have to worry about choosing the wrong kind of envelope! Candy Chand has had wonderful success in e-mailing queries. "Don't be afraid to try; the worst thing you will hear is 'no.'" E-mail queries can also get a response in minutes—Candy has sometimes heard back almost instantly. Sure beats checking the mail every day for a sign of your SASE!

SASEs and Other Ways to Hear Back

Remember the definition of "unsolicited submission"? It's one that the agent did not ask you to send. Because you are sending something that was not requested, it is up to you to cover the cost of getting a reply. Always include an *SASE* with your correspondence. That way the agent can easily reply.

If you want to know whether your query arrived at its destination, include a small, self-addressed and stamped postcard that the agent can just pop into the mail. Write something like this:

> Yes, the attached query letter was received in my office on _____.

Bookmarks

What is an **SASE?** It's short for a "self-addressed, stamped envelope." Never send a query letter or proposal without one. The publishing industry would go broke if editors had to pay to return all the unsolicited material they receive. If you haven't included an SASE and the agent or editor isn't interested, your stuff goes straight into the recycling bin. Harsh, but true.

You can also send your query letter via FedEx or UPS. This is more expensive than the good old U.S. mail, but it also lets you track your letter and ease your mind about whether it ever arrived. (Two-day express mail is considerably less costly than next-day air.)

Do not call an agent's office to ask whether your query letter arrived. You will appear anxious and unprofessional.

Bookmarks

As in most businesses, assistants make the world go 'round. **Assistants** are the unsung young folks who open the mail, sort the mail, answer the phone, and otherwise keep an office running. Chances are, your query will be seen first by someone's assistant. Editorial assistants, literary agents' assistants, production assistants—be nice to them all. Today's assistant might be tomorrow's editor-in-chief.

But They Asked for It!

You met an agent at a writer's summer camp who encouraged you to send your proposal? Congratulations. But please don't assume that the agent remembers the invitation. Remind him in the first line of your query letter: "We met at the Mendocino Writers' Conference, and you asked that I send the following proposal." An agent might meet a hundred writers at conferences throughout the year (and talk to another hundred on the phone). So don't be hurt if he doesn't remember you or your book. And don't forget to include an SASE with your query.

Voicemail

And if you are anxious about a query that you've mailed to an agent or editor, should you ever—*gasp*—call them to check up? Try not to. We understand the impulse, but for unsolicited queries the protocol revolves around written correspondence. If you do break down and place a call to check up, please leave a pleasant message. Sheree has received more than one hostile voicemail message from an anxious writer demanding to know if a package has arrived or when they might hear a response. The folks that left those messages received their rejections swiftly!

The Rules

Now that we have given you the rules, please believe us when we say it is in your best interest to follow them. If you try to get around them, if you try things that you think are clever or devious, it can backfire. At the very least, an agent might think you are annoying. In the worst-case scenario, you could come off as a nut—and agents are not very eager to sign up nuts! Let them know that you have done your homework, that you know how the routine works, and that you will follow the rules.

Having said that, we must confess that sometimes people do break the rules and succeed because of it. And sometimes people win the lottery. But as a first-time writer, you improve your chances tremendously by playing it straight.

The Least You Need to Know

- Query letters should be one page long and should contain a brief description of the book, the market, and the author.
- Practice being brief by editing your writing down to one powerful paragraph.
- Don't use a query letter to air your grievances with anyone.
- Unless you include an SASE with your query letter, you might never hear an answer.
- A good query letter states its purpose up front in the first paragraph.
- Be businesslike. Don't try to be clever or witty; don't use scented paper or fancy typestyles.

Chapter 8

Bulletproof Nonfiction Book Proposals

In This Chapter

- ◆ What goes into a book proposal
- ◆ Building a book proposal, step by step
- ◆ Selling your idea
- ◆ Selling your market
- ◆ Selling yourself as an author
- ◆ Choosing the best sample chapter

Congratulations! You wrote a great query letter, and an agent or editor has asked to see your book proposal! Uh, now what do you do?

The Art of Proposal Writing

In a book proposal, you are proposing an idea for a book. You *propose* to do it because, in most cases, you haven't actually written the book yet!

You Mean I Don't Have to Write the Book First?

We'd like to let you in on an industry secret. Here is how most professional nonfiction writers work:

♦ First, they come up with an idea for a book.

♦ Next, they write a book proposal 20 or so pages long.

♦ Then they send it off to their agent and wait.

If a publisher decides to publish the book, the writer sits down in front of the computer and writes the book. But if there are no takers, the professional writer comes up with another idea and starts the process over again.

That's right. To sell a nonfiction book and get a contract from a publisher, you don't really have to write the book first. You can write it later. First, you have to write a good proposal.

> **Hot Off the Press** _____
>
> Some proposals are long, some are short, but Jennifer thinks she wrote the smallest one ever. It was on a mini-sticky note. Many years ago she'd written up a long list of personal goals, one of which was a reminder to "wear more cashmere." Jennifer liked the way that phrase sounded so much that she wrote it on the tiny yellow note and stuck it to the side of her computer. Fast forward to the summer of 2001, when an editor who'd seen that note on her computer years before called and asked her to turn the idea into a book! Say hello to *Wear More Cashmere: 101 Luxurious Ways to Pamper Your Inner Princess* (Fair Winds).

But When Should I Start the Proposal?

Don't even think about querying agents or editors until you have written at least some portion of your book proposal. Not only will it give you a more solid sense of what you are doing (and help you distill it into a good query), but it also cuts down on the lag time between when an agent or editor says, "I'd love to see your stuff," and when you can actually send it. So get a jump on things and start now.

Building a Book Proposal

Here's a short list of what you should include in your book proposal. It'll give you a quick *overview*. Then read on for a longer description of each key element. If you have trouble understanding any elements, don't panic. In the back of the book, there's an entire sample book proposal for you to read.

Read through this list once, and then sit down and begin to write your own version. A book proposal should develop before your very eyes.

The parts of a book proposal are as follows:

◆ A cover page with the title, your name, your address, and your phone number

◆ A three- to five-part pitch

◆ A detailed table of contents

◆ A sample chapter of the book

◆ Attachments such as recent news articles about the topic or recent news articles about the author

Bookmarks

Be prepared to answer the question, "What is the overview of your book?" An **overview** is another term for the synopsis. In the movie business, they call it a "take-away." What will your reader take away with him after reading the book? Write it out in one succinct sentence.

Slush Pile

Remember how businesslike your query letters should be? A book proposal should be equally businesslike in appearance—no fancy graphics, colored paper, or elaborate typestyles. Your writing skills are on display here, nothing else.

Your Cover Page

This is a great first step. It takes only about five minutes to do it, and once you have made a cover page, you can consider yourself on the road to building a book proposal. Flip to Appendix C in the back of the book and take a look at the cover page for the *Exit Strategy* book proposal. Follow that same basic design, and fill in your own title, name, and address.

If you are sending off the proposal to an agent who requested it, put your name and address on the cover page. Once you have an agent and she is shopping your book to editors, she'll put her own name and address on your proposal's cover page.

After you've made a cover page, print it out and hang it on the wall next to your computer. Whenever you are feeling discouraged, glance up and see your title and your name in large type!

It is important to note that we just mean a plain cover page for your proposal, not a fancy, highly designed idea for your future book. As you will learn in later chapters, authors (and even editors!) have little control over the actual cover, so you should not invest time, energy, or money into this part of the proposal.

The Pitch

Ever heard the sales term *pitch?* In a book proposal, you are trying to pitch a book idea. The pitch section of the proposal can be broken down into five smaller parts:

- The idea
- The market
- The competition
- The publicity and promotion potential
- The author

Remember all that work you did while writing your query? Those long paragraphs describing the book idea, the market, and the author? Pull them out now and see what you can use.

What a Great Idea!

First, describe the idea behind the book. What kind of a book is it? What kind of information will it contain? Describe your book in one tight sentence, and then elaborate on the idea for several paragraphs. Co-author Sheree tells her clients that this is their chance to describe the contents of their book "enticingly and thoroughly."

Bookmarks

Some folks out there are known as **proposal doctors,** also known as book doctors. You can hire one of them to help you write your proposal. They are mostly former editors or longtime writers, and you will see their advertisements in the back of writers' magazines. You might also ask an agent for a recommendation.

Off to Market

Now describe the market for your book. Who are the millions of potential readers? Why will they be interested in your book? The market section should contain as much hard data about *demographics,* trends, and other facts as you can get your hands on. Remember to avoid using the sentence "Everyone should read this book."

The market section of your proposal could also contain information about possible non-bookstore outlets for your book. Where will these millions of potential readers be found? In gardening stores, lingerie shops, or hospitals? Let the publisher know if there are specialized sources of distribution that target these folks.

Bookmarks

Publishers love **demographics**. Publishing is an inexact science, and the more an author can cite demographics about population statistics, the size of an age group, or personal income levels when describing the potential audience for his book, the better the agent, editor, and publisher can sleep at night.

Compete with the Best

This is an easy section to write. As a matter of fact, you've already done much of the work. You've spent hours wandering the aisles of your local bookstore. At last you get to display the knowledge you gained!

To create the competition section, list all the books already published with which your book will compete. The purpose of this section is to establish that you know what else has been done in your area and that you believe your book fills a need that exists. Describe these books at length, but also be fair and balanced in assessing what you perceive to be their weaknesses. Do not attack. Remember the advice of former Hyperion senior editor Laurie Abkemeier from Chapter 6? Never use the competition section to slam other books. You never know who will end up reading your book proposal!

A secondary purpose of the competition section is to highlight books that, instead of competing with your proposed book, complement it. Complementary books can help you establish that a book like yours will succeed. Flip to the sample proposal in the back of this book to see how this works. Check out the section that describes best-selling small business books. This helps you to use the success of other books to build your case.

This is also a good place to point out how your book could cross over and succeed in two markets at once. Publishers love the dazzling idea that one book might sell to two different types of people, for example, that a Christian fiction book like the *Left Behind* series might someday grow so large as to burst out into the mainstream market, or that a money workbook for couples could work in the finance niche as well as in the relationship section.

La Publicité

The publicity and promotion section is of critical importance in today's publishing market. All publishers want to know how hard the author plans to work, how many media contacts the author already has, and whether this topic lends itself to *publicity* and *promotion*. So the more you can supply here, the better. How do you find this stuff out? By paying attention to how often the media writes about your topic or about the audience that your book targets.

Publicity Opportunities

Using *Accurate Arthritis Answers* as an example, quickly come up with some of the different places that this book could get publicity:

♦ National magazines targeted to older Americans (such as *Modern Maturity*), and the national network of small newspapers for seniors

♦ The morning news shows, such as *Today* and *Good Morning, America*, which frequently devote time to issues of health

♦ Nationally syndicated radio health shows, which are growing in popularity

♦ Health editors at all major newspapers and magazines

♦ Newsletters in retirement communities, such as the various Sun City communities around the country

> **Bookmarks** _____
>
> What's the difference between **publicity** and **promotion?** The two words sometimes seem to be interchangeable. The bottom line is—the bottom line! Publicity is free. Promotion (which can mean advertising) usually costs money.

Is It Especially Timely?

Are there special times of the year when your book could be promoted? Talk about the potential for gift or seasonal promotions. Is there any major event (such as an upcoming election, or a hot new movie) that your book ties into? Mention it.

Bulk Sales?

This is also a good place to mention any possibilities you see for large sales of the book to groups, businesses, and organizations. Publishers are very interested in pursuing large, nonreturnable sales. Using the arthritis book again, here's how you could say it in a proposal:

> The pharmaceutical manufacturer behind one of the major drugs used to treat arthritis has expressed a willingness to purchase 2,500 copies of *Accurate Arthritis Answers* to use as a premium. The author also intends to seek out other large group purchases for the book.

If you already have a solid commitment for a large buy for your book, be sure to mention it. If you plan to buy a large number of the books yourself (to give away to clients or sell at speeches), mention that also. Publishers are interested in protecting their investment, and this kind of information could help tip the balance in your favor.

A Stamp of Approval

Have you approached any big-name authors or professionals who are willing to give you endorsements for your book? Let the publishers know who you plan to approach, and if you have existing ties with these folks. Deepak Chopra is your brother-in-law? Colin Powell lives next door? Write it down! If you do have close personal or professional ties to big-name folks, approach them now. It is even better to have an endorsement in hand when you are in the proposal stage. This, too, could help tip the balance in your favor.

Let's Hear About You!

Finally, you'll need to include information about you, the author. Here's where you can really let loose and brag about what you have accomplished in life: awards, honors, education, experience—pile it on. Let everyone know about your writing experience, publishing history (if you have one), and professional success. Do you have local, statewide, or national recognition in your field? Talk about it here. Try to position yourself as someone uniquely qualified to write this book.

Are you a skilled public speaker or presenter? Do you hold seminars or classes that relate to your book? The publisher needs to be reassured that you are not only a qualified author, but that you can also be an effective public image for the book. If you have professional photos on hand, include them. But don't send candid snapshots that would undermine your authority.

Now that you understand everything that goes into the pitch section of your proposal, you're ready to move on to the other sections.

Do You Need a Partner?

While working on this section of your proposal, please take the time to seriously consider how strong your credentials will look to the editor who is considering them. Are they as strong as they should be or could be? Might you have a better chance at selling this book if you teamed up with another expert in the field? Keep an open mind to the possibility, as that might well help you sell the project.

Detailed Table of Contents

That's right, you'll need to include a detailed table of contents. Not only should you list each and every chapter, you also should include a short paragraph to describe each chapter or section. This is sometimes referred to as a chapter summary. Describe not only the purpose of each chapter, but also some of the content.

Sample Chapters

Including a good representative sample chapter is important. Not only is the writing itself important, but so is the topic. A well-chosen sample chapter can be a powerful thing. Just as the query letter was a way of introducing yourself to a stranger (and presenting yourself in the best possible light), so, too, is the sample chapter. It gives you the opportunity to influence the way you are perceived. It's important that the chapter you include is representative of the rest of the book in style, content, and length. It's not unusual to include Chapter 1, but if Chapter 1 is not representative, replace it with one that is. Better yet, include Chapter 1 plus a later representative chapter. We'll give you a great example.

Write What They'd Enjoy Reading

When we were trying to get the contract to write the first edition of this very book, *The Complete Idiot's Guide to Getting Published*, we needed to write and submit a sample chapter. With all the possible aspects of getting published to choose from, which do you think we chose? Publicity. We wrote a sample chapter about book publicity and how important it is for authors to work hard to publicize their books. We included lots of information about how hardworking authors can make a big difference in the sales success of their books.

Send an Upbeat Message

Why did we choose that topic? Because we wanted to send a positive message to the publisher: that these two women, Sheree Bykofsky and Jennifer Basye Sander, know what they are doing. They understand how to make a book sell. They will work their tails off to make this book succeed.

Why choose a chapter with a negative tone (like one that talks about the high rate of book returns, or the changes afoot in the publishing business) when we could do something positive? Not only was the chapter on an upbeat topic, but it positioned us as go-getters. Hey, we got the contract, didn't we?

So what should you choose for your sample chapter? Choose something that will help the reader. And the reader, in this case, is not the general reading public, but the agent or editor reading your proposal. Give that person a sample chapter that will make him feel great or learn something new. Don't choose a chapter that will leave him depressed and reaching for a box of tissues. Here is an excellent opportunity to make him feel good about you and your ideas. Look at your material and see if there is a section there that will get the editor or agent nodding their head in recognition or agreement. Help them say "yes" to you!

The Kitchen Sink

The very last thing that goes into your proposal is important: evidence of your credibility and that of your book. Here is an opportunity to include all the media attention you and/or your topic have gotten and that you've been saving up. With an impressive bundle of clippings, you can establish yourself as an expert, and you can establish your topic as big.

Newspaper and Magazine Articles

Did we say *recent* articles? It is important to include only articles from the last five years. If all your clips date from years ago, an agent or editor will wonder what happened to your career in the meantime.

It is also important that the articles you include about your topic be recent. If you include dated material, it might appear that the topic itself is old news and that the book would not sell.

Be careful about the quality of the clippings you send. Ripped, smudged, or messy-looking clippings will do you no good. You are a professional, and you need to look like one. Make sure that you include only clear copies that are readable, neatly presented, and of a reasonable length. It is better to send nice new copies rather than large original clippings from a newspaper. And because you will be making many copies of your proposal, it is cheaper than buying up 20 copies of the newspaper on the day you appeared.

Slush Pile

No gimmicky presents should accompany your proposal unless they relate to the book itself. So a proposal for a book on chocolate truffles probably won't be harmed by sending along a box of samples. But don't send a box of truffles with your proposal for a book about world peace.

Video Clips

Videotapes of you being interviewed on a major television program are great to include as well. Short clips are best, though. Don't go overboard, as agents and editors will rarely watch an hour-long video. A professionally edited and labeled video clip is best. Worst is sending the wrong tape, like the one of your children in the bathtub. Be sure to label your tape clearly with your name and address, in case it gets separated from your proposal.

Hot Off the Press

"It sometimes seems like agents are on the frontline of weirdness," agent Natasha Kern says. "We get even more kooky stuff from strangers than publishers do. What are these people thinking when they send off such things? One guy sent me a picture of himself in his underwear. Come on!" One prospective author sent Sheree a pair of used shoes. So not only should you not send silly gifts to agents, but refrain from sending overly personal things. Agents are looking for talented, hard-working authors to represent, not for relationships.

Proposing Your Self-Published Book

If you have a self-published book that you are now trying to sell to a publisher, you must include a copy. Also include a brutally honest description of the sales and distribution of your self-published book. Did we say "brutally honest"? We mean it. Be sure to specify not only how well your own edition sold, but where and how you sold it—whether out of the trunk of your car or at Barnes & Noble. Under no circumstances should you fudge, puff up, or exaggerate how well it sold. Trust us, if you lie, you will be caught. And that will be the end of your chances of selling the book. It may work to your advantage if your book sold well to a limited audience (for example, through your newsletter) but never made it to the major bookstore chains. That way, if a publisher *does* release your book, it will appear fresh to a bookstore buyer, not seem like old news.

More than one self-published book has sold successfully to a major publisher. Two big examples are Robert Kiyosaki's *Rich Dad/Poor Dad* and Richard Paul Evans's first book *The Christmas Box*. Both sold well in their self-published editions and then received substantial advances from publishers.

Time to Get Writing!

Do you have a good handle on what goes into a book proposal now? We have included as an appendix the entire book proposal for one of co-author Jennifer's books, *Christmas Miracles*. Was it a successful proposal? Heck, yes. This proposal was so well received that the rights to this book were auctioned for a healthy six-figure advance. So get to work on your proposal, and you, too, might hit the jackpot!

The Least You Need to Know

- A book proposal is a 10- to 20-page description of the book, with supporting information.

- Professional nonfiction writers write a book proposal first; if it sells, then they write the book. You can do the same.

- The more compelling the information you provide about the market, the greater your chance of finding a publisher.

- Choose a sample chapter on a topic that will leave the reader (the editor or agent) with a good feeling.

- Include clean copies of recent newspaper and magazine articles about yourself and your topic.

- Do not send gifts or attention-getters with your proposal.

Chapter 9

Fun with Fiction

In This Chapter

- ◆ You've got to write the whole book first!
- ◆ Ready, set, query
- ◆ Writing a novel synopsis
- ◆ Now you've got an agent on the line!
- ◆ Summarizing your novel

When writing nonfiction, you can sell your book before you write it. No such luck with fiction. Fiction is a different ballgame with a more complex set of rules. It's harder to play and harder to win—but the rewards are enormous. The most successful novelists become, in effect, the brand names of the book business: King, Grisham, Rice, Crichton, Patterson, Steel. As the late best-selling author James Michener used to say, "You can't make a living [writing novels] but you can make a killing." Win in the very competitive field of fiction, and you can win big.

In this chapter, we'll tell you how to write query letters and book proposals for fiction. But before we do, let's look more in depth at the wide world of fiction.

So I Have to Write the Whole Book First?

Yes, to sell a work of fiction, you have to write the entire book first. Why? Because fiction requires more craftsmanship.

To write nonfiction, you need to know how to organize information in a clear and entertaining way. But writing fiction requires a mastery of myriad fiction techniques. From pacing to character, plotting to dialogue, more skill is required to pull it off. Moreover, a novel has a beginning, a middle, and an end—and lots of complications along the way. Publishers can't tell from an outline and a sample chapter alone if you can sustain a narrative and keep readers turning the pages for 250, 500, or maybe even 1,000 pages.

You have to supply them with proof, which is in the completed manuscript. You need to have written an entire novel before you can approach an agent to represent you. Agents, too, need to know that you can keep it up for hundreds of pages. Then, with masterpiece in hand, you can prove you've written a page-turner. You might become the successful novelist that you—and your mother—always dreamed you could be.

Want Support? Mingle with Other Writers

Writing may be a lonely business, but getting published doesn't have to be. Join a writers' organization so that you can keep abreast of new markets and trends and make valuable contacts with agents and editors.

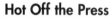

Hot Off the Press

"Belonging to Sisters in Crime has meant so much to me," says Terris Grimes, award-winning mystery book author. "The other writers are so open, so encouraging. Without their support, I wouldn't have had the starch to go on and finish my first book. It's important for creative people to get together in a group—if only a group of two!"

If you are completely antisocial, don't despair. Many of the organizations in Appendix B have online chapters you can join. You can cybernetwork without leaving the privacy of your own computer.

You can also sign up for a writing class at your local college, which will help you make friends and contacts even as you polish up your writing skills. Here again, you don't have to leave home if you don't want to; there are a number of writing classes and seminars available online, run by writing organizations, local universities and such online "distance learning" centers as www.ed2go.com.

And Then I Have to Write the Whole Book, Again?

You and your mother are not alone. Agents and publishers like nothing better than successful novelists. Like the Energizer Bunny, successful novelists just keep on going and going and going. They sell, sell, sell. New York literary agent Ethan Ellenberg, who represents fiction writers in all genres, puts it this way: "A successful novelist can write 10 or 20 books over 10 or 20 years."

That's the long haul, and the long haul is what publishers are looking for when it comes to fiction. It takes time and money to build an audience for a new novelist. Publishers are willing to spend that time and money when they believe that they are building a new brand name for their house. Brand names attract a huge audience, whose loyalty sustains through book after book after book.

Once that audience exists, though, the sky's the limit. People who read fiction read their favorite writers, i.e., their favorite brands. And when they find a new favorite writer, they read everything that writer ever wrote—as well as everything he or she goes on to write in the future. This makes successful novelists an excellent investment for publishers. It more than makes up for the initial investment required to build an author's name.

But Can You Do It Again?

That's why it's not enough to show the publishing world that you can write one great novel: You have to convince 'em that you can do it over and over and over that you, too, are in it for the long haul and that you can keep 'em turning pages through 8 or 12 books over 10 or 20 years.

Most important, you have to convince 'em that you aren't just a good writer, but that you're also a good storyteller.

The Never-Ending Story

Literary agent Don Maass, author of 14 novels as well as *The Career Novelist: A Literary Agent Offers Strategies for Success*, advises aspiring novelists to make the distinction between good writing and good storytelling. Artful language does not make good storytelling. Conflict does.

"John Grisham is not known as a great stylist, but he's a great storyteller," says Maass. "Take the opening scene of *The Firm*. It's just a job interview, but it's riveting because of the conflict. In a Grisham novel, there's conflict on every page, and conflict keeps readers turning the page."

Forget Dickens!

According to Maass, the biggest mistake many fiction writers make is to rely on nineteenth-century storytelling techniques—techniques that no longer engage today's fiction reader.

"I see so many manuscripts that begin with long, rambling descriptions, descriptions that would be great in a novel published in 1890, but not in a novel published in this era of MTV," says Maass.

What works today is the novel that is written cinematically. Film and TV storytelling has become the vernacular for audiences the world over. Not only will cinematic storytelling resonate with your readers, it will also attract film and TV interest, which not only increases your appeal to prospective publishers but ultimately increases your potential audience exponentially.

Elmore Leonard, author of dozens of best-selling novels over more than thirty years, admits that it was the film version of his novel *Get Shorty* that made him truly famous.

"When I meet somebody and I tell them I'm a writer and they've never heard of me, I ask them if they've seen *Get Shorty*. 'Oh, yeah,' they'll say, 'great movie.'"

With the success of *Get Shorty* the movie, Elmore Leonard won a new audience—an audience far greater than the book audience. The movie also brought Leonard more readers, making him a bigger brand-name author than ever. (For more on adapting novels to the screen, see Linda Seger's *The Art of Adaptation* or catch the Bravo TV show, *Page to Screen*.)

Writing in a cinematic way will help you get your start in the book business, and set the stage for crossing over into other media as well.

Read, Read, Read

So where do you go to learn twenty-first-century storytelling techniques? Surprise! Go to a bookstore.

"The best course is also the least expensive," says Maass. He advises his clients to study today's great storytellers. "Read, study, and analyze. Then write your own powerful stories—stories with conflict on every page. Tell the best damn stories that you can."

We'll take Maass's advice one step further. Read books about writing written by writers you admire. We like *Novel Ideas: Contemporary Authors Share the Creative Process*. It includes long interviews with best-selling authors like Tony Hillerman and Wally Lamb and goes into great detail about plot, dialogue, developing characters, and of course, dealing with editors!

Writing Is Rewriting

Joyce Carol Oates likens writing the first draft of a novel to "building a house." The second draft, she says, is when "you decorate it."

Just as a house is not a home until you've moved in, furnished it, and invited friends and family over, a manuscript is not a novel ready for public viewing until you've rewritten it. Be prepared to do at least three drafts—a first draft to get the story down; a second draft to refine the story, capitalize on its strengths, eliminate its weaknesses, and layer meaning and theme; and a final polish for language and style.

As we've noted, writing good fiction isn't easy. Don't panic if you know your work needs revising, but you have no clue where or how to begin. There are people out there who can help you figure out what you need to do to make your story shine.

Take It to the Next Level

The days of Maxwell Perkins are over. Gone are the editors who discover a diamond in the rough in the *slush pile*, and then spend months, even years helping the writer rewrite until the manuscript is ready for publication. Editors today don't have the time or the energy for that sort of intensive editorial work that their predecessors like Perkins gave to such raw young luminaries as F. Scott Fitzgerald, Thomas Wolfe, and Marjorie Kinnan Rawlings.

Bookmarks

The **slush pile** is where all the unsolicited manuscripts are piled, waiting to be returned.

If you're thinking that agents have taken over where editors have left off, think again. While it's true that some agents do develop close working *editorial* relationships with their authors—Al Zuckerman and Ken Follett come to mind—most do not. Agents are first and foremost salespeople; their job is to sell your work, not edit and revise it.

Still, you can find professionals who can help you make sure that your manuscript is publisher-ready before you send it out the door. Find an experienced editor who will critique your work, suggest revisions, and help polish your prose. Ask your writing friends and any publishing professionals you may know in the book business for referrals; you can also look online and in industry publications. Be sure to choose an editor who has experience in your genre. Remember that word-of-mouth is the usually best recommendation; ask for references. Rates vary, but you'll find ballpark ranges for editing fees in the Writer's Market, at the National Writers Union and online.

Ready, Set, Query

Okay, so you, the great storyteller, have written a great novel with an engaging protagonist. There's conflict on every page. The ending not only satisfies your readers, but it leaves them screaming for a sequel. You've pounded out several hundred pages that readers won't be able to turn fast enough—and rewritten those pages until they sing.

Congratulations, you wrote a novel. Now take that 12-pound doorstop and put it away where you can't see it (and the dog can't eat it).

What? After we insist that you write the whole novel first, now we tell you to put it away?

Exactly. The last thing anyone in publishing wants to do is read a 12-pound manuscript from an unknown writer. Agents and editors are drowning in them. All those publishing cartoons you've seen in *The New Yorker*, the ones with the editor sitting behind a desk mounded high with papers, are true. You have to sell these people on the idea of reading your hefty tome. That's where your query letter comes in.

Targeting your queries should reveal better results that the shotgun approach. Seek out those editors and agents most likely to appreciate your story—and query them first. You'll find their names in the acknowledgments pages of your favorite books, and/or the books most like your own. You can also find them in industry publications like *Publishers Weekly* and the online Publishers Lunch, both of which feature deals made in the fiction business. Find out who's representing/buying novels like your own—and put them at the top of your to-be-queried list.

Did you read Chapters 7 and 8? They were good introductions to what comes next, especially for you.

Introducing the Mighty You

Your query letter is your major sales tool. It's a one-page letter that sells an agent on taking a chance on you. Your query must convince your quarry to invest several minutes, hours, and even days evaluating your novel—all this on the off-chance that the time invested will pay off. Remember, no one pays agents a salary. They invest hundreds of hours looking at stuff in the hopes that they can find a writer who will someday bring in the dough.

All that in one page, huh? It can be done. The trick is to keep the query simple, sweet, and sell, sell, sell. Here's how you break it down.

First Paragraph: What Kind of Book You've Written

You've written a 55,000-word mystery set in Jamaica at a Club Med titled *Dead Men Don't Date*. Skip the cute introductions; get straight to the point by describing the genre, your concept, and a sentence or two about the plot. The only exception is if you've met the agent at a writers' conference or you've been referred by a mutual friend or colleague. If so, mention that first. As with every business, publishing is a business of people. Any kind of personal connection counts.

Second Paragraph: What Your Book Is About

Dead Men Don't Date is a story about young, unpublished romance novelist Melissa Manhattan, who escapes the cold, slushy, January streets of her native New York City in search of sun, sex, and a multibook contract at a writers' conference in Aruba— only to wake up and find the publishing industry's leading sleaze-bag agent dead in her king-size Club Med bed. Through a combination of wits, pluck, and an uncommon knowledge of deadly voodoo poisons, our girl Melissa solves the murder, saves the life of the biggest independent romance publisher in the business, and lands a six-figure contract as well as a very attractive and well-connected publicist—not to mention bringing the murderer (a disturbed ghostwriter driven to the edge after years of putting his sexy prose into lesser writers' mouths) to justice.

Third Paragraph: Why Only You Could Write This

You grew up in New York, where your mother worked as a secretary at a big publishing house. You spent your summers in the Caribbean helping your father with his life's work, the cataloging and classifying of voodoo poisons. You have met a sleaze-bag agent and personally know two ghostwriters committed to mental institutions for the foreseeable future.

Fourth Paragraph: Other Impressive Stuff

You studied creative writing in college and wrote your master's thesis on "The Importance of Poisons in Agatha Christie's Poirot Novels." After school, you worked for a couple years as a reporter for the *Bronx Cheer*. You have published a number of short stories in the mystery magazines, both print and online. You serve as president of your local Sisters in Crime

Slush Pile

You won't make it very far if you do any of the following: hand-write your query letter, fail to send it to an agent who represents fiction, spell the agent's name wrong, or spell anything wrong. And please, don't say "fiction novel." It's repetitively redundant.

chapter. You are already hard at work on book two of the Melissa Manhattan series, *Dead Men Don't Call You Back*.

Fifth Paragraph: How to Reach You

You would be happy to send a copy of the manuscript for review; feel free to contact you at home or at work anytime. You have also enclosed an SASE—as well as your cell phone number and e-mail address. You look forward to hearing from them.

How Hard Can That Be?

Writing an effective query letter ultimately depends on salesmanship. For some reason, many people who can write great novels cannot write a decent sales letter. So if you feel that your efforts to sell yourself and your work on paper fall flat, don't despair. Enlist the help of a copywriter friend or colleague to help you punch up your pitch. If you don't know anyone with that skill, hire someone. Look in the Yellow Pages or online for freelance advertising copywriters.

Remember, this one-page query letter is your foot in the door. It's worth investing more than a little time and money on perfecting your query. So when the door opens up a crack, you want to slip in a Gucci loafer, not those old sneakers you wore to paint the front room.

Also be sure to enclose an SASE, and sign all the query letters yourself.

An Invitation for a Proposal!

You come home from a hard day at work to see the message light blinking on your phone. Could this be the call? Has your query letter hooked an agent?

"I'd really like to see more," the agent says. "Can you send me a proposal?"

A proposal for a novel? If you read the chapter on nonfiction proposals, you now know all the different types of information that goes into one of those. But what on earth do you put into a fiction proposal?

Very little, actually. Here is what goes into a fiction proposal:

- A synopsis of the novel
- The first 50 pages of the novel, or the first 3 chapters, whichever is longer
- Information about the author

Unlike a nonfiction proposal, you won't have to spend countless hours analyzing the competing titles. Novels are generally understood to stand on their own, not to compete directly with similar novels on similar themes. You won't have to do research and include data on the market for the novel. The market is understood—it's people who read fiction.

So let's see how to put together a *synopsis*.

Bookmarks

Before an agent or editor will read your whole novel, he will want to read your synopsis. A **synopsis** is a 10-page long summary of your novel, written in the present tense, in the third person. It spells out the plot of your novel in an effective and readable way.

Summarize, Please

Why do you need to write a synopsis if you've already written the whole novel? Here again, it is a question of time. Agents and editors aren't going to plow through your 12-pound manuscript to see if your plot is full of holes. They can figure it out by skimming a 1- to 10-page synopsis. They also don't have room in those cluttered offices for an extra 30 chapters when they can tell in 50 pages or less that your characters play like cardboard cutouts and that your pacing is wildly uneven.

Like the query, writing a synopsis is an art all its own, with its own set of rules.

Hook 'Em Again?

Entertaining and scintillating? How can you condense an entire novel into a few pages, much less be entertaining and scintillating? Granted, it's not easy to breathe life into such a stilted narrative, but it can be done. Many writers spice up their synopses with snippets of dialogue and small bits of scenes. Whatever you can think of doing to add flair to your synopsis, do it.

Approach the writing of your synopsis as if you were writing a treatment for the movie adaptation of your novel. Not only will a cinematic-style telling ensure that your synopsis is engaging and compelling, it will make it all that easier to sell the film rights later.

Sample Synopses

Did you join the local writer's group for your genre? Do you attend workshops as part of a romance writers group or a mystery writers group? Or do you meet with a group of local writers at the Starbucks down the street to swap tales? Ask your friends if they have sample synopses you could see. Study these synopses, and then write one for your book that outshines them all!

If they're interested, some agents, like co-author Sheree, will request the whole manuscript in lieu of a proposal. Even then, it's necessary to include at least a one-page synopsis and bio. Sheree likes to request the whole book for several reasons: (1) so she can finish the book while it's still fresh in her mind if it's got her hooked after Chapter 3, (2) so she can be sure the novel is complete, and (3) so she can be sure the novel keeps her attention through the end.

Exclusivity

There is a lot of confusion about this topic. When an agent asks for exclusivity, it means she wants to be the only agent to consider your manuscript. If an agent does ask for exclusivity, be sure that she gives you a reasonable time frame for a response. Ask exactly what she expects, and make sure you understand her terms, as each one might be different. Sheree usually offers a four-week turnaround for a proposal or manuscript in exchange for an exclusive first look at a manuscript. Giving an agent exclusivity does not mean that you are then required to use that agent if the agent likes your manuscript. She is still going to have to click with you. The agent should show some passion for your project, should offer you terms for representation that you find reasonable, should be able to give you references, and should be able to do whatever is reasonably necessary to make you comfortable that the agent is the best person for you. If not, on to the next!

The Least You Need to Know

- ◆ With fiction, you must write the entire novel before trying to get an agent or a publisher.

- ◆ Be sure to rewrite and polish your manuscript before sending it out. If you need professional help to take your first draft to the next level, hire an experienced editor to advise you on the rewrite.

- ◆ Write your novel in a cinematic way to increase its marketability.

- ◆ Never send the entire manuscript unsolicited; try first with a short query letter.

- ◆ Your query letter should include a short description of your novel.

- ◆ Your proposal should include a 1- to 10-page summary of the novel, and either the first 50 pages of the manuscript or 3 complete chapters.

Part  3

Romancing the Stone: How to Get a Book Contract

Whether your goal is to find an agent first or to go directly to a publisher yourself, the information is all here. You'll find great tips on how to find agents, and even how to get agents to find you! But if that doesn't work, you'll learn the protocol for approaching publishers without an agent. Whether with children's publishers, university publishers, or even self-publishing, there is much to be learned about the different styles of publishing books.

We'll also help you understand two critical areas of the publishing process: what goes on in an editorial meeting, and how to understand a standard publishing contract.

Chapter 10

What's an Agent for, Anyway?

In This Chapter

- ◆ Why writers use agents
- ◆ Why agents and editors do lunch
- ◆ How agents negotiate contracts
- ◆ Some common contract pitfalls
- ◆ How agents help you stay on the publisher's good side

You've written a tantalizing query letter, and your bulletproof book proposal is put together. The outline for the book (or the entire novel itself) is solid and waiting for a buyer. You're ready to go. But wait! You worked darn hard on all this—why should you cut an agent in on the deal now? Because writers write, and agents sell.

Whether you write fiction or nonfiction, it's hard enough going about the business of writing without also having to deal with the actual business end of it. Very few writers are really equipped to both let their imaginations soar on the blank page and at the same time concentrate on trying to market their work.

Here are a few quick reasons that writers use agents:

◆ Contacts

◆ Contracts

◆ Money

◆ Guidance

Friends in High Places

Agents devote much of their time to cultivating contacts with editors and publishers. They do lunch, they circulate at book parties, they attend conferences, they share cabs. Agents make it their business to get to know *acquisitions editors* at all the major publishing houses. Agents learn what kinds of books each and every editor likes and, more important, just what kind of book each editor never wants to see again!

Bookmarks

The editors who are responsible for bringing in new books are called **acquisitions editors**. They are often called senior editors, but they may also be editors or editors-at-large. The titles vary from house to house and generally depend on the level of responsibility or the amount of experience an editor has.

Each publishing house has its specialties. Some large houses publish a vast array of books on a vast array of topics. Random House, for instance, has a mind-boggling number of imprints, each with a different personality and focus. A smaller publisher such as Avery, on the other hand, is known for alternative health titles. Agents keep track of who publishes what, who went out of business, and even which publishing companies seem to be nicer to their authors than others. This is the sort of specialized knowledge that an agent can use to sell your book to the right publisher. And editors do jump ship a lot. They change jobs, change careers, go on maternity leave, and quit to write their own books. A good agent tracks the circulation patterns of all the editors while remaining a constant contact for the author.

What Gets Done When Agents and Editors Do Lunch?

Lucky for agents—particularly poor, starving agents—this is the only business around where the buyer wines and dines the seller. This expensive practice alone should help convince you of the important role that agents play in the publishing business.

Publishers value the knowledge, judgment, and wisdom of agents enough to ply them with meals. Just as authors can't effectively do their job of writing while also being their own agents, publishers can't do their jobs of acquiring and editing while at the same time screening a million writers and projects.

When an editor agrees to take a look at a project that an agent is representing, she knows that this is a professional project worth considering. The editor is relying on the fact that an agent is not likely to take on a project (investing hours of his own time, office help, and supplies) that he doesn't believe to be of the highest quality. Editors rely on agents to do quite a bit of the screening and selecting for them.

> **Experts Say**
>
> But if agents and editors are friends, how can they negotiate contracts? "In my experience, many agents do become my friends over a period of time," says Susan Schwartz, former senior editor at NTC/Contemporary Publishing Group. "But I knew them as agents first, so that relationship is primary and doesn't change. It is a professional arrangement, and we behave accordingly."

What do they find to talk about during these long publishing lunches? That is where all your hard homework, all the information you dug up about the audience, the market, and the potential for your book comes in. The agent works to sell the editor on the potential of your book, combining her knowledge with the information you've supplied. In the publishing business, unwritten books are the stuff of dreams. Who knows where the next big thing will come from? Every agent, every editor, and every publisher hopes that she has found it.

A Hope and a Prayer

Does a book have an intrinsic value? Well, no. The value of an *intellectual property* is determined purely by taste (the editor's) and perceived need. It isn't like a diamond or a vacuum cleaner, something that has an expected value in the marketplace.

> **Bookmarks**
>
> What is an **intellectual property**? A house owned by a college professor? No, it's a legal term for, according to the *Random House Legal Dictionary*, "copyrights, patents, and other rights in creations of the mind; also, the creations themselves, such as a literary work, painting,

A book is more like Jackie O's toilet brush or Mark McGuire's seventieth home run baseball: It's worth whatever someone is willing to pay. So over lunch, agents get editors excited about the books they have for sale. Agents also listen closely as the editor describes the kind of books he hopes to find.

"Is That the Best You Can Do?"

Well, the lunch meeting between your agent and the prospective editor was a great success. The agent sends the proposal over, the editor reads it, and eventually the editor calls your agent to make an offer. This doesn't happen that same afternoon, however.

Bookmarks

P and L stands for a profit and loss statement, which takes into account all the money that must be spent on a book, balanced against the money that can be expected from potential sales. It is hoped that the P column outweighs the L column by a desired profit margin.

Profit or Loss?

In Chapter 14, you'll get an inside look at what happens during editorial meetings. But before then, we'll just say that the editor needs to get the support and approval of a whole bunch of other folks—and to do what's known as a *P and L* (profit and loss statement) before he makes that call to your agent.

This profit and loss statement is used to estimate in advance what a publisher can expect to earn from the publication of a book.

Any Other Takers?

Agents often meet with several editors to raise interest in a project from several publishers. Let's pretend that the agent has submitted your brilliant proposal to editors A, B, and C. Editors C and B are polite, but editor A is the only one who calls the agent with an offer. Editor A wants to make sure, then, that he is not "bidding against himself." If there is only one bid on the table, the agent does not have much leverage to get it raised. Agents do have a trick or two up their sleeves to try to maximize the publishers' offer and get the best possible deal for their author. This process is referred to as an auction and can take place over the course of an afternoon or a few tense days.

Let's not forget that an agent's work is done on "spec"—his income is solely based on *commission*. No sale, no commission; low sale, low commission. Your agent earns no money at all from representing you until your book is sold to a publisher. Then, depending on your agreement, she receives anywhere from 10 to 15 percent of your royalties and 15 percent of your advance. So it is possible for an agent to work long and hard, only to earn nothing if your book is not sold. You can see why an agent will always try to get the best deal possible for the author—because it is at the same time his deal, too.

Bookmarks

Literary agents work solely on **commission**, a percentage of the book's income.

Money, Money, Money

So the editor wants your book. Great. You get the call from your agent and begin dancing around the room shouting, "Show me the money!"

Just how much money can you expect?

This is a sticky subject. Sadly, most American writers have rather small average yearly incomes. Around $10,000 a year is typical, and that may reflect a number of different income sources (magazine and newspaper articles, freelance copywriting) in addition to book royalties.

How much money you can expect depends. We've seen first-time advances for most nonfiction books range anywhere from as low as $5,000 to as high as $100,000. You may only hear about the mega advances, but the reason for that is they are unusual. That makes them news. At a single meeting, a major publishing house might allocate $2 million to acquire five books—with $1.9 million going to a single title. A smaller publishing company might allocate as much as $50,000 to acquire 5 or more titles. If you really have a great background—a platform that includes a large speaking schedule, a newspaper column, a high-profile name, or a tremendous idea—the number will reflect that.

Experts Say

Life in New York has become so frantic that the traditional leisurely lunch hours have become a time to cram in as many meetings as possible. According to *The New York Times*, some agents and editors are doing multiple lunches in an effort to find that big book before someone else does. How does it work? A big agent will set himself up at the table, meet with one editor over the salad course, another editor over the main course, and yet another editor for dessert and coffee!

Megamarkets

The number could also be higher if you establish a ready market for your book. With *Christmas Miracles*, co-author Jennifer was able to establish how well Christmas books sold, how well books on miracles sold, and how well inspirational short-story books such as *Chicken Soup for the Soul* did. All that research paid off—as did the passionate pitch made by her agent, Sheree, at a Women in Publishing Christmas party.

Advances for Fiction

Advances for first-time novelists are generally on the low side, but if your book is perceived as a best-seller candidate and an auction ensues, the advance could go off the charts. From time to time, an unknown writer hits the million-dollar jackpot. It happens.

> **Bookmarks**
>
> The money paid to an author upon signing a contract is called an **advance against future royalties.** That's money up front that will have to be earned back once the book is available for sale. An author's royalty account starts as a negative figure that reflects the advance. Once the royalties earned surpass the amount advanced, an author begins to receive more money.

Double Indemnity

When agents negotiate contracts, the size of the advance is just one of many complicated issues. In Chapter 15, you'll walk through a typical publishing contract piece by piece.

Rely on Your Agent

Although agents negotiate contracts on behalf of the author, the agent does not sign the contract. The author does. But you shouldn't sign the contract until the agent is happy with it, until you have read it completely, and until you understand it. Your agent is there to explain the quirks of the contract. Don't be afraid to ask about any and all details.

Publishing agreements are sticky wickets, but thankfully (for agents and authors), they are all pretty much the same. An experienced agent is aware of the traditional traps and loopholes. Nobody, including most lawyers, knows publishing contracts like an agent. Agents know just when to push and when to back off.

Let's Do Another One, Just Like the Other One

Agents sometimes maintain "boilerplate" contracts with the publishing houses with which they do business. What does this mean to you? On other contracts, the agent has already gotten the house to agree to more free copies or a better royalty rate on special sales, or he's eliminated the option clause (which ties up the first look at your next book). The agent then has a boilerplate that can be used with that house for future contracts. The editor likely will knock these things out of your contract, too.

After the Deal Is Done

So your contract has been negotiated and signed. You and your editor have a direct relationship. Your editor will now guide you through the publishing process. Is your agent's job finished? Not by a long shot.

An agent is an experienced publishing player. He can help you learn the ropes so that you, too, will be an experienced player. After the contract is filed in a drawer, the agent will take on these tasks:

- Learn how to get the most from the publicity department

- Examine your royalty statements

- Make sure that you get paid properly

- Sell subrights and licenses for your book

- Assist you and the editor in solving any major problems that might arise in revising or finishing the manuscript

- Be your book's greatest advocate

Slush Pile

So your agent has gotten an editor interested? An offer is on the table and a contract is in the works? *Mazel tov.* But don't ever pick up the phone and call the editor directly about a contract issue. This will make both your editor and your agent angry. Relax, and let your agent do his job.

Experts Say

Author and former lawyer Tim Perrin says that whenever you receive a first offer from a publisher, you should always say, "Oh? Is that all? I was thinking more like ...." Then name a figure substantially higher than what you've just been offered. "It's never failed for me," says Perrin. "I don't often get double or triple the amount first offered, but I always get a substantial increase. I make more money in those 10 seconds than I do in any part of writing."

Good Cop/Bad Cop

And the best part of all is that your agent can be the bad guy. As an author, you want to be loved by your editor. You want to shy away from any kind of behavior that could damage your relationship with your editor (more on this later in Chapter 19). But what if you aren't happy?

Your agent can do the job! Call and tell him your concern, and ask him to speak on your behalf. You can sit back and let your agent air your complaints in such a way that you don't jeopardize your relationship with your publisher. Your agent is the bad cop.

The agent will do the yelling (about the crummy cover design, the lack of a publicity campaign, or the slow royalty checks) while you sit back and bat your eyelashes.

Publishers are people, too. Even if your book is the best thing since *Gone with the Wind*, those with the power to help you will not put forth their best efforts if you alienate them. At any given time, a publishing house has lots of different books to peddle, so don't give it a reason to spend less time on yours. Your second most important job as a writer (after writing the best book you can) is to make the publisher love you and your book. Be as pleasant as you can. Let your agent do the unpleasant things.

Should You Get an Agent

Now you know the full story. An agent's role goes far beyond brokering a profitable deal with a publisher.

We're not saying that you need an agent because co-author Sheree is one (and we're not saying that because Sheree is Jennifer's agent, either!). We're both writers, and we know a lot of other writers. We have seen all that can happen to writers in the rough-and-tumble world of book publishing. Get yourself a good agent, and you will have less to worry about.

Even in-house editors, like Jennifer, who know the ins and outs of the publishing business, use agents when they become authors.

How the heck do you find an agent? Move on to the next chapter, and we'll show you where they hide!

The Least You Need to Know

- Agents do many things, from negotiating a contract to guiding you through the publishing maze.

- Agents get to know editors and what kinds of books they want to publish.

- Books are intellectual properties and are worth what the highest bidder will pay. An agent is better placed to handle the bidding.

- Standard boilerplate publishing contracts favor the publisher, not the author. An agent knows the ins and outs.

- Agents can help you maintain a good relationship with your editor and publisher.

Finding and Working with an Agent

In This Chapter

- ◆ Where do they hide, those agents?
- ◆ Choosing among the many
- ◆ Fiction or nonfiction?
- ◆ Agent etiquette
- ◆ Landing a live one!

With any luck, we convinced you in Chapter 10 that you may need an agent, particularly if you are a first-time author and want to sell your book idea to a large national publisher. If you've decided that's the way to go, in this chapter, we'll tell you how to find a good one.

Members of the Club

So how do you tell if an agent is the real thing? A large percentage of established agents in the business are members of the Association of Author's Representatives (AAR). This is the largest professional association of literary and dramatic agents for authors. Its address is PO Box 237201, Ansonia Station, New York, NY 10023. To get a list of all its members, send your request with a self-addressed, stamped (totaling 55 cents) envelope and $7 to cover photocopying and handling, or take a look at the association's free website at www.aar-online.org.

Hot Off the Press

In its Canon of Ethics, the members of AAR pledge loyal service to their clients' needs. A member's accounts must be open to the client at all times with respect to the client's transactions, and members promise not to represent both buyer and seller in the same transaction. The AAR believes that the practice of agents charging clients or potential clients for reading and evaluating literary works (including outlines, proposals, and manuscripts) is subject to serious abuse that reflects adversely on the profession. Current and future members may not charge for reading and evaluating literary works and may not benefit from the charging of such fees by any other person or entity.

What will this list tell you? That the agents listed are what they say they are: experienced literary agents. To become a member of the AAR, you must be a well-established agent with several contracts negotiated on behalf of authors with major publishing houses. In addition, you must agree to abide by a strict Canon of Ethics. You must also pass a rigorous application and screening process.

Hot Off the Press

"Book doctors should respect your confidentiality," says Jerry Gross, a book doctor himself. If you use a book doctor, no one needs to know about it. Other than the confidentiality question, what else should you ask a book doctor before hiring one? First and foremost, make sure that he is skilled in your area. "If you are writing a sci-fi novel, make sure that the book doctor has written sci-fi novels, too. You don't want someone with an expertise in romance novels." Ask for references—and check them! And always be suspicious of someone who "guarantees" that if you work with them, they will get you an agent or a publisher.

Just How Much Is This Gonna Cost?

It costs nothing to have an agent who's a member of AAR read your material. Other agents may charge reading fees. Most of the reference books that list agents will note whether they charge a reading fee, and if so, how much.

> **CAUTION**
>
> ### Slush Pile
>
> Rather than paying reading fees to an agent, hire yourself an independent editor, or sign up for a writing class if you want your writing evaluated. Agents will either represent you or not represent you. We don't think you need to pay someone to evaluate your work in exchange for representation. And by all means, do not pay an agent a fee to represent you or to place your manuscript with a publisher. Agents collect commissions, not fees.

Reading Fees? No

The fact that an agent charges a reading fee does not necessarily mean that he is taking advantage of you. In fact, if you ever got a glimpse at the towering stack of unsolicited material that floods into agents' offices every day, you might understand the idea behind a reading fee. Remember, agents don't make any money at all until they sell your project.

But the AAR believes that reading fees can easily lead to corrupt practices (like charging for books they might never read, or charging for needless editing or ghostwriting on a book they knew was not salable), so do try to stay away from paying a reading fee.

> **CAUTION**
>
> ### Slush Pile
>
> You owe it to yourself and your book to be rigorous in your evaluation of a potential agent. Do most of your early research through books and any personal sources you might have. Don't call and ask agents for their biographies or the names of potential clients until they have offered to represent you. Once they have offered to represent you, it is perfectly proper to ask questions.

They're Agents, Not Readers

Not only do most literary agents not charge reading fees, but they also do not provide "reader's reports." An agent will simply tell you whether your manuscript is suited to his agency. If the manuscript doesn't interest him enough to represent it, he certainly won't take the time to tell you what he thinks is wrong with it. But if he does want to represent your book, he will take the time to help you make it better.

The hard truth is this: If all the agents that you approach who don't charge fees turn you and your project down, it is pretty likely that the publishers are going to have the same reaction. So if this happens, spend your money on a good book doctor, a writing class or seminar, or an independent editor. All these will help you to improve your work and its chances of someday being published.

Where to Find Help (!)

Many good book doctors and freelance editors can help you with your proposal, and agents sometimes can give you the names of such people. So might members of local writers' groups. Then there's the Editorial Freelance Association (EFA), a nonprofit organization whose members are all freelance editors. Check out EFA's website at www.the-efa.org, or call 212-929-5400. Another good group of editors can be found at wordsintoprint.com.

Screening Agents

Are all good agents members of the AAR? Are all members of the AAR good agents? Many good agents are not members of the AAR and don't charge fees. But evaluating them may prove difficult without checking with an association.

After an agent has offered to represent you, but before you sign up, feel free to ask for names and phone numbers of other clients. The agent should happily let you speak to some of his clients to get a better sense of who they are. If an agent is reluctant to hook you up with any other clients, take this as a red flag.

Not sure what kinds of questions you should ask an agent before agreeing to let him represent you? Here are a few questions that will help you sound him out:

- How long have you been in business as an agent?

- Do you have specialists at your agency who handle television and movie rights?

- Do you represent other authors in my area of interest?

- What is your commission?

- Do you issue 1099 tax forms at the end of the year?

- What kinds of books have you sold lately?

Where to Look for Agents

So where else do they hide, these agents? Co-author Sheree would like to say that all the good agents have offices in New York City (guess where she has an office?), but she would be lying. New York agents might have an easier time accessing New York editors face to face, but excellent agents live all around the country. Agents outside the Big Apple make frequent trips into New York. They pack their appetites in their carry-ons and gang up their breakfasts, lunch, dinner, drinks, and coffee dates with as many publishers as they can.

Besides checking the membership list of the AAR, there are several other ways to find agents.

Look in a Book

Three great books list agents: *Literary Market Place* (*LMP*), *Writer's Guide to Book Publishers, Editors, and Literary Agents,* and *The Writer's Digest Guide to Literary Agents.* We talked about the *LMP* in Chapter 4; it's an expensive professional reference. Though it's full of information, only one of the many sections in it is devoted to agents. The agent listings in the *LMP* don't give any information beyond name, address, and phone number, and whether the agent is a member of the AAR.

The *Writer's Guide to Book Publishers, Editors, and Literary Agents* is put together by an actual literary agent, Jeff Herman. He's been doing it for the last 10 years or so, and he includes lots of personal and professional information about the agents he lists. Each agent listing includes the agent's description of the type of book he or she likes to represent, and the type of book he or she never wants to see again. If you are just beginning your search for an agent, Herman's book is great. Be sure to get the most current edition available because the listings change every year.

The Writer's Digest's Guide to Literary Agents lists more than 500 agents who "sell what you write." It's concise, is kept up to date, and is an excellent resource not just for finding agents, but also for learning about the publishing industry.

Face to Face

A great way to find an agent is through a rec-ommendation from a friend or colleague, particularly a published friend or colleague. But what if you don't know any other writers? Get thee to a writers' conference!

In any given month, somewhere around the country, a writers' conference is being held. Most organizers of writers' conferences arrange to have a few agents on hand for you to meet. These meetings are invaluable. Not only do

Bookmarks

When authors write to a number of agents at one time, this is called a **multiple query**. You are approaching a number of agents at once to try to get them interested in requesting your proposal, chapters, or manuscript. This is an accepted practice in publishing.

they give you a chance to stick out your hand and shake with a live agent, but you also can often arrange for personal appointments with agents to discuss your project. This is time that you wouldn't be able to get from them on the phone with a cold call. If you are serious about writing, writers' conferences are never a waste of time. They're especially useful for authors who write in particular genres—as there are conferences that specialize in genres, such as mystery, romance, and sci-fi. The Guide to Writers' Conferences & Workshops at www.shawguides.com is a fabulous source for writers. It provides more than 600 detailed conference and workshop descriptions, including upcoming dates, faculty, and programs. In Appendix H, we've listed some conferences, many of which co-authors Sheree and Jennifer have addressed.

> **Hot Off the Press** _____
>
> When you do get a chance to meet an agent at a writer's conference, how does it work? It can be likened to speed dating, in which you have a limited amount of time to make a good impression. Most appointments are for 15 or 30 minutes, and you should arrive with your best material in hand and a well-practiced speech about your project and why it should be published. Like a speed date, this is not the time to go into heavy background on your life, but rather stick to what will sell your project and you as a potential client. It also gives you a chance to see agents up close and get a feel for who you'd most like to work with.

"I'd Like to Thank My Agent"

Don't know any writers? Can't get to a writers' conference? Well, you can open a book, right? That is a great place to find agents! Take a book, any book, off the shelf. Open it to the acknowledgments page. Not all books have such a page, but many (if not most) do. This is where the author thanks his family for their patience, his editor for her guidance, and his agent for all those lunches.

> **Experts Say** _____
>
> You've heard us mention it before: Many editors end up becoming agents. But does anyone else ever make the leap? Well-known agent Esther Newberg was quoted in *The New York Times* (with her tongue firmly in her cheek) as speculating that even ex-presidents might consider the career. "And frankly, that's what I hear Bill Clinton is going to do when he retires. And that's the real reason he bought a house in Chappaqua."

Looking in the acknowledgments is a great tactic, particularly when you need to find an agent who represents books in your area. Writing a health book? Look inside the health books that you admire. Writing a romance novel? Check out recently published romances. This method helps you find the agent that might be open to your type of writing. Does the author thank everyone in the world but her agent? Hmmm … must have been an oversight.

Eeny, Meeny, Miney, Mo ...

So you've looked inside your favorite books. Your list has arrived from the AAR, and you met eight great agents at a writers' conference last weekend. You've highlighted, cross-checked, and pondered the selections. You know which agents represent your area, and the list is longer than Madonna's little black book. Do you have to just choose one? No! You're in luck. It is perfectly acceptable to send queries to more than one agent at one time.

Still, you want to be somewhat selective about whom you send your precious queries to. What if they all responded at once, and they all said "Yes"? Select your hottest prospects first.

Exclusive Territory

When an agent does respond and request more material from you, she might also ask for an "exclusive" for a limited amount of time (see the later "You Hooked One!" section for more on exclusives). Three to four weeks is standard. What does this mean? It means that for the next three to four weeks she can study your material closely and not have to worry that you might be swiped out from under her by another agent.

If an agent chooses you, do you have to choose her? No. But realistically, if someone does want to represent you and offers you a reasonable author/agent agreement (and if she doesn't seem obnoxious), well, why not? Don't try to interest an agent that you really don't want. You will waste both your time and hers.

The Good Agent

The best things to look for in an agent include these:

- An established reputation
- A reputation for selling books in your field

Slush Pile

No matter how brilliant you think your book idea is, if you don't have the written material to back it up, you will fail. Do not approach an agent or a publisher with an idea for a book until you have something in writing—your writing!

♦ Accessibility by phone (once she's become your agent)

♦ A manner that lends itself to comfortable communication

♦ A passion about her work—and about yours

If you can't find all these qualities in an agent who responds to you, move on down your list until you do.

Are You Really Ready?

How do you know when you are ready to begin querying agents? You're ready if you have the following: a well-written query letter and a polished proposal for nonfiction or a polished manuscript for fiction. If these elements are in place, get started!

Fiction

If it's fiction you're writing, don't even think about querying agents until you are satisfied that your novel is the best it can be. You'll hear from time to time about first-time novelists selling a novel for a million dollars. It happens, but rarely. What you might not realize, though, is that although this is the first book that writer has sold, it is probably not the first book he has written. Many writers write 2, 3, or 10 novels before selling one.

Novelists write and write, regardless of whether they'll get published. True novelists usually get published, eventually. But don't send something to an agent just because you worked hard on it. Send it because it's good. Don't ask an agent to decide whether it's good; ask discriminating colleagues, teachers, and editors for their honest opinions first. Take praise from family and friends (who may be biased or who don't want to hurt your feelings) with a large grain of salt.

Sometimes novelists need to put their novels aside and let them sit for a while. Then they go back to them with a fresh perspective and reevaluate them. Very often authors come back to their very first novels years later and say, "Oh my gosh, what was I thinking?"

Nonfiction

For nonfiction, you can submit before you've got the entire book written. As you learned in Chapter 8, nonfiction is usually sold on the basis of a book proposal, a table of contents, and a representative sample chapter. If a publishing house likes what it sees in a proposal and decides to publish it, you have a deal. There are several models for paying out advances—some publishers will pay half the advance upon signing a contract and half upon receipt of an acceptable manuscript. Others might break that up into smaller sums for milestones like a third on signing, a third on completion of the first half of the book, and a third upon delivery of manuscript. A manuscript is deemed acceptable when it matches the promises in your proposal, as reflected in the contract description.

When you have a good nonfiction proposal together, go ahead and start querying agents. If you haven't yet started your sample chapter, don't worry. Start it soon, but don't let it hold you back. If an agent is interested in your query and then asks to see more, you don't want her to have to wait too long. She might forget you!

> **Slush Pile** _____
>
> Although most nonfiction books require only a book proposal, there is one instance in which you will need more. Creative nonfiction books that are literary memoirs (such as *Angela's Ashes*) require a more fictionlike approach. You can't sell creative nonfiction with a bare bones nonfiction proposal. Like a novel, you might need to write the whole book or a substantial portion first.

Try, Try Again

What if an agent looks at your proposal and tells you it still needs more work? She might tell you exactly where she thinks it is weak and how to improve it. Or she might think your proposal is so weak that you need to hire help, and she might suggest that you work with a book doctor (see more on book doctors earlier in this chapter and also in Chapter 8).

Big Name, Superb Credentials

You might not have to wait until a proposal is done before querying agents. If you have such superb professional credentials, such as a recognizable name, you might not have to wait. Write a strong query letter and see what kind of reaction you get from agents. It might be that an agent will be able to link you up with a co-writer for the project. The agent might also be able to guide you in the proposal process.

Shopping Yourself

If you decide to try to place your book first without an agent, don't shop the project to all the publishers in town and then try to find an agent after you have a stack of rejection letters in hand. No matter how good your project is. Agents can't go back to the same publishers; if a publisher has passed on a project already, an agent will feel awfully foolish when the editor points it out—and it will come back to haunt you. Come clean with agents about which publishers have passed.

CAUTION

Slush Pile _____

If you use a book doctor or other kind of professional in preparing your proposal, and the book finds a publisher, you need to make sure that your finished book does not disappoint the publisher. If the publisher bought your project based on a proposal that had help, make extra sure that your book itself meets or exceeds the expectations set in that proposal. Don't promise one thing and deliver another. Many publishers have been burned by books that didn't match the quality or content of the proposal. In cases of extreme differences in the quality of writing between the proposal and the finished manuscript, the publisher has the right to hire a book doctor to fix it and charge the cost to you.

Return to Sender

Don't send your unsolicited query letter via certified or registered mail. The agent will think he's being sued! Seriously, you don't want to look overcautious or paranoid. Portray yourself like the professional you are.

Once again, we will remind you of the importance of including a self-addressed, stamped envelope with your correspondence to agents. It is a simple step that can make all the difference in hearing back. If you leave out the SASE, the agent will assume that you need no reply if the agent isn't interested. If that's the case, it's better to say so than to look sloppy.

Hold My Calls, Please

Unless (and until) you have an agent/author agreement with an agent, do not try to call a prospective agent on the phone. It will backfire. Approach agents the way they want to be approached: with a query and an SASE.

Agents need to evaluate your writing, not your speaking. So give them what they need and more: a great query letter that will pique their interest right away.

You Hooked One!

An agent received your query letter, read it, and then picked up the phone and called you! Hurrah! This is a good sign. But don't jump the gun and start writing your Pulitzer Prize acceptance speech yet. When an agent is intrigued by your query, she might call you to find out more about the project. She might be calling to learn more about you as a person.

If the agent does want to go further, she might ask for an *exclusive*. Remember, this is when you assure her that she is the only one considering your project for a particular length of time. It is hard to say no to an agent on the phone, and that's why it is so important for you to have done your research before deciding which agents to query. You don't want to go to the dance with the wrong partner!

Bookmarks

When only one agent is considering your proposal, this is called an **exclusive** submission. If an agent asks for an exclusive submission, be sure to set a time limit. Three to four weeks is reasonable.

Another Darn SASE?

When an agent responds to your query and asks to see more material, include an SASE with your proposal. There is more at stake here, in fact. You are sending a lot of material, and you want it back if the agent decides to pass. To be sure that your package was received, send it via an express service such as FedEx or UPS. You can track it by phone without calling the literary agent and looking anxious. The good old U.S. mail is just fine, too. According to statistics, 99.9999 percent of all mail is delivered properly.

For packages that weigh more than one pound, include return postage, either loose stamps for the proper postage or a check to cover the cost of an express service.

The Least You Need to Know

♦ Members of the Association of Author's Representatives abide by a professional code of ethics and don't charge a reading fee.

♦ Find an agent through the membership of AAR, directories that list agents, or writers' conferences.

- Looking in the acknowledgments section of books in your genre that you admire could lead you to a great agent, too.

- With nonfiction, query agents when your proposal is finished; with fiction, query when your novel is finished.

- Always include a self-addressed, stamped envelope with any correspondence to an agent.

Chapter 12

What You Can Expect from an Agent

In This Chapter

- ◆ When an agent calls to represent you, what then?
- ◆ The agency/author agreement
- ◆ Is it okay to call now?
- ◆ Dealing with rejection letters
- ◆ Every author's first question
- ◆ How agents sell books

Was that a dream? Did an agent actually call and say, "I want to represent you"? You wrote a good query letter and you have a great idea, so stop pinching yourself! And put down that champagne glass—you have more work to do.

99 Percent Ready

It is rare that the manuscript or book proposal that you sent is 100 percent ready to go. Chances are, the agent will want to discuss some fine-tuning and changes. At the very least, you'll need to change the cover page to your manuscript or proposal. Remember, it has your name and address on the bottom. Now that you've got an agent, you'll need to drop your own information and add his.

CAUTION

Slush Pile

Spelling mistakes are unacceptable under any circumstances. Even with the advent of "spell check," there is just no excuse for finding misspelled words in your manuscript or book proposal. But be careful—even spelling checkers can work incorrectly. Read your manuscript for spelling and usage first—then use spell check.

"I Really Like It, But ..."

Fixing the cover page—that's no problem. But is this agent passionate about your project? Does she believe in your book? It is imperative that the person who is going to represent you to publishers feels confident about your book's prospects. If the agent has any doubts going in, you want to know about it.

Let's say that the agent does love your project, but maybe she also has some changes she needs you to make before sending your book out to publishers. After all, what an agent sends out is her calling card. She must maintain a good reputation with publishers to stay active in the business. You must make your work as perfect as possible.

Be Open to Changes

The agent might feel that the competition section of your proposal needs work. This might mean that you need to strengthen your facts or do a quick double-check to make sure that you haven't left out major titles.

She might also feel that you've been too hard on the competing titles and might risk alienating the publishers of those books you've maligned (who might have otherwise become your publisher).

Your new agent might also make recommendations on your author biography section. Perhaps you've been too humble about your accomplishments. Or perhaps you've been a touch arrogant and need to tone it down.

Your Best Interests Are at Stake

Whatever the agent suggests, feel free to discuss it with her. This is very important. Discuss all changes. If an agent makes suggestions to your manuscript (about combining chapters, say, or dropping a section), you don't have to agree. Do not make any changes to your work that you don't feel 100 percent good about. If you can't get the agent to see things your way, or vice versa, then perhaps this is not the agent for you. True, you've both wasted your time, but thank heaven you discovered it early.

On the other hand, the agent does have quite a bit of experience in this area. Do try to be open-minded and understand what is being suggested (and why). The agent has your best interests in mind and is trying to make your project as salable as possible because you really have only one shot at it. If the agent sends out a project that wasn't quite ready to go and it is turned down by everyone who sees it, that is the end of the road. Publishers seldom want to see the same project twice.

Love at First Sight

Now let's say that you and your agent are completely simpatico. You see eye to eye about the book and agree on what is necessary to touch it up and make it ready. The conversation you had about your book energized both of you. You like the agent's manner. You can talk to her. She listens. Great, so what's next?

Call Other Authors

The agent might suggest that you call one or two of her other clients for a reference. This is a great way to learn more about what the agent is like to work with on a long-term basis. Take the numbers; it wouldn't hurt to call. In fact, if the agent doesn't offer this, you should bring it up.

Great Expectations

This is also a great time to find out more about how that agent works. Ask the agent to describe how she plans to sell your book. What is the process? And what more does she need from you? Here are a number of good questions to ask:

- Will you need to make copies of your proposal or manuscript? How many copies?

- How many publishers does the agent plan to contact?

- Will you get copies of the rejection letters?

- Does the agent call the publishers to let them know your proposal is coming?

- Does the agent plan to submit to several publishers at once, or only one at a time (exclusively)?

Are there any wrong answers to these questions? Not really. But it is better to ask in advance about how the agent works than to grumble about it later.

Who Does What?

The answers to this question might be found in the agent/author contract. This is an agreement that the agent will send to you after you have agreed that he may represent your book.

Most times, the agent/author agreement covers just the one book. Ideally, an author hopes that one perfect agent will represent him forever. Just as ideally, agents long for clients whom they can represent profitably forever. But at this stage of the game, take it one book at a time.

In many ways, this is a trial run with an agent—an engagement, not a marriage. Maybe you're really just dating for a while. Hopefully, the relationship will turn out well—the agent will sell your book, and you two will get along famously. But you'll also want to continue to monitor the relationship after your book is successfully sold. Is the agent still communicating? Is she still passing along information as she receives it? If not, maybe the relationship should end.

Read the Fine Print

Examine the agent/author agreement carefully before you sign it. Make sure that you understand all the terms and that they are acceptable to you. (You might want to look at the sample agreement in Appendix D.)

Office Fees

One of the things that you might notice is that there is typically a charge for expenses such as postage, messengers, copying, and other office expenses. What's up with that?

Most agents require that the author pay for these expenses. This charge is not to be confused with the reading fees discussed in Chapter 11. Some agents put a cap on such expenses. For instance, co-author Sheree caps these fees at $150 per book. Realistically, however, it could cost an agent several hundred dollars to sell a single book.

How are these fees collected? If your agent sells your book and receives an advance check from the publisher, the office fees will be deducted (along with the agent's commission) before a check is sent on to you. And if an agent hasn't had any luck selling your book after trying for a year or so, don't be surprised if you receive a bill in the mail one day.

So make sure that you know what the fees could be. If the agreement doesn't mention office fees, ask.

"Hello, It's Your Author!"

You shouldn't call agents during the query process, but now that it's official, go ahead and call. You have a right to expect reasonable access to your agent, not to just shoot the breeze, but to be kept informed of everything the agent does on your behalf. Expect progress reports from time to time.

Your agent will be pleased if you respect his time. Call only when you need to, and try to group your questions together. Better yet, send a fax (or e-mail) with all your questions, and ask your agent to call you.

Do we make agents sound scary? They aren't really. But they are busy people who, like us all, have developed particular ways of working. You will get along nicely with your agent if you just accept that fact.

So What Do You Think?

Up to this point in your writing career, you have been in control. But from the time an agent starts to try to sell your project, the agent is now pretty much in control of what happens.

Here is what you hope is happening: The agent is calling editors to pitch your book. He's talking you and your book up as he lunches with editors. Throwing humility to the winds, he has all the top editors clamoring to see what you've written. He has written a glowing cover letter, which accompanies your proposal as it goes out to publishers that request it.

Time in a Bottle

How long does the process take? It takes several weeks for editors to respond. The cover letter that your agent sent along with your material might have requested a response within a certain time period. Sometimes agents include a sentence similar to this: "I'd like to have all offers in by January 30." But even with a clock ticking, editors tend to move slowly. (In Chapter 14, you'll get a glimpse at the inner workings of a publishing house to better understand the process.)

What is your agent doing while the days slip by without an answer? Making follow-up calls to check that the proposal arrived. The real purpose of the phone calls is to remind editors of their early interest in the project, of course. But so as not to appear pushy, more subtle tactics are employed.

Ante Up

If a publisher calls to express an interest in acquiring your book, the agent will once again work the phones. Calls will be placed to all the publishers that received the proposal, and the agent will say: "Publisher X is interested in that book you liked so much, and I wondered if your house was still interested." This way, the editors are once again prodded into action. And such news might result in a larger offer because the second (or third or fourth) bidder has to beat what is already on the table.

> **Bookmarks**
>
> When an editor declines to pursue a book project, she sends out a **rejection letter.** Rejection letters sent directly to authors say little more than "no thanks." But rejection letters sent to agents might contain more information about why the editor turned it down.

The Rejection Blues

Realistically, most responses will be in the form of *rejection letters.* Even the best writers get rejection letters, so if it's any consolation, you're in fine company.

A Day in the Life of an Agent

What exactly do agents do all day? Let's peek in on Sheree's typical day:

Today was a typical day. It started out with a pile of papers on my desk and phone calls from yesterday that needed to be returned. Soon the big bag of mail arrived. I paused to see if there was anything particularly interesting, and yes, I struck paydirt—literally. Right on top was the telling envelope that revealed an acceptance check for a book I thought would never see the light of day—a book on astrology. I rubbed my eyes in disbelief. If my post office hadn't been affected by anthrax last year, I might have kissed the envelope. Two years ago, right before the book was due, the author had a serious accident (now please don't ask why the author didn't foresee this; she actually is an impressive psychic, I can attest). Anyway, two years ago, the author was unable to give the original publisher a new deadline that she could meet, and they cancelled the book. Recently, the author completed the book and that publisher didn't want to see it ever again. I quickly sold it to another publisher, who is excited about publishing it. It will give me great pleasure to refund the first publisher dollars from this new advance, especially because they might have long ago written off the possibility of ever retrieving a dime. But I'm proud that my author is ethical and thrilled that she is recovered. She truly deserves this book to be a best-seller.

No time for reverie, though; publishers called to ask questions about projects and register their interest; others called to make offers (my favorite calls). As Tim Perrin wisely advises, whatever they offer, pause and say, "Is that all?" There were a few contracts to negotiate, a few authors with requests ("Where are my contracts?" "Should I hire a publicist?" "Did you see that horrible cover?" and the ever popular, "When is the publisher sending the [expletives deleted] money?")

One thing I love about being an agent is successfully troubleshooting problems—well, in hindsight, anyway. It's extremely rewarding to save books from the cutting-room floor and keep authors and publishers from shooting each other.

A famous radio disk jockey whose career I followed all through high school and college called to see how I liked his proposal (based on my ideas). My associate and I did have some feedback for him, as we were as eager as he was to get this into shape quickly so we can begin the process of submitting it to publishers. That is one of the special pleasures of being an agent. I'm not talking about hobnobbing with celebrities and teen idols; I'm talking about being in a position to come up with an idea, seek out an expert, and bring that idea to readers in the form of a book. Richard Roeper's *Ten Sure Signs a Movie Character Is Doomed* is based on my idea, and just last week I saw an installation at a museum in Milwaukee that inspired a book idea. I searched out the artist on the Internet (that was easy!), sent him an e-mail, and, wow, I got a positive response. He is interested in working with me. *Gulp.* I'm glad I wrote to him before I realized how important he was. His lengthy bio listed Emmys and other prestigious awards. Lucky I hadn't been too intimidated to contact him. Most agents are continually on the lookout for high-profile folks they can approach with ideas.

As usual, several editors called with a shopping list of titles in search of authors. I am so pleased that they think of me when they have such projects. I have placed at least 30 great authors with series books at the request of the publisher. Many if not most series titles (like the one you are reading!) come to fruition this way.

After I looked through the mail, read some queries and rejections, and glanced at some requested manuscripts, I fired up the computer to check my e-mail. There it was: the usual 100 letters of which only a small portion could be deleted out-of-hand. Here's something interesting. My Chinese agent is asking if we'd like to accept two offers from Chinese publishers for two of my authors. Hmmm ... we just double-checked and saw that these two authors had already published with this agent in China. What's up? Well, it turns out that there are at least two languages in China and the rights are sold separately. So we are, happily, free to accept these offers. What do you know? A book can be sold in 10 countries and in 11 languages (at least).

As you might guess, my to-do list (I'm a Virgo) is miles long and the phone is ringing. Remember, my day looks like this, and so does the typical day of other agents in the business.

Kissing the Boo Boo

An agent can help you overcome the sting of rejection letters. Plain and simple, those letters hurt. They hurt you as the author, and no matter how many rejection letters your agent has seen in her career, they hurt her, too. Talk about it with your agent.

Those Wicked Letters

Should you even see your rejection letters? Yes. Here is what you can learn from them:

◆ How many publishers have seen your work

◆ Which publishers have seen your work

◆ What kind of a relationship your agent has with publishers

◆ What kinds of criticism your project is receiving

All this information will help you get better and will help increase your chances of getting published in the future. Are all the letters saying the same thing? If all editors say that they don't see a market for your book, that might tell you something. If all the editors say that there are too many similar titles already out there, that, too, might be sending you a message. And if it makes you feel better, pin your rejections up on the wall and toss darts at them.

Slush Pile

Rejections do hurt. But don't respond with a rebuttal in writing or a nasty message on the phone. You can easily make enemies in the publishing world with such loose-cannon behavior. Your agent will not be pleased, and editors will not be pleased. Try a big bowl of ice cream instead.

One of Sheree's clients once asked for the original copies of two of his rejection letters. In one, the publisher said that the proposed book was "too specific." In the other, the publisher said that the book was "too general." He framed the letters side by side in his office. You'll be pleased to know that this story has a happy ending: Another publisher thought that his proposal was just right, and his book was published!

No matter what you wind up doing with them, try to learn from those letters—and learn to deal with rejection. Consider it a personal growth experience.

Going Once, Going Twice ... Sold!

What if several publishers let your agent know that they plan to make an offer for your book? To get the best price for it (in other words, the biggest advance), your agent will plan an *auction*.

Here is how an auction works:

- ◆ Your agent will choose a date and alert the interested publishers.

- ◆ Your agent may establish a *floor*, a minimum bid, or reserve the right to decline unacceptable bids.

- ◆ On the day of the auction, your agent will call the editors for their bids. (Not all editors will end up bidding.)

- ◆ As the number rises, the agent will continue to call editors and inform them of the latest price.

- ◆ At the end of the day (or days), the editor with the highest bid gets your book.

Bookmarks _____

When an agent has all interested publishers submit their bids on the same day, it's called an **auction**. This is the best way to get a high advance. The agent might also specify a minimum bid, called the **floor**.

An auction day can be very exciting for both the agent and the author. You'll find it hard not to call your agent every few minutes to check on things. Let your agent call you, though. She needs to keep those phone lines clear for editors with big checkbooks!

"How Much Can I Expect?"

This is the dreaded first question every new author asks an agent. And it's a question that's impossible to answer. The size of an advance depends entirely on the perceived size of the book's audience. It depends on how much the publishing house loves your book. It depends on how unique your book is. It depends on how many publishers are interested in your book. It depends on the timing of your book, too, and how many competing titles there are out there.

Other factors that can affect the size of an advance include whether the publishing industry is on an upswing or a downswing. The size and power of the publishing house that wants to buy your book figures in, too. Another factor may be whether that publishing house had a good year or a bad year. It may also depend on whether the publisher had a fight with his spouse or whether it is raining outside. Who knows?

Nibbles

If an editor is interested in your book, chances are she'll call your agent before making a formal offer. This lets the agent know that you've hooked at least one fish!

Chapter 14 is filled with material about how editors pull together information before making an offer, but in this chapter, let's just say that the first offer is never the best offer. Your agent will work hard to try to get the offer increased.

Reeling 'Em In

As the author, you should be included on the action surrounding your book. Your agent will want to keep you abreast of interest, offers forthcoming or on the table, and any anticipated closing date. You should definitely be included in the conversation about money. This does not mean that you, too, will talk to the editor. Money talk goes on between an agent and an editor; it does not include the author. But you do get to approve the final deal—congratulations!

Breaking Up

You worked hard to get yourself an agent, and you did get one! Now that agent has sold one or two of your books, and you are feeling … well, feeling like maybe you want to get a new agent. Like any relationship in life, dealing between writers and agents don't always work out smoothly forever. So can you change agents?

Yes, you can change agents. Most relationships between writers and agents go from book to book. If you want to change in between books, it should be fine. However, changing agents while a deal is being negotiated is *verboten*. And even if you've changed agents, the publisher will continue to send monies through the agent of record for a book as long as that book is in print.

The Least You Need to Know

- Know what you can expect from an agent who wants to represent you.
- Familiarize yourself with an agent/author agreement.
- An agent might ask you to make changes to your work, but you don't have to agree.
- Rejection letters sometimes have much useful information you can learn from.
- The size of an advance is totally unpredictable, but what is for certain is that your agent will work to get as large an advance as possible.

Chapter 13

Submitting Directly to Editors

In This Chapter

- ◆ If you can't get an agent—or don't want one
- ◆ University presses, small publishers, and niche publishing
- ◆ The world of children's books
- ◆ Basic submission guidelines
- ◆ Should you self-publish?
- ◆ Publishing electronically

What do you do if you can't get an agent? Or what if you simply don't want to use one? Can you try to work directly with a publisher without the extra layer of an agent? Sure. In this chapter, you'll discover how to work with editors directly and some of the specialized situations in which agents aren't required. You'll also learn how to make a professional submission without an agent.

It is entirely possible to get published without the help of an agent. Many writers have done it. In fact, there are some areas of the publishing business in which agents rarely, if ever, are used. Where? At university presses, scholarly publishers, regional publishers, some small presses, mid-list nonfiction, and many children's publishers. Are these the only areas in which you can try without an agent? No, you can try to approach anyone on your own, but these are the parts of the business that might be most open to you working alone.

Let's take a quick look at the world of academia first.

The Ivy Leagues

University presses are a world unto their own, with specialized methods of editorial selection and approval. Acquisitions editors who work for university presses crisscross the country attending professional conferences of all sorts—literary, anthropological, medical, sociological, and the like—to stay on top of what the issues are and who is tops in the field. When they familiarize themselves with the leading scholars in their field of publishing specialty, the editors cultivate relationships with them in the hopes that these experts will someday write for them. To put it bluntly, in most cases you don't call such editors; they call you.

> **Experts Say**
>
> "Once a university press editor asks for your proposal, it should be an exclusive submission," a professor told us. "Etiquette dictates that, even if you never hear back, you wait at least six months before trying another publisher. Multiple queries are all right, but the in-house review process is so long with the proposal that you need to give them the exclusive."

You can submit without being "summoned." How do you do it? First send a query letter to the acquisitions editor describing yourself and your book, and then wait for the editor to respond. All the same rules for writing query letters (as you learned in Chapter 7) apply. Do not leave out your self-addressed, stamped envelope. University presses have even less money than other publishers and surely cannot afford to pay the postage on all the unsolicited material they receive!

Curriculum Vitae

An editor at a university press will take a long, hard look at your educational and scholarly credentials. If you do not have the right ones to back up your book, the chances are slim that a university press will take you on.

If an acquisitions editor does respond to your query, she might ask you to send in a "prospectus." Don't panic—that's just a book proposal by another name. Why the world of scholarly presses uses it is unclear; perhaps it just sounds more scholarly.

Readers and Referees

Unlike a trade publisher with its pub board and editorial meetings, folks outside the university press primarily judge the fate of a proposal.

If the editor likes what she sees in your prospectus, and if your credentials are up to snuff, your material will then be sent to a reader. *Readers* are also known as *referees*. These are well-known professors and other experts who are qualified to judge your material from a professional standpoint. As the editor is seldom academically qualified to pass judgment on a manuscript, readers perform this critical task.

How many readers or referees will see your material? Perhaps only one, or as many as three or four. It depends on the topic and the input from the first reader. Readers might sometimes recommend your book "with reservations." The editor will then go back to the author and ask for changes or a response to the reservations.

Bookmarks

University presses use **readers,** or **referees,** to help with the acquisitions process. These folks judge manuscripts in their fields of expertise. They either are paid a fee or are paid in kind with free books from the press.

Read More About It

The average print run from university presses is lower than a trade publisher, but you might find that university presses have a longer-term commitment to keeping their books in print.

An excellent way to learn more about the world of university presses is through a book published by the Modern Language Association. Known as the *MLA Style Manual and Guide to Scholarly Publishing,* this is the standard guide for graduate students preparing theses. Over the years, it has grown to include information on how to get published.

At a recent annual conference of the Modern Language Association many in the academic world decried the difficulty of having their scholarly work published. Do fewer presses, fewer opportunities to publish, yet the same "publish or perish" atmosphere exist on campus? Is academic publishing on the verge of disappearing, as so many at the conference fear? Not likely, but it is a specialized industry in which it is very difficult to succeed.

Small Can Be Good

Some of the success stories coming out of small publishing companies show that small can indeed be beautiful. Don't kid yourself—New York is not the only place where book publishing gets done. There are thriving presses all over the country, from Tennessee and Louisiana to Washington and Vermont, and from New Mexico to Colorado. One of the strongest-selling business books in recent history, *The Millionaire Next Door,* didn't come from Random House or Simon & Schuster. It came from the Longstreet Press in Atlanta, Georgia. The long-time best-selling career guide *What Color Is Your Parachute?* comes from Ten Speed Press in Berkeley, California. Both *small publishers?* Technically, yes.

"Mini-majors," a new term in publishing, refers to publishers such as Running Press in Philadelphia; Adams Media, based just outside of Boston; Chronicle Books in San Francisco, and Workman Publishing in New York. They're not big publishers with sales of hundreds of millions of dollars, but they're independently owned medium-size companies with solid sales in the $20 million to $50 million range.

Bookmarks

How small is small? Instead, ask how large is small, as the case may sometimes be. The term **small publisher,** or **small press,** is used loosely but generally is applied to publishing houses with sales of less than $10 million a year. Mini-majors are publishers with $20 million to $50 million in annual sales.

Small publishers and the mini-majors are generally more open to dealing directly with authors than the New York houses are. And it can be somewhat less intimidating for a first-time author. Many a big-name author (including Deepak Chopra) got started with a small publisher before achieving fame with a larger house (much to the chagrin of the smaller publisher, who took a chance on an unknown).

When you work with a publisher that has a small staff, you can sometimes have a closer relationship with the editor, publicist, and other people working with your book.

Small publishers are seldom in the business of paying big advances, so cast aside your dreams of the big bucks up front if you are pursuing this route. The occasional small publisher might only offer authors a one time payment for work-for-hire, but this is rare.

Before you can get your foot in the door to a small publisher, though, you need to introduce yourself in the same way you would to an agent—with a compelling query letter.

The Name Game

The best way to get your query letter read is to address it to an actual editor. How do you find out who the editors are at these small presses? Here are three ways:

◆ Look on the acknowledgments page of other books from that publisher; authors often thank their editors.

◆ Look in the *Writer's Guide to Book Editors, Publishers, and Literary Agents;* or in the annual *Writer's Market* published by the same folks who do the *Writer's Digest* magazine.

◆ Call the publishing house and ask which acquisitions editors acquire books in your genre.

Query an Editor

The query letter you should use with a small publisher is essentially the same as outlined in Chapter 7. The only difference is that you're not trying to sell an agent; you are trying to sell an editor.

Review the advice in Chapter 7. Remember to keep your query letter short and to the point. But also remember that the purpose of a query letter is to sell yourself and your project. Talk up the market, and talk up your commitment to seeing the book work. Also include an SASE.

Will you hear back from an editor at a small publisher? Yes, if you have included an SASE. How long it will take to hear back is anyone's guess. But if you neglect to include an SASE and your query doesn't interest the editor, you will never hear back. Your letter will be tossed, and you will wonder forever if it ever even arrived. Resist the temptation to call and ask whether your query letter got there. Even at small presses, an editor's day is hectic, often with no time to return phone calls about unsolicited queries, proposals, and manuscripts.

Negotiating on Your Own

If an editor responds to your query and requests a copy of your proposal or your manuscript, you are one step closer to success. What happens then is described at length in Chapter 14. The acquisitions process for a small publisher is the same as that for a large publisher.

Experts Say

Have you been dropped by your agent, who was unable to sell your project after a year or so? You're not alone. Mark Victor Hansen and Jack Canfield were dropped by their agent, too, just before the *Chicken Soup for the Soul* book sold to Health Communications. "Biggest mistake he ever made," they laugh.

If the small publisher makes you an offer, then what? You can negotiate on your own, but if you decide to do so, you'll need to learn a lot in a hurry. An excellent book by Mark Levine, called *Negotiating a Book Contract*, can help you.

Chapter 15 walks you through some of the basic points in a publishing contract. Some editors are also quite patient in explaining contract points to first-time authors.

An Agent, at This Point?

If you have an offer in hand, getting an agent should be no trouble now! Those same folks who weren't interested in helping you before would be happy to help you now that there's an offer on the table. But do you need an agent?

> **Hot Off the Press** _____
>
> Lewis Buzbee, a San Francisco writer and college professor, sold his book *Alone Among Others: The Pleasures of the Bookstore*, to Jennifer at Prima Publishing on his own, without an agent. What did Jennifer find most compelling about Lewis' proposal? The fact that he included letters of support for the book ideas from publishers' sales reps. These are folks who have a terrific sense of what sells and why, so early approval from this group carried a great deal of weight in her decision. Could you pull this off, too? Get to know booksellers, sales reps, anyone in the publishing world who might help you get a leg up in the process if you are doing it on your own.

If you don't think you can do a good job of negotiating on your own behalf, perhaps you should get an agent involved. At this point, the editor may be happy to refer you to an agent she's worked with before. Ask if the agent is willing to take a lower commission, though, since you got the deal on your own.

If the publisher tells you that it doesn't like to work with agents, be on your guard.

The Hunt Is On

Small publishers and mini-majors sound great, but how do you find them? They're right there on the shelf next to the big boys! As you spend time in bookstores familiarizing yourself with the players in your category, you will begin to spot the small publishers on your own. Many of them are listed in *Writer's Guide to Book Editors, Publishers, and Literary Agents*, and in *LMP*.

If you're game, give it a try; small publishers just might be right for you.

Tight Niches

A discussion of small publishers has to include the "niche" publishers, the ones that specialize in one tight niche market. A niche market can be anything from mountain-climbing books (The Mountaineers Press) to books on the occult (Samuel Weiser, Inc.), and from Northwest travel books (Sasquatch Books in Seattle) to Southern travel books (Pelican Publishing Company). The more familiar you become with your area of specialty, the more you will notice niche publishers who cater directly to your market.

Don't spin your wheels trying to interest a large publisher when you can go directly to a small niche publisher that specializes in your area. These are the experts in the marketplace and will understand right away whether your book is marketable and how best to do it. Niche publishers are very careful about the books they publish. The decision process will be slow, but if your book is published by a smart niche publisher, the sales could be steady for years to come.

Once Upon a Time ...

Children's books are another area in which you can deal directly with a publisher. Keeping in mind that children's books include both picture books (written with an author and illustrator) and YA (young adult) novels and series. Some agents specialize in representing children's books, of course, but a large portion of children's authors do not have agents.

How do you approach a children's book publisher about your idea? With a query letter! Look for the names of editors in *Writer's Guide to Book Editors, Publishers, and Literary Agents* or the more specialized *Writer's Guide to Children's Book Editors, Publishers, and Literary Agents*, or call the publisher to ask for the names of its acquisitions editors and their areas of specialty. But if you do call, just get the name from the receptionist and politely hang up. Resist the urge to ask to speak to an editor directly at this point. Remember, the early stages of getting published are all done by written letters, not phone conversations. You must first prove that you can write.

Bookmarks

There are several different types of **children's books**: illustrated books, easy readers, and chapter books. Illustrated books are the lovely big picture books that small children love to "read" over and over again. Easy readers are books of the "see Jane run" variety, and chapter books are longer books for more experienced readers.

CAUTION

Slush Pile

Do not send an illustrated manuscript to a children's publisher. Illustrated manuscripts go first to the publisher's art department to be evaluated, not to the editor. If it doesn't meet with the art director's approval, it is rejected. Your actual words themselves will never be seen or read. Submit only a manuscript. In children's publishing, the publisher traditionally matches authors with illustrator, rather than buying a complete package from an unknown.

You may also call the company and request its submissions guidelines. When you receive the guidelines, follow them down to the letter. Do not get fancy and decide to try another approach. Guidelines have been developed over many years of publishing experience and should be heeded.

Be warned, however, that many children's publishers have ceased accepting unsolicited manuscripts altogether. These companies still will accept query letters from first-time authors, though. There are many aspects of the children's book publishing industry that can be quite different than regular publishing. If you plan to try to get a children's book published, a wise move would be to pick up a copy of *The Complete Idiot's Guide to Publishing Children's Books* by Harold Underdown and Lynne Rominger.

Experts Say

"I recommend so many writers to the Society of Children's Book Writers and Illustrators, it should pay me a commission!" laughs author Debra Keller. "The benefits of membership are tremendous: a list every August of all children's book publishers, the names of their editors, the submissions guidelines, and what they are looking for." You don't need to have been previously published to join. Contact the SCBWI at 323-782-1010. They also have a helpful website at www.scbwi.org.

Poetry

Poetry is still one more category that usually does not require an agent—and most agents do not represent poetry. If you would like to have your poetry published, our best advice is to scour the writer's shelf in the library or bookstore, and read more than one book on getting poetry published. Identify appropriate magazine, journal, and poetry book publishers, and query them according to their specific guidelines. Some books list appropriate publishers, but an even better technique is to read books and magazines of poetry. Ask poetry teachers as well as published poets for advice. Don't get discouraged before you start. Poetry gets published all the time—just not very often via agents.

To Self-Publish or Not to Self-Publish

If you've had no luck with agents and no luck submitting directly to publishers, what options are left? Is the only way your book will ever see its way into print if you pay for it to be printed and bound?

Self-publishing is an old and honorable pursuit, and many of the literary world's glossiest names have published their own work at one time or another. Think we are just trying to make you feel better, if this is your only option? Nope, this is the actual truth. Margaret Atwood, Virginia Woolf, Pat Conroy, Ken Kesey, the list could go on forever. But how can you decide if it is right for you? After all, writing a book is an art. Self-publishing a book is a business.

A Means to My End?

To decide if self-publishing is the right route for you, go back to a question in Chapter 1: Why do you want to write a book?

Which of those goals can be satisfied by self-publishing your book? Pretty much all of them except fame and fortune. Sure, it has happened that a self-publisher has gone on to fame and fortune, but it is a fluke.

Do You Have What It Takes?

Not everyone is cut out to be a self-publisher. It requires lots of money, creativity, ingenuity, dedication, and entrepreneurial zeal. Do you have what it takes? Asking yourself these five questions might help you find out:

- Is publishing my book so important to me that I am willing to pay thousands of dollars to see it happen?

- Am I willing to accept the fact that I will probably never see that money again?

- Once my book is published, am I willing to invest countless hours attempting to distribute, publicize, and market my book?

- Am I thick-skinned enough to take it if my book is criticized, ignored, or rejected by booksellers and/or the media?

- Am I persistent enough to keep going if I get that kind of treatment?

Hot Off the Press

Christopher Paolini is, at 19, a young man from Montana on his way to the top in the New York publishing world. His fantasy novel, *Eragon,* was bought by Alfred A. Knopf in a deal reported to be in the half-million-dollar range. How'd that happen? He self-published the book and then made more than 70 appearances around the country during 2002, from elementary schools to bookstores. His family helped him produce and sell the books, and by the time Knopf bought the rights they "couldn't handle things any longer on our own, so it was a case of perfect timing," Paolini says.

Speaking of Speaking ...

One of the best reasons to self-publish a book is to augment your speaking career. If you are already giving talks to rooms full of people, it might be quite easy to sell them a book you just happened to bring with you. Skip the headache of bookstore distribution, and keep all the money. Sounds great! And it can be done with a self-published book. We'll talk more about the speaking and writing circuit in a later chapter.

Several excellent books are already available on how to self-publish a book. We really don't have enough room here to do a thorough job of covering the process, but here's a quick look at the steps you will need to go through.

1. Find a copy editor and a proofreader.

2. Get the book designed and typeset.

3. Have a cover designed.

4. Find an affordable short-run printer.

5. Arrange for your book's distribution.

6. Market and publicize the book.

Experts Say

Why not learn from the best? Best-selling author Mark Victor Hansen periodically teaches a popular weekend seminar called Mega Book Marketing University. And he should know—millions and millions of people bought his *Chicken Soup* books and his financial self-help book *The One Minute Millionaire* was a best-seller right out of the gate. For information on scheduling, or to purchase an audio of the event, check out his website at www.markvictorhansen.com or call 949-759-9304.

Proof Positive

If your self-published book is a success, can you sell it to a larger publisher? Certainly! You have to stop selling it yourself then. If you can show a solid record of sales success with a self-published book, both agents and publishers will take you very seriously.

On the other hand, best-selling self-publishers have sometimes just stuck it out for the ride instead of selling to a larger publisher. They might also ride it to the very top in order to cut a bigger deal with a large publisher. *Rich Dad, Poor Dad* spent month after month on the business best-seller lists at the end of 1999 and into 2000. The author continued to publish under his own imprint, pocketing the larger portion of the proceeds himself instead of taking a royalty arrangement from a publisher. The book itself attempts to teach lessons in wealth-creation—apparently the author had learned the lessons pretty well because when he finally did sell to Warner Books, he made quite a bundle!

Oh, Don't Be Vain!

Self-publishing is a fine and honorable pursuit, but we think vanity presses are a rip-off. We recommend staying away from anyone called a "subsidy publisher," or anyone who acts like he's willing to publish your book as long as you pay the costs.

The contract from a vanity press looks just like a standard publishing contract, but with one critical difference: A clause states that you have to pay for producing the book. If you are offered something like this, run!

The Electronic Edge

Many adventurous writers are experimenting with new forms of self-publishing: e-books and on-demand printing. Companies such as Xlibris (which is owned by Random House, so they know a thing or two about professionally produced books) have set up systems whereby writers can either make their materials available online to prospective purchasers, or print up smaller quantities than would be possible with most printers.

Like traditional self-publishing, though, it remains the responsibility of the author to create sales for what he has written. Just because your work is available online as an e-book doesn't mean that a reader is going to buy it, unless you somehow create demand through publicity.

These companies have even more to offer: online classes and seminars taught by publishing professionals. Check out the website at www.xlibris.com.

As with the rest of the online world, what happens there changes with blinding speed. So even if this route never occurred to you, go and check out these companies anyway. Who knows what services they are offering today?

You're on Your Own

You now know many of the circumstances in which you can try to get your work published without an agent. When submitting on your own behalf to any kind of publisher (whether a children's publisher, a niche publisher, or a small publisher), be as businesslike as possible. Review the chapters on queries and proposals before you begin to compile your materials, keeping in mind that you are directing your information to a book editor, not an agent.

An editor has the same concerns as an agent: the potential market for the book, the author's credentials, and the uniqueness of the idea. Just as an agent's career depends on finding successful authors, so, too, does the editor's career flourish when she finds great writers whose books sell well. Editors are looking for new writers. Help them find you!

Selling your work on your own really can work sometimes. California inspirational writer Candy Chand has sold four book projects on her own by querying editors directly. She has an uncanny knack for guessing the in-house e-mail addresses for editors at big houses and sending off query letters. Sometimes she gets rejected in minutes, but believes it saves time, money, and heartache. It could work for you, too.

The Least You Need to Know

- It is possible—and quite common—to approach university presses, children's publishers, and small publishers without an agent.

- Learn the names of the editors, and approach them directly with short query letters.

- Respect the system: queries first, and proposals later (if requested). Do not try to call editors directly before they've had a chance to review something from you in writing.

- Once you have a deal in hand, you will be able to get an agent, but ask for a reduced commission.

- Self-publishing requires both money and dedication, but it can be emotionally rewarding and can perhaps help boost your career.

Chapter 14

Behind Closed Doors

In This Chapter

- ◆ Getting past the first hurdle: the editor
- ◆ The pub board meeting
- ◆ Competition and sales projections
- ◆ Production costs and P and Ls

So far, on your mission to get published you wrote a great query letter and a superb book proposal. An agent called you up and offered to represent you. Or no agents called and you decided to take up the task yourself. Twelve copies of your proposal have been sent to twelve editors at the twelve publishing houses best suited for your book. Your fingers are crossed, and you are saying your prayers nightly. What happens now?

Hurry Up and Wait

Several things could happen:

- ◆ The editor opens her mail one day and discovers your proposal. Intrigued after reading just a few paragraphs, she sets it aside on a stack of material she plans to take home and read more thoroughly.

♦ Your agent may have placed a call to the editor to get him excited about the proposal in advance. It arrives in the mail, and the editor thinks, "Ah, yes, this is the book Mr. Agent described. I must take a look at it right away; it sounded perfect for our *list*." He glances at a few pages and sets it aside on a stack of material he plans to take home and read more thoroughly.

Bookmarks

The word *list* is used to describe the books that the publisher or editor plans to publish in the near future. "It's on our list," an editor might say, or "We have a few holes on our list that need filling"—these phrases are music to an agent's ears. Perhaps *your* book is just perfect for their list! The list is usually a pre-planned template of books (or types/price) of books that editors have committed to their bosses and their bosses have committed to their bosses for planning purposes. Any given year, an editor will be responsible for bringing in a set number of titles for the list (or plan).

♦ Your agent might have gone to lunch with the editor the day before. Over a spinach salad, your agent pitched the editor a number of book projects from several clients. The editor expressed an interest in seeing one or two of them (including yours!), and the agent messengers them over that same afternoon.

The editor sets it aside on a stack of material she plans to take home and … you know the rest.

However it got there, your proposal is now inside the doors of a publishing house.

Experts Say

Editors don't read much at the office. Yes, they do read query letters, but most of the real reading gets done at home. "As an acquisitions editor I broke the straps on four book bags in one year alone from the weight of the manuscripts I carried home every night," says Danielle Egan-Miller, a Chicago-based literary agent and former editor. Longtime editor Renee Wilmeth has now adopted the habit of using a big leather laptop briefcase, filled with manuscripts instead of a laptop!

"Sorry, Not Right for Our Needs at This Time"

Sadly, the story could easily end right here. The editor might not put your proposal on the stack that she plans to take home. Perhaps she took a look at your proposal and then put it in her reject pile.

Why? Well, for any one of a number of reasons. You might not make it as far as the editorial meeting for these reasons:

♦ It is clearly not appropriate for that publishing house—your book is about the history of fighter pilots, and this publisher publishes only vegetarian cookbooks.

♦ The publishing house already has a book on that topic, and it hasn't sold well.

♦ The publishing house already has a book on that topic, and the author of that book plans to do more in that area.

♦ The editor doesn't think that a large market exists for your book.

Most rejection letters do not include any actual reason why your book was rejected. The standard line is "Thank you, but this is not right for us." Why don't editors write more? Two reasons: They don't have the time to analyze, critique, and then write to you; and they don't want to invite a response or rebuttal from you. Try to take your rejection letters in stride.

Who knows, you might end up selling your book eventually to that publishing house anyway. Candy Chand (who has such luck selling projects on her own) sold her book *Ashley's Garden* to an editor at Adams Media after a different editor turned it down.

Hot Off the Press

Publishing is a people business, and the people who work in publishing are people just like you. Sometimes they are tired, cranky, and not in the mood to buy books. If your book proposal has been rejected by an editor, do not take this as a sign that your project is doomed and will never be published by anyone. Who knows, perhaps it just was a bad day at the office when your material crossed their desks. Keep trying, and go on to the next publisher.

Consider This

But if your book does make it onto the stack to be read further, then what?

Editors do quite a bit of investigating before bringing your proposal to a meeting. An editor might call your agent to ask questions or request more material. An editor might call you directly to learn more about you, the market for the book, and your plans to promote it. Editors might also do more hands-on investigation: prowling around bookstores to examine the competing titles, asking friends in the industry how well that category is selling, or cruising the Internet to see if there is much interest in the topic.

If the editor likes what he sees in the proposal, what he hears from you, and what his own research turns up, the next step is for him to present it to his colleagues and superiors for possible publication.

Slush Pile

The phone rings, and it's an editor asking about your book. Although the questions may all relate to the book itself, the editor might have another motive. How well you present yourself on the phone is critical to your book's future success. Editors want authors who can handle themselves easily with interviews and the media. If you are tired, distracted, or otherwise unprepared to sound good on the phone, it is better to beg off and reschedule the conversation.

Committee Decisions

As powerful as many of them are, editors do not make the decision to publish a book on their own. That decision rests with a group of people sometimes called the *pub board* or the *editorial board.* The editor who likes your book is only one voting member of this group. Other members usually include some combination of other editors, the publisher, and folks from the sales, marketing, and publicity departments. The process works something like this:

Bookmarks

Unless it is a one-person publishing house, your proposal will be presented to an **editorial board,** or **pub board.** This is a group of people who collectively make the decision about what titles to publish.

◆ An editor is intrigued by your proposal and decides to present it to the pub board.

◆ The editor brings your proposal to a meeting.

◆ The editor makes a short presentation about your book and attempts to drum up interest and enthusiasm.

◆ The editor answers questions from other members of the group. Sometimes the editor needs to do further research and will present the book in more detail at a future meeting.

So that's it. The fate of your book can be decided in about 10 minutes. But if you get past this point, then what happens? Does the editor call to say that he wants to make an offer? No, not yet.

Hot Off the Press

"Editors had to do a lot of homework before presenting a title for a publication decision," explains Carol Hupping, former executive editor of Peterson's. They had to fill out a long "proposal to publish" form. It included an overview, content description, a chapter outline, strong selling points, the editor's take on the market, descriptions of competing titles, and an author bio. The editor also had to provide the specs for the book: information on the proposed size and shape of the book, number of pages, and whether it had photos or illustrations. Each presentation took about 10 minutes, although the discussion might stretch to a half-hour.

How's It Gonna Sell?

Even if an editor has successfully lined up support in the meeting, there is still more work to be done. Remember, publishing is a business, and in business, the bottom line is king. So the editor has to work up the numbers to see whether publishing your book will pay off. How is this done?

Editors often ask the sales department for help. Experienced sales folks can help the editor figure out what the typical orders would be for the proposed book. How many copies would Borders buy? Barnes & Noble? Target? Small independent bookstores across the country? They add up all these numbers and hope that the result is big.

Slush Pile

The power and influence of the publishing sales department has grown in the last decade. Although in years past, the typical sales department wouldn't find out what was on the list until the sales conference, it is now often included in the front-end decisions about what to publish—either just before or just after the book is approved. If the sales department doesn't think it can sell a book to its customers, the book does not get published. End of story.

The publicity department may also be polled at this point. The editor will talk with the publicity folks about whether the topic of the book (or the name of the author) lends itself to publicity.

The editor might also pay a visit to the production department to check on the typical production costs for a book of this type.

All these numbers are plugged into the P and L, the profit and loss statement. If the numbers look good, the editor reports back to the pub board. And then maybe, just maybe, the title will be approved and the editor will get the go-ahead to make an offer.

The Meeting Begins

Let's take a close look at what goes on in one of these meetings. This will give you a good idea how all the information you dredged up for your proposal comes into play.

It is a Tuesday afternoon at Big Publishing Company, Inc., and all the members of the pub board are gathered in a conference room. The editors carry armloads of book proposals and other materials. In any given meeting, the fate of 10 or more books is decided. Each editor has high hopes for the books he has decided to champion.

Batter Up!

Editor 1 leads off with her first proposal: a book of affirmations and prayers for breast cancer survivors. She describes the focus of the book, the reason that the world needs this book, the qualifications of the woman who put it together, and the impact the book could have on the women who read it.

The sales manager speaks up with a question: "How many books already exist on this topic? And just how large is the market? What are the current figures on breast cancer occurrence?"

The editor has carefully read the proposal and knows the answers to those questions because the author did her research well. It was all right there.

The publisher wants to know: "There is a strong title already on the subject from another publisher. How will this book be different enough to find an audience? I worry that the bookstores won't see a need to order another similar title."

Once again the editor answers the questions and concerns with authority. The author of this book has researched the competing titles, talked to bookstore managers about the need, and lined up the support of a major breast cancer survivors group. A solid proposal has all the answers.

So the pub board is interested in considering this title. What happens then? The editor spends the next few days making the rounds of the departments to gather more information on how much it would cost to produce this book and how many copies they can expect to sell. She calls the agent or the author with any questions about the proposal that she couldn't answer herself. She distributes copies of the proposal to those interested in reading.

When the editor has rounded up all the answers, she once again makes a short presentation at a pub board meeting. If the numbers are right, the group will decide to go on to the next phase: making an offer to publish the book.

Next Up!

Editor 2 gets a turn. He begins his presentation on a book about the history of base-ball cards. "This will be the first-ever book on the topic," he says proudly, pointing with confidence at that claim in the proposal.

"Oh, come on!" says the publicity manager. "I am a collector myself and own at least two books on the history of baseball cards."

The editor stammers and flips quickly through the pages of the proposal, looking for something to salvage the situation. "Ah, but this is the first time that the cards them-selves will be organized by player position rather than team! That is really unique!"

"Just like the book I have on my shelf," the publicity manager snickers.

Another book bites the dust.

Hot Off the Press

The worst thing you can do in a book proposal is lie. If you lie or fib about your qualifications, if you lie about the competing books, or if you lie about the sales his-tory of your other books, you are headed for disaster. Editors never forget and will certainly not forget if they are made to look foolish with information that you sup-plied. Think you can try to fool one editor at one house and then move on to the next if that fails? Don't be surprised if your first editor moves, too. A bad reputation spreads quickly and is hard to shed. Always play straight.

Let's Pretend

You can see how critical the information that you provide in your proposal is to your future success. When compiling a proposal, pretend that you, too, are a member of a pub board. Put yourself in that person's shoes, and try to anticipate all the negative or hard-hitting questions that might be asked. Then supply the answers in your pro-posal. Give the editor something to work with.

Second Chances?

Is there ever a second chance? If an editor flops with your proposal once, can he ever try it again? Seldom, but it happens. It has nothing to do with begging or pleading on your part, though.

If the editor has truly fallen in love with your book project, he might go back to square one. He might poke around some more in the marketplace, ask more questions of friends in the industry, and try to gather ammunition that will convince the skeptics that this book would succeed. If the information he gathers is compelling enough, and if his own commitment to the book is strong enough, it just might work the second time around.

But if the answer was "No" and the editor doesn't have the heart or the interest to re-pitch the project, you have probably come to the end of the road—the end of the road with that publisher, anyway. Even though it worked for Candy Chand and *Ashley's Garden*, we don't recommend trying another editor at the same house.

Congratulations are in order, though. Only a tiny fraction of book projects ever make it to the pub board stage, so you have succeeded. Keep trying. If one editor was interested enough to pitch it, another one will be, too.

They Like Me! They Really Do!

What if the answer is "Yes"? Go ahead and pop open the bottle of champagne. The editor succeeded with the pub board and got the go-ahead to make you an offer—way to go! Now what happens?

The editor will call you, or your agent, if you have one. The conversation will sound something like this: "I've got good news! We'd like to publish your book. I'd like to make you an offer of an advance against future royalties of …."

Money, Money, Money, Money

The editor doesn't make the decision to publish on her own, nor does she decide the size of the offer on her own. In the pub board discussion or in a one-on-one with the publisher, all decision-makers determine the range of the advance. The editor then has the authority to call either the agent or the author (if there is no agent involved) to make the offer.

Understand that a smart editor will never make his or her highest offer first. This is particularly critical information to have if you are working without an agent. If the editor has been approved to offer $18,000, she might first offer $15,000 to give herself room to go up. It's a basic negotiating tactic. So brush up on your own negotiating skills and ask for more.

The Numbers Game

The size of the advance could vary from small to large. Who knows? There is no way to predict exactly how much you'll be offered. If you have an agent, chances are that she will immediately ask for a larger figure (remember, the more you make, the more your agent makes). If you don't have an agent, should you ask for a bigger number, too?

It never hurts to ask, but ask for a reasonable increase over what is being offered. You might also risk looking like an egotist if you counter with what the editor thinks is an unreasonable sum. And you only risk being told "No, we won't go any higher." On the other hand, if you are just thrilled that someone wants to publish your book, take the offer.

> **Hot Off the Press**
>
> Some editors like working with first timers, but first timers who are willing to learn how publishing works. The first timers (typically arrogant business guys) who think they can come in and make publishing work like other businesses are frustrating—this includes contract terms, processes, marketing, etc.

Other Considerations in the Offer

Do you need to bone up on negotiating techniques in order to deal directly with an offer? Thankfully, publishing isn't a particularly cut-throat business. In the chapter on contracts we will walk you through each clause and let you know which ones are easiest to negotiate and change.

Congratulations, you are getting published!

The Least You Need to Know

- Editors present proposals to a pub board made up of representatives from several different departments.

- If the sales department is not enthusiastic about a book idea, it will seldom go any further.

- The better the information in your proposal, the easier it is for an editor to gain support for your book.

- Never lie, exaggerate, or exclude important information from your proposal; it can only hurt you.

- If you get a "Yes," you'll be offered an advance, which you (or your agent) might be able to negotiate upward.

The Party of the First Part

In This Chapter

- Boilerplate contract clauses
- "Half-and-half" advances
- The 12 major flex points
- Rights, royalties, and remainders
- Bonuses and other contract sweeteners

An offer is in and a contract is coming. Your book project is becoming more real by the moment. Someday you really will be able to walk into a bookstore and see your book on the shelf.

But first, you have to sign a contract.

We are not lawyers. After working with hundreds of contracts over the years, however, we do have a fairly good handle on what it all means. In this chapter, you will learn the meaning behind many of the standard clauses found in a publishing contract. Then we'll give you the inside scoop on which clauses we have found to be more negotiable than others.

Whereas and Therefore

Regardless of the size of the publishing company, most contracts are essentially the same. Some are considerably longer than others (40 pages is the longest we've seen), but the basic points are the same.

CAUTION

Slush Pile

So you don't have an agent. Do you need a lawyer? Actually, most lawyers have little knowledge about the quirks found in publishing contracts. An editor will not be pleased to hear from your lawyer, either, if he or she is not familiar with a publishing contract. To find a lawyer who specializes in publishing, contact the Author's Guild (see Appendix B).

What is the purpose of a book contract? A publishing company wants to publish a work that you wrote and needs to have a legal document that does the following:

- Gives the company the right to publish and sell your material in an agreed-upon territory

- Outlines the monetary arrangements

- Establishes your right to grant the company the rights

- Spells out the responsibilities of the author and the publisher

- States a time length for the agreement

Pretty simple, isn't it? Then why does it take so many darn pages to establish those simple facts? Is that because lawyers bill by the hour? Perhaps. But the business world grows more complicated by the decade, and new legal issues crop up all the time. Let's take a close look at 15 major clauses in a publishing contract.

Most all points are negotiable. And editors will tell you which ones are not (like the indemnity and warranty clauses). So if you want something, ask for it. You might not get it, but at least you asked—and you might get something more than you had before. Negotiating a publishing contract is all about choosing battles—be prepared to let a few things go, and decide in advance what they will be. We'll fill you in on which points are the easiest to get changed.

The Work

One of the early paragraphs in a contract will define what is generally called the "Work." This, of course, is your book. Your book will henceforth be referred to as the "Work." You get to be the "Author." The company is forever known in contracts as the "Publisher."

In this paragraph, the subject matter of the work will be defined. If you are writing a novel, it will be defined as a work of fiction, and the general focus of the book will be mentioned. If you are writing a nonfiction book, the work will be described as "a Work of nonfiction whose subject matter is as follows ...." The expected length of your finished manuscript will also be stated.

Why is this here? The publishing company needs to make sure that the book you turn in is the book that it had in mind when it signed you up. This clause protects the publisher from signing you up to write a novel about the Civil War, only to have you turn in a nonfiction memoir about your childhood in New Orleans.

Copyright

Standard publishing contracts state that the publisher will register the copyright to the work in the name of the author. Beware of any contract that asks you to assign all rights to the publisher, or one that stipulates that the publisher is the copyright holder. Unless the author gives the right away, he or she owns the copyright by virtue of having written the material. In fact, the minute that you put pen to paper and write something original, it is copyrighted material without you even so much as filling out a form.

Tentatively Titled

This section of the contract might also contain a zinger, a phrase that refers to the book as "tentatively titled." Tentatively titled? But you thought of that title years ago, and it is all over your queries and proposals. How can the publisher refer to it as tentatively titled?

Sorry, but most publishing contracts allow the publisher the right to change the title of your book. Some will state that the title can be changed only "by mutual agreement."

Your delivery date (the day that your manuscript is due) will also appear in this early section of the contract.

> **Experts Say**
>
> As the author, you are not selling your book rights to the publisher; you're merely licensing the rights. When you license a right, you continue to own it for the life of your copyright, which is 95 years. The publisher may exercise certain rights that you grant him only for the term of the license. Once that term has expired, those rights revert back to you.

The Advance

Ah, the money part. This is where the publisher spells out exactly how much of an advance you will receive. The language will read something like this: "As an advance against all monies accruing or payable to the Author under this Agreement, the Publisher will pay to the Author the sum of ____, payable as follows …." Payable as follows?

Regardless of the size of your advance, do not expect to receive it in one lump sum. Those glittering sums you read about in the paper—like the millions that retired politicians like Rudy Giuliani are offered—aren't paid out all at once either. One arrangement is for two payments: one payment on signing the contract, and the second tied to the completion of the final manuscript. (Some of the big ones have final payment tied to publication.) The language and terms for the final payment vary widely, with some publishers paying when you turn the manuscript in on your delivery date, and other publishers not paying until the manuscript has been edited. Those are the most common advance payouts, but not the only ones. A few publishers have gone to three payments of one third each, with the final payment upon publication of the book. Others pay one third upon signing, the second third upon receipt of one half of the manuscript, and the final third upon receipt of the remainder of the manuscript. If it's your first book, they might tie a payment to completion of revisions.

Why won't they just write you a check for the whole sum? The publisher needs to know that you will follow through and turn in a manuscript on the topic and in the style that you promised in your book proposal. The best way to do this is to hold back part of the money until that happens. The publisher also wants to make sure that what you turn in is publishable—hence, the second payment is generally linked to receipt of an acceptable manuscript.

Grant of Rights

This is where you, as the author, grant and assign the rights to your work to the publisher. This is what gives the publisher the legal right to publish and sell your book. In addition to the right to sell your book in bookstores and other retail outlets, this clause may also grant the publisher the right to do these things:

◆ License the work to book clubs

◆ Sell the English-language book in foreign countries

◆ License foreign-language editions of the work

◆ Produce or license electronic versions or multimedia versions

◆ Produce or license audio book versions

- Produce or license hardcover, trade paperback, or mass market paperback versions

- License newspaper and magazine excerpts or serializations

- License movie rights

- License commercial or merchandising rights (maybe even coffee cups and T-shirts)

- Produce other sundry items, such as Braille versions or a play based on your book

Sounds like a lot of rights, right? This is a complicated section, one that agents love to tackle in detail. Publishers believe that they should be granted all these rights to be given a chance to earn back the money invested in your book—and they often have whole teams of people focused on selling these rights—called *subrights*. On the other hand, agents like to retain as many rights as possible on behalf of the author to obtain extra income for both of you!

There is some flexibility in this clause. Although most rights categories call for a 50/50 split of monies received between the publisher and the writer, you can negotiate the percentage with the editor. The most common change has to do *with first serial rights* (this is when a section of the book appears in a magazine before the book is published and available in stores, authors can sometimes get 90/10, with the 90 in their pocket!). Be aware, though, that the less money the publisher receives, the less likely they will try to market those rights.

Royalties

In the royalty section of the contract, the publisher defines exactly what the author will receive from the sale of the book. There are two different ways to calculate royalties:

- As a percentage of the retail price printed on the book

- As a percentage of the publisher's net, the actual cash the publisher receives from the sale of the book after discounts have been deducted

Bookmarks _____

The publisher's standard contract is referred to as a **boilerplate contract**. It's the standard contract that's always used, and it has not (yet) been modified with any changes that you might request.

There are two major types of royalties: retail (based on the cover price of the book) and net (based on the after discount price of the book). Royalties based on the retail price usually range from 7 to 15 percent or more. Royalties based on net may start higher, at 10 percent, and escalate from there. Your contract should clearly state what type of royalties you will receive for each copy of your book sold. Whether a publisher pays net or retail royalties is a policy set by their financial advisers. Changing from net to retail is not typically a negotiation point.

The royalties clause might also be where you will find information on what share (or "split") the author will receive of any subsidiary rights income if any of the rights that the publisher is granted earlier in the contract (book clubs, mass market paperback, and so on) are sold.

You will also find information on how many free copies of the book the author will receive once it is published, and whether the author can buy more copies at an author's discount.

Delivery of Manuscript and Corrections

The hard, cold truth is revealed here: the date by which you must turn in your completed manuscript. It might be a few short months, or it might be years away.

What happens if the date arrives and the publisher does not receive your finished work? The contract will include language to the effect that the publisher has the right to terminate the contract, generally upon written notification of the author by the publisher. If this happens, the contract states, the author will be obligated to repay the publisher any sums advanced to the author.

The contract will also include language that allows the publisher to reject the work as unpublishable, or to request specific changes to the manuscript. The contract should state a process by which the author can address the changes. If the publisher still feels that the manuscript is unacceptable, the contract can be terminated.

Once again, this is included because the publisher needs to be protected against receiving a shoddy product. In the case of nonfiction books, the publishing house probably made its decision based on only a proposal and a sample chapter. If the book ultimately turned in does not offer the proper information or isn't written professionally, a publisher will pull the plug.

Other Deliverables

The contract will outline the publisher's expectations regarding photographs, illustrations, maps, and charts. Who pays and when it needs to be turned in will be spelled out in this section.

Options

Publishers are taking a chance on your book. If it becomes a success, the house might want to publish more of your work. In the *option clause*, the contract will state that the publisher gets the first crack at your next work, the book you write after the book under contract. The language gives your publisher the exclusive right to consider your next work and describes how long the publisher has to make an offer. It may also say that if your publisher bids on the next work, you cannot sell the next work to another publisher for a lesser sum. It will also specify the earliest date that the next work can be submitted for consideration.

Bookmarks

Most contracts contain an **option clause** for the author's next work. This means that the publisher gets first crack at the next book you write, or the next book of the same type.

The clause might also cover competing works. The publisher will not want you to publish a similar book with a different publisher that would compete with this one.

The option clause and the noncompete clause can sometimes cause trouble for working writers. Later in this chapter, you'll find some ways to deal with this issue.

Author's Representations, Warranties, and Indemnity

In this clause, you, as the author, are assuring the publisher that the work is original and that you have the "sole and exclusive right to make the grant of rights set forth herein ...." You also are assuring the publisher that you are not slandering, libeling, or invading anyone's privacy with your work.

If legal action arises from the publication of your book, this clause allows the publisher to stand aside and point directly to you. "He's the one you want, he wrote the words. We just printed the darn thing." This clause might also outline the legal procedure if a lawsuit arises. Some publishers carry libel insurance; some do not. This clause is also going to point out that in the case of a lawsuit, the publisher will manage the defense and provide the legal team. This is because most large publishers have legal teams who know publishing law inside and out and are going to have the best idea how to handle a situation.

Although you might or might not agree with the wording in these clauses, this section of the contract is often not up for negotiation.

Obligations of the Publisher

You have promised to deliver a manuscript by a certain date, and in this clause the publisher promises to publish the manuscript by a certain date. Other than exceptions mentioned in the contract (such as labor strikes, acts of God, or other circumstances beyond the publisher's control), if the publisher does not publish it, what then? There should be language that allows the author to terminate the agreement and keep the advance.

Accounting

You have already been informed about the amount of royalties you will receive, but when exactly will this be paid to you? The contract will have a paragraph that outlines the schedule. Some publishers pay twice a year; some pay only once a year. This section should also include language on what happens in the case of overpayment (if the publisher's accounting department accidentally sends you too much money!) or if audits are requested by the author.

Overstock, Out of Print, or Reversion of Rights

If your book goes out of print, or if the sales dwindle down to nothing, what then? The answers will be found here. Most contracts state that if the book goes out of print for a particular length of time, the rights revert back to the author.

This clause also gives the publisher the right to sell your book at *remainder* prices, if need be.

Bookmarks

When a book ends up being sold at a steeply discounted price, it is called **remaindering.** Books are sold for pennies on the dollar to remainder companies (who then sell them back to bookstores for the bargain tables). Before a book is remaindered, most publishers offer the author the chance to buy copies at bargain prices.

Assignment

Once you sign the contract, your heirs will be legally bound by it as well. This means that if you die, the publisher still has the rights to the book. This clause also allows the publisher to assign the rights to your book to a new company if your publisher sells the business.

Bankruptcy

This clause covers the possibility of the publisher's bankruptcy, not yours. Your book rights are an asset now, and according to most contracts, if the publisher goes bankrupt, the author may buy back the rights to the book or the publishers assets will be sold. But it may leave the publisher the right to sell any remaining copies of the book in inventory without paying any royalties.

Agency Clause

If you are represented by an agent, there will be an agency clause in your contract. If you are not using an agent, this clause won't appear.

The agency clause names the agent as the person to whom the publisher should send all monies accruing to this book. The agent will then subtract her percentage and pass the balance on to you. As long as the book remains under contract to this publisher, the agent will receive the royalty check. What happens if you and your agent someday have a falling out and part ways, or if you decide to change agents? You are committed to the agent stated in your contract. You won't be able to call the publisher and ask them to start sending checks directly to you or your new agent. The checks for this title will still go to the agent listed in the contract unless both you and the agent send a letter to the publisher.

Electronic Rights

The term *electronic rights* is very broad. Several things are meant when one speaks of electronic rights, so it is important to look at each right individually:

- **Verbatim electronic rights.** The right to make a book available online, noninteractively, or using a handheld device such as an e-Rocket book. This is also known as "electronic display rights."

- **Database.** An electronic collection of writings (such as an anthology or a cookbook).

- **Interactive.** An electronic version of the book that is enhanced by a third party (the publisher, for example) with material such as audio or video elements or illustrations that allows the reader to manipulate the text. Publishers increasingly either are insisting on keeping this right or are retaining the first option of exploiting it. Even when an author does keep this right, it is important not to compete with the published version of the book. The publisher might get mad and might have cause to litigate, and it is not necessarily beneficial to the author.

◆ **Print on demand.** This refers to short-run printing. New technology has made it possible to use an electronic file to print a small number of copies of the book as and when they are needed, relatively inexpensively. In the past, it was very expensive to print a small number of books; even a thousand was considered small. Now books can be printed one or a few at a time. When publishers control print on demand, they either use it to authorize wholesalers or retailers to print copies as needed, or do so themselves. When authors control print on demand, they can publish books themselves through services such as those offered by Xlibris. Authors cannot hold back print on demand, however, when they sell to a publisher. It is really only useful once the rights to a book have reverted back to the author.

Is It Worth It?

For the average unpublished writer, self-publishing, whether through electronic print on demand or otherwise, will not bring you income, nor will it establish you as a successful writer—and you may end up with a garage full of books. Print on demand, therefore, seems to be most valuable to published authors whose books no longer generate enough sales to warrant standard print runs, but who have found an audience. Another value to print on demand applies to promotional speakers or people who make a living giving seminars: These authors can sell books from a table in the back of the room. This is a cheap way to make professional-looking books available.

> **Hot Off the Press** _____
>
> Rosetta Books, run by a New York agent, ran into trouble when they began to issue e-book versions of old classic titles. Random House wasn't pleased, as they felt they had the right to issue old version of books by writers like Kurt Vonnegut. But the contract doesn't cover electronic rights, because back then, the argument was, no one even knew of such a thing. After much legal tussling Random House and Rosetta finally settled by agreeing to work together to produce the e-books. The perfect ending.

So Is Anything Negotiable?

Hey, most things in life are negotiable, including (sometimes) contracts. As we mentioned before, we've each spent hundreds of hours working with publishing contracts, so we know a thing or two about where publishers might be willing to make changes. Don't take this as legal advice, but rather as guidance from two learned colleagues.

Here are the 12 major flex points:

♦ Who pays for the index

♦ Who pays for illustrations, photos, and similar parts

♦ What sales territory the publisher has the rights to

♦ Various subrights issues

♦ Commercial and dramatic rights

♦ How many free copies the author receives

♦ The delivery date

♦ The author's expense budgets

♦ High-discount/reduced royalties clauses

♦ Joint accounting

♦ Next work and option clauses

♦ Reversion of rights

We have seen publishers make concessions in these clauses many times. Let's examine them closely.

Who Pays for the Index?

Most contracts call for the author either to provide the index or to pay for a professional index. Ever tried to do an index? Forget it. We recommend asking that the publisher pay for the index, or at least split the cost with the author. Indexing can cost several dollars a page, so the bill can be steep. If the publisher won't pay the entire amount or won't split the cost, ask for a cap on the cost. If you end up having to pay for the cost of the index, make sure that it comes out of your future royalties so that you don't have to pay for it out of your advance or out of your pocket.

Who Pays for Illustrations, Photographs, and Other Such Things?

For books in which photographs play a central part, the cost is usually borne by the author. When designing the book, if the publisher thinks that photographs will add to the book (food photography, for instance), the publisher should pay. Illustrations that decorate the book usually are paid for by the publisher, but illustrations for necessary charts are paid for by the author.

Make sure that you understand who pays for what, and feel free to ask the publisher to pay a larger share. Sometimes the author needs to deliver only what is known as scrap art: rough sketches of suggested art for the publisher to have drawn professionally.

The Sales Territory

The publisher will, quite literally, ask to publish the book in every language throughout the whole world—not just the United States and Canada, but tiny territories you've never even heard of. It wants the right to publish the book in the English language throughout the whole world, and it also requests the right to license foreign publishers to translate the book into other languages.

Some publishers do exploit these foreign rights well; others routinely distribute in the United States and Canada and let all the other territories languish. If you have an agent, your agent might want to keep foreign rights on your behalf and try to sell them directly to foreign publishers, so she will try to retain this right for you.

When publishers license translation rights, they split the monies received from foreign publishers with the author. If you don't have an agent, at least ask if there is any flexibility regarding the split. Some publisher's contracts call for a 50/50 split between the publisher and the author on the money from the sale of these rights, but you can always ask for a better cut. "How about 75/25, with 75 percent going to the author?"

Bookmarks

When an excerpt from the book appears just before the book is published, this is a **first serial**. Any excerpts that appear after the book has been published are known as **second serials**. These strange-sounding terms come from the word *serialization*.

Splits and Serials

As with the size of the territory, there are two questions with regard to serial rights. One, who controls the rights? Two, what is the split? If you have an agent, she might want to try to keep control of the *serialization* rights. But if you (or your agent) don't have the contacts to try to sell *first serial* rights to a magazine or newspaper, you might as well let the publisher's rights department try. But again, ask about the split. It is not unusual for the author to receive 90 percent of the money from a first serial rights sale.

Commercial and Dramatic Rights

These are the movie and play rights. Do you see your book as a perfect movie-of-the-week? Or as the basis for a Broadway musical? Then either fight to control these rights all yourself, or reduce the publisher's split.

Free Author's Copies

Most publishing contracts give the author a scant 5 or 10 free copies. Hey, you've got a big family! Your mom wants one, your great-aunt, your old next-door neighbor …. You need more free books, and you can probably get them. This is an easy place for an editor to give up a little something. Ask for 25, anyway, and see what you get.

Publishers usually are generous with free copies used for publicity or review purposes, so if you have good opportunities for promoting the book yourself, ask for some free publicity copies.

Try to get at least a 50 percent discount on the cover price for any additional books that you want to buy. If you plan to give lots of speeches and sell books, try to get an even better quantity discount. Bear in mind that you will have to pay the freight on these purchases, and that books are heavy objects. You need to factor in the freight costs when deciding what makes up an attractive per book purchase price.

The Delivery Date

By the time you get to the contract stage, the publishing company might already have a pub date in mind. But you can always try to get a little extra time here—a few weeks or an extra month or so. Be kind to your editor, though. If you don't need the extra time, don't ask for it.

Expense Budgets

These are fairly rare. Expenses are assumed to be the authors' responsibility—that's what an advance is for. Sometimes cookbook authors get baking allowances to help with the cost of buying ingredients. And sometimes the authors of anthologies or compilations can get a *permissions* budget. It never hurts to try, though.

Bookmarks

If you are using material to which you do not own the copyright, you need to secure the proper **permissions**. To quote or reprint from newspaper, magazines, or other book, you must contact that company's permissions department. Sometimes there is a fee involved, which generally falls on the author.

High-Discount/Reduced Royalty Clauses

These are tough. Publishers claim that the deep discounts so prevalent today have cut into their margins and that they need to reduce royalties to stay in business. Agents (and authors) claim that it reduces royalties to practically nothing. Always try to get some concessions in this area. Publishers will also ask for reduced royalty rates on small print runs. You can try to negotiate the size of the print run that triggers this.

> **Slush Pile** _____
>
> This chapter is not all you need to negotiate a contract. If you don't have an agent, then consult a literary lawyer, or at least a good book, such as *Negotiating a Book Contract*, by Mark Levine. The Author's Guild in New York can also be a good resource, if you wish to join.

If your royalties are based on net and not list price of the book (see the section on royalties, earlier in this chapter), you or your agent may want to ask for a higher starting royalty rate. Or perhaps ask that the royalty rate escalate as the book sells more copies—for example, a starting percentage on the first 10,000 copies sold, a higher percent on the next 5,000 copies, and the highest percentage on all copies sold in excess of 15,000.

Joint Accounting

Joint accounting? What's that mean? It means nothing on your first book. It means a great deal if you publish a second book with the same publisher, however. With joint accounting, all monies from both of your books go into the same big pot. So if you haven't earned out the advance on your first book and your second book does really well, the publisher will ding your account for the negative royalty balance on the first one. We think each book should stand on its own, and we recommend asking to get this clause eliminated.

Options Clauses

If you and your publisher get along well, you will want to work together again. If you don't get along, you don't want to be legally bound to offer it your next book.

If you are a working writer with lots of books in the works and in various stages of publication, this needs to be stated in the contract. Some contracts actually seek to prevent you from signing another contract with another publisher until this book is published—and publication can be months (even years) after you've completed the manuscript. If this is a problem, speak up.

Electronic Rights

Unfortunately, as the field of electronic publishing is changing so rapidly and rights appear to be more lucrative, publishers are becoming less willing to budge from their very stringent boilerplates on the matter. They want to keep a great big bag full of rights. Following is an electronic clause that we feel is fair to the author.

"Electronic book" rights, which for the purposes of this agreement shall be limited to the right to digitize, reproduce, transmit, display, download or otherwise transfer, manufacture, publish, distribute, and/or sell the verbatim text of the Work, or a portion thereof, in an electronic format in any media and by any means, on any platform now known or hereafter developed, but without enhancement (such as video, extrinsic illustrations, audio or any other contributions not present in the printed edition of the Work). Any such display, transmission, or transfer of more than a single chapter of the Work must be encrypted to prevent unauthorized reproduction. Publisher acknowledges and agrees that such grant of electronic display rights does not include any grant of electronic version or interactive multimedia rights, and that such rights are expressly reserved to Author.

> **Experts Say**
>
> Publishing lawyer Bob Stein says, "Authors should look very, very carefully at all electronic rights clauses to ensure that they are compensated for any uses made or authorized by the publisher." He adds, knowingly, "Publishers vary considerably in their willingness to negotiate these provisions."

Reversion of Rights

Some contracts state that as long as the publisher keeps the book in print somewhere (even if it's available only in New Zealand), the rights will not revert to the author. It is generally in the best interest of the writer that the rights to the book revert when the book is out of print in book form in the United States. Ask and see.

It's becoming more important to note that the availability of print on demand copies or electronic copies have the potential to keep a contract in effect forever if it is not expressly excluded from the definition of "in print."

Publishers might say that this is beneficial to the author, but it prevents the author from having the book reissued by another publisher who might promote it, which actually might happen if a new book by the author becomes successful. It also hinders the author's ability to re-use the material in other, newer works on the same subject. In any case, it is just as easy for an author to make her book available through print on demand as it is for the publisher, and the author can keep 100 percent of the profits without having to earn out an advance.

If you can neither keep the print on demand rights nor get the publisher to exclude print on demand from the out-of-print clause, then at least request vociferously that a clause be added stating that unless the book sells a certain number of copies (for example, 250) in a royalty period, then the work shall be considered out of print. Many publishers are finding this to be a fair compromise.

The Least You Need to Know

- A publishing contract grants the publisher the right to publish and sell your book.

- You should receive a small payment, a royalty, on every copy of your book that is sold.

- Exactly what rights are granted to the publisher is open to negotiation.

- Under most contracts, the publisher has the final decision regarding the book's actual title and the cover artwork.

- Some contract terms are more negotiable than others, such as free copies to the author, first serial rights, and merchandising rights.

- If you plan to negotiate on your own, get help from a literary lawyer, or get a good book on publishing contracts. The family lawyer probably won't be much help here.

Part 4

War and Peace: Working with a Publisher

Congratulations, you've got a publisher! But now what happens? In this part, you'll get a complete overview of the actual book publishing process and learn about how to work effectively with all the players. From meeting deadlines to formatting disks, to keeping an editor happy to understanding the retail book process, it's all here.

You'll also learn the basics of book publicity, a critical element in the future success of your book.

Chapter 16

I Signed a Contract— Now What?

In This Chapter

- ◆ Deadlines, deadlines
- ◆ That first advance check
- ◆ The sizzle for your steak: sales materials
- ◆ Why haven't I heard from my editor?
- ◆ What's going on with my book?
- ◆ The loud ticking of the clock

Now you've done it—you've signed a book publishing contract. That means now you will have to produce a manuscript. No more talking about how someday you plan to write a book; now you have to. In fact, you are legally obligated to write one. This was the very thing you sought so hard, but now that it has happened, it can be intimidating.

Allow us to repeat what we believe is the central message of this book: The book publishing business is a business, and to succeed in book publishing as an author, you must be businesslike.

You wrote a businesslike query letter. You put together a businesslike proposal. You conducted contract negotiations in a businesslike manner. Now you must continue to behave in a professional manner during the next phases of the process. No artistic suffering, no writer's block—and the dog can't eat your manuscript. Remember to use professional behavior at all times and in all interactions with your publisher.

Deadlines Loom

Deadlines can sound so final—and they are. When a contract specifies a deadline for a completed manuscript, it is not just an arbitrary date. It's a date that needs to be met because of these reasons:

♦ You need to maintain a good working relationship with your editor and publisher.

♦ Your publisher has to plan for the publication of your book in advance so it can be sold and marketed.

♦ If you do not meet the deadline, your chances to be published might disappear.

Think back to those idyllic days when you first decided to write a book. You were completely in charge of the schedule for the project. You decided when you would sit down and write, when you would wander down to the bookstore for a low-fat cappuccino and a little bit of research, and when you'd finish up the query letter.

But those leisurely days are behind you. Once you sign a contract with a publishing house, you may no longer do things at your own pace. You must meet the deadline specified in the contract. You also have to think about something else—meeting the exact *word count* or *page count* specified in your contract. Ask your editor if they have a page count formula you can use so that you'll know when you have hit the mark.

Bookmarks _____

Some contracts will specify a **word count** for the completed manuscript. This is the minimum number of words that your manuscript should contain to live up to the contract. Some contracts might specify a **page count,** the minimum number of pages that must be in the manuscript. And sometimes there is a maximum word count or page count, which means that you don't promise *Life's Little Instruction Book* and deliver *War and Peace.*

Ready, Set ...

Why is meeting deadlines so important? The minute a book is scheduled for an upcoming season, the following wheels are set into motion:

- ♦ The book is scheduled for publication.

- ♦ The catalog copy writers begin to write.

- ♦ The cover designer begins to design.

- ♦ The accountants begin to forecast costs and expenses.

- ♦ The sales department starts planning the best way to sell your book.

- ♦ The publicity department begins to think about publicizing your book.

- ♦ The subrights department begins to think about who they can sell foreign rights to or which magazines might pay to excerpt.

- ♦ Your editor makes plans for editing your book.

So as you can see, this is no longer just a solitary endeavor for you, your imagination, or your computer. A large structure has just been put into place that depends on the timely arrival of your fully completed manuscript.

We'll examine some of these things more closely in later chapters so that you have a better understanding of the sales process, the publicity process, and the editorial process. But for right now, keep that image in your mind—the image of a cast and crew of several people all waiting anxiously to begin working on your book.

This image is not meant to scare you. But on those days when you just don't feel like working (even if you know that it will set the project back a week or two), remember what is happening inside the publishing house. The entire house is expecting you to meet a deadline.

> **CAUTION**
>
> **Slush Pile**
>
> Bear in mind that if you need to ask for an extension on your deadline, the reason is immaterial. The editor doesn't really care if your computer crashed, your house was destroyed in a mudslide, or there has been a death in the family. This sounds cruel, but it is true. One excuse is no better than another. If the book is late, the editor is in trouble. It doesn't matter why.

More Time, Please?

You tried hard to meet the deadline, but the book just won't be done on time. What can you do? You can ask your editor for an extension on the deadline—that is, an officially sanctioned excuse note.

"Don't wait until the last minute to ask for an extension," warns editor Steve Martin of Sage Publishing. "Better to recognize your need for extra time as early as possible and ask accordingly." If you don't warn your editor that you won't make the deadline and then call the day your book is due … well, this is not a good thing. No editor wants to hear bad news at the very last minute. Plan ahead, but don't count on an extension. Never ask for an extension of an extension. And try to get your editor to put the extension in writing. Read your contract. Be aware of what will happen if you ask for more time. At many houses the failure to meet a new deadline can be grounds for cancellation.

Slush Pile

Editors don't cut checks; the royalty department generally does. Understand that no matter how sympathetic your editor is that you have not yet received a check, she cannot write one for you. She might be able to walk down the hall and ask, nudge, or lobby, but she cannot write the check. So don't hold your editor responsible for the fact that the check hasn't arrived yet.

Where's My Advance?

You signed a contract promising to deliver a completed manuscript by a certain date. The publishing company signed that contract, too, and promised to send you an advance. But it's been weeks, and the money isn't here. You have to meet a deadline; shouldn't there be some deadline they have to meet, too?

Welcome to the world of business. The simple answer is "no." The company should be timely, but it can take many months sometimes to see the first of your money.

It seems awfully unfair, doesn't it? Yes, but try to be businesslike about it. If you have an agent, let your agent nudge the editor about when the first payment will arrive. If you don't have an agent, tread as gently on the topic as you can. You are just starting out in your relationship with your editor—don't jeopardize it now. Should you threaten to stop working on the book until you get your first check? Once again, the simple answer is "no." Yes, it stinks that you are working hard to meet a deadline and that the money hasn't yet shown up. But it is better for your book (and your career) to keep working. If you threaten to stop working, you will hurt only yourself.

Hot Off the Press _____

When does a contract become a signed contract? Most publishers send a contract to you to sign, then you send it back for them to "countersign." It might have to be countersigned by more than one person in-house. Once the contact is countersigned by the publisher, they process a check request for your "on signing" advance. They'll also send you copy of your contract. Your contract then will go to the royalty department, where they will set up an account for your new book and process the check. Depending on the department and size of publisher, this entire process can take up to four to six weeks.

The Sizzle for Your Steak

You and your editor have had a conversation or two about your book, and she has asked you for quite a bit of material. This might seem to you as unimportant stuff. Shouldn't you concentrate on writing and not have to worry about sending off the bunch of newspaper clippings and magazine articles she's asked for?

As you learned a few paragraphs ago, much is happening at the publishing house while you work away on your book. One of those things is hype.

The fate of your book may depend on several things:

♦ How excited the sales people are

♦ How sexy the catalog copy is

♦ How jazzed up your editor is

Bend Over Backward

While you're working hard to meet your manuscript deadlines, you also need to work hard to supply the things that these folks need—particularly when they need it. If someone from the publicity department calls for a copy of the newspaper profile that you included in your proposal, get another copy made and send it. Don't ask to get a copy from your editor. If someone from the editorial department calls and asks about where you went to school, answer the question. Don't tell the caller that the answer can be found in your proposal.

Will You Say "I Love It"?

Your editor (or the copywriter, or the publicist) might also ask you about endorsements. Your proposal bragged about an endorsement or two, and now you need to produce them! Why do they need endorsements so long before the book is being published? Endorsements aren't just used on the back of the book or in advertisements—they are sometimes used in catalog copy as well. (The catalog and book covers are usually produced six to eight months before your book is published. If your book will be publicized with bound galleys four months before publications, your publisher will need cover quotes and other materials even months earlier.)

You need to spend time and energy rounding up endorsements for your book, often both professional and celebrity ones. But you will be amazed at how the words, "I'm under contract to Publisher X to write a book …" helps you open doors and get responses to requests for endorsements. You'll find that this is a great time to expand your personal and professional network. And never forget that most folks *love* to see their name in print!

You're Excited, They're Excited

Understand that publishing people will ask you all kinds of silly questions and will ask for all kinds of silly stuff. Just smile and provide the answers and materials they need. The easier you make it for them, the more excited they will be about you and your book. Conversely, the less cooperative you are with them, the more their excitement will dim.

> **Bookmarks**
>
> The word-of-mouth publicity created before a book is actually published is the **buzz**. You want a lot of buzz for your book, from the publicity department to the sales department. The more buzz, the better.

The more enthusiasm that builds around you and your book, the better your chances for strong sales. And you can help to create the excitement and enthusiasm by supplying your publisher with as much information as possible to create a *buzz*, the impression that you and your book are destined for greatness.

> **Experts Say**
>
> "There were two different periods of silence while I wrote my book," says Ellen Reid Smith, author of *E-Loyalty: How to Keep Customers Coming Back to Your Website* (HarperBusiness). "First, it was unnerving that I was almost finished with the book and the contract still hadn't arrived. Then you turn the book in and the silence starts again. You worry that maybe they hate it because you've heard nothing; then weeks later they call to say they love it!"

But I Haven't Heard from My Editor in Months!

You are working diligently to meet your deadline. You have created a writing schedule, and you sit down to do it every day, regardless of whether you feel creative. You take your contract deadline seriously. So why haven't you heard from your editor in a while? Has she forgotten about you?

No. No one will forget about you. But yes, there may be long stretches when you will not hear from anyone.

Another reality check from the world of publishing: Your editor is responsible for many books at once, perhaps as few as a dozen or as many as 30. It depends on the size of the publishing house and how many editors are on staff. What's more, all the books the editor oversees are in different stages—acquisitions, contract negotiation, manuscript review, typesetting, publicity—so her attention is sometimes fragmented.

Speaking as longtime editors, we can assure you not to worry about the long absences. If an editor leaves you alone for a while, take it as a sign of trust. The editor trusts that you are a professional who is working away at home, not needing constant encouragement and reinforcement from her. Editors adore writers who don't need constant attention.

What's Going on with My Book?

You are writing easily and are pleased with the progress you've made so far. Your check for the first half of the advance arrived, and your editor has expressed his confidence in your ability to do the job. Let's leave you alone for a moment and check in to see what's happening at the publishing house.

You aren't alone. It may seem that way as you write deep into the night, with your computer screen glowing in the darkness. But you are not alone. Much is happening with your book.

- ◆ Editorial and marketing are finalizing the title of your book with any subtitles or taglines.

- ◆ Copywriters are producing copy for the catalog which the sales reps will take with them to sell your book.

- ◆ Cover designers, art directors and marketing folks are designing a cover for your book.

What's in a Name?

You learned in Chapter 15 that the publisher has the final say over your book title. If the publisher does change your book's title, it will not be a casual decision. The title of your book will be discussed again and again. In every meeting on any marketing issue—from catalog copy to cover design and everything in between—the title will be reexamined.

Slush Pile _____

You might find yourself talking to someone from the publishing company who knows very little about your book. Perhaps it's the copywriter, or a publicity person, or an editorial assistant. If this happens (and it probably will), don't be snippy. Understand that yours is just one of many books. Be polite, and use this as an opportunity to educate, not attack.

When a group of people cluster around a table to see the sketches for your book's cover, the title will be questioned.

When a group of people sit together to examine the sales department issues for your book, the title will be questioned.

When your book is presented to the sales department (more about that in a future chapter), the title will be questioned.

Why does everyone care so much about what your book is eventually named? Because a good name can make a book, and a lousy name can kill it. When these same folks aren't obsessing over the title of your book, they are probably obsessing over the subtitle, which is equally critical to the success of your book.

Catalog Copy

Using your own book proposal as a basis, a copywriter is struggling away to describe your book in 100 words or less for the catalog that the sales representatives use. On rare occasions, a copywriter may call the author to learn more about the book. The more he knows, the easier it is to choose the most important points that must be included in the 100-word description.

Hot Off the Press _____

Books are cataloged and sold by seasons. Winter season is typically for books that publish January through April, spring/summer season is for books that publish May through August, and fall season is for books in September through December. When a publisher schedules a publication month for your book, they will take into account any "seasonality" or if there's a time during the year that books on your topic are more popular. For example, January is big month for weight loss and fitness books, September is the big month for cookbooks and gift books, and July is usually the big month for back-to-school.

Judging a Book by Its Cover

Another busy person at the publishing company is the cover designer. This person's title might vary somewhat, from art director to cover coordinator. But somewhere, someone is working on designing a cover for your book.

The same group of people who met to decide whether to publish your book might also be getting together to discuss the cover ideas. Or it might be a group that includes more folks from sales and marketing and fewer from editorial. Regardless of the group's makeup, its task is a critical one: to decide how to best convey your book's message in such a way that it accomplishes these points:

◆ The cover is eye-catching and unique.

◆ The title can be read from a distance.

◆ The purpose of the book is immediately clear.

This is easier said than done. The proper solution for each book is different.

Will these cover folks include you in their discussion? Possibly. Another harsh fact (are there more?) is that, as with the title, the publisher has the contractual right to determine what the cover will say and what it will look like. As the author, you might be included as a courtesy (this is called "consultation"), but it is not guaranteed.

The Good, the Bad, and the Ugly

What if you don't like the title? If your editor sends you a copy of the cover-in-the-works (not all do) or you read the catalog copy and you think it stinks, do not react immediately. Count to 10. Count to 20 if you still aren't cooled down. Never make a phone call to your publishing house in the heat of the moment.

The best way to convey your thoughts about the cover is on paper. Write a measured, professional letter in which you offer alternative suggestions. Don't just offer criticism in your letter. Make useful suggestions, too. Jennifer received a thoughtful e-mail from two of her authors not long ago with their thoughts on the cover. They made professional suggestions regarding the type size and colors in the cover and also pointed out that as a married couple they preferred their names read somewhat differently than shown—critical information they needed to pass along, and it was appreciated.

If you have an agent, let the agent know how you feel about the cover. With your agent to back you up, the publisher just might make some changes.

The Clock's Ticking

But enough about these other people—let's get back to you and your computer again. The time is ticking away, and the deadline looms closer ….

Although this is a book about getting published, not about actually writing a book, we can't resist offering you a few suggestions. Here are nine ways to meet a deadline:

- Write every day, even if it is for just 15 minutes.
- Set small goals, and reward yourself when you meet them.
- Turn off the phone, fax machine, television, and radio.
- Take yourself away for a weekend to write in solitude.
- If you find yourself stuck on writing, go do research for a little while instead; then come back to your writing.
- If you are stuck on Chapter 3, work on Chapter 5 instead.
- Write your ending first, and fill in everything that comes before it.
- Call your mom and ask her to scold you into writing.
- Find a buddy writer, or join a group, and report regularly on your progress.

Remember the old writing adage: If you write just one page a day, in one year you will have a 365-page book. We hope that your deadline leaves you that much time!

The Least You Need to Know

- Maintain your businesslike attitude, particularly about meeting manuscript deadlines.
- If you're going to miss a deadline, give your editor as much warning as possible; don't wait until the last minute to ask for an extension.
- Long before your book is published, you will need to provide material for the sales, marketing, and publicity departments.
- There'll be long periods of time when you don't hear from anyone at your publisher; don't worry, you've not been forgotten.
- While you are writing the book, other people are also working on your book, including the cover designer and the catalog copywriter.
- Keep seeking endorsements for your book while you are writing.

Chapter

17

Saying Good-Bye to Your Baby

In This Chapter

◆ The best software; proper formatting

◆ Garbage in, garbage out

◆ What about the pictures?

◆ Why do they need so many copies?

◆ I'd like to thank my first-grade teacher …

◆ Bye, bye book!

You met your deadline, and with pounding heart you prepare to send off your manuscript. Is there a right way and a wrong way to submit it?

To keep your editor happy (and don't you just love the phrase "your editor"?), you need to submit a clean and polished manuscript prepared according to the rules of the publishing house. These rules are known as the manuscript guidelines.

Go with the Guidelines

Typical *manuscript guidelines* stipulate things such as the following:

- What type of word-processing software is acceptable, such as the most current version Microsoft Word or Word Perfect

- What type of disk to send (floppy, ZIP, or CD) or how to submit by e-mail or ftp server

- How many printed hard copies of the manuscript to send

Disks? Formats? Say what? If these terms are unfamiliar to you, you might be—dare we say it—computer illiterate. In this age of cyberspace and hard drives, a writer needs to know the basics of word processing, the Internet, and file formats. Traditionalists might object, but even the die-hards are submitting electronically these days. As in other parts of the business world, publishing has embraced technology, too.

Bookmarks

Manuscript guidelines (or *author guidelines*) pertain to the actual disk preparation, formatting, and hard copy requirements of the final manuscript. These guidelines vary among publishing houses and sometimes among editors within a house. Make sure you have a copy of the manuscript guidelines in hand before you start to prepare your manuscript.

Why not simply pound out your masterpiece on your trusted old Underwood manual typewriter and then pay someone to input it on a computer for you?

You could. But by the time you pay a typist to not only input your manuscript but also make any corrections that come up later in the editing and production phases, heck, you could buy a pretty fancy computer—and hire someone to train you. Your publishing house most likely has an optical scanning service available to convert your manuscript, but you will probably be charged for the cost of preparation.

E-Mail, Anyone?

Submitting your manuscript on a disk might not be enough. Today, you will most likely be asked to communicate and even submit electronically, via e-mail or ftp. So you're going to need a modem and an e-mail account. Moreover, if you are e-mailing your chapters, you might be asked to follow guidelines similar to these:

- Create an individual file for each chapter of the book. Do not write your entire book in one file.

- Save the files as an attachment to an e-mail. *Do not* cut and paste text into the e-mail message area.

- Save all files as Microsoft Word or compatible (per your publisher's instructions). To ensure that your editor can read your files, send a test file using only one chapter.

- If at all possible, avoid submitting incomplete files. If you must update a file after it has been submitted, talk to your editor and get instructions on the best way to do this.

- Make sure you're using an Internet provider that lets you send and receive multiple files. If you love your AOL account, you might want to investigate setting up another account just for your manuscript, as AOL will only let you send or receive one attachment per e-mail. Many writers have Hotmail or Yahoo! accounts for this very reason.

- To reduce the number of e-mail submissions and maximize the number of files submitted per e-mail, you might want to utilize compression software such as WinZip (or Stuff-It if you're on a Macintosh).

Hot Off the Press

Submitting your manuscript by e-mail? Don't submit and just assume your editor has the files. A project editor at Prima Publishing told us about the stressful time an author e-mailed his entire manuscript at the very last minute on the day it was due in a text format that was unreadable. The author had left on a month-long trip traveling to an inaccessible part of the Middle East and was unreachable. "It caused quite a panic for a day or two," remembers the editor, "but luckily his assistant also submitted a disk a few days later. Whew!"

Sound complicated? It might seem so at first, but look at e-mail submissions this way: They cut down on the cost of postage (and those trips to the post office) and allow for *nearly instant* confirmation that your files have been received. If you're still confused, consider investing in a simple book on Microsoft Windows, the Internet, or the word-processing program of your choice.

Slush Pile

Andy Rooney, Danielle Steel, and a few die-hard newspaper columnists still use old manual typewriters. But don't think that you, as a first-time writer, can turn in a typewritten manuscript. Those days are behind us now. Plug in your computer and get typing!

The Best Software

By definition, the best software is the software stipulated in the manuscript guidelines. But when you first started writing so many months (or years) ago, who knew what publisher you would end up with and what kind of software that publisher would require or recommend?

Your best bet, then, is to stick with the largest and most popular programs—Microsoft Word or WordPerfect. Most editors work on PCs, not on Macintosh. As a general rule, the more current the version of your program, the better.

Experts Say

"Getting wired means having access to e-mail and the Internet," says freelance editor Paula Lee. "Don't worry, be happy—you'll soon learn that the Internet is a writer's best friend."

If you're submitting electronically, your publishing house might even have many editors edit the files electronically or "online." Programs such as Microsoft Word have features that allow editors to track their changes, make comments, and edit your manuscript so you can see very clearly any additions or deletions. It's worth it for you to become familiar with the revision features in your software. You will most likely need to use it.

Hot Off the Press

Working with a co-author or several contributors? It might go quite smoothly computer-wise, or it might not. In our case, it was a bit of a hassle in the early years. Jennifer, who wrote in an old version of Word for Windows, couldn't read her co-author Sheree's files written in WordPerfect. We tried saving files and then e-mailing files in a variety of different file formats, but no luck. So we resorted to long faxes flying back and forth. Thankfully, we and our equipment have improved over the years and it is now easy to send files back and forth. If you are not writing alone, one author needs to take the lead in preparing the manuscript. Work this out before you get too far into the project to avoid misunderstandings and future complications.

Proper Formatting

Back in the days before computers, *formatting* was pretty straightforward. Your editor would ask you to submit your manuscript neatly typewritten (with a new ribbon!), on standard, white, 8½ by 11-inch high-quality bond paper. Margins were to measure one inch all around, and text was to be double-spaced with half-inch indentations.

It was quite simple, actually. The tricky stuff such as italics, bold, *headings*, and the like, were left to the typesetter.

Bookmarks

Formatting refers to the set of instructions that determines the way the printed words appear on the page, including things such as margins, indents, type size, and fonts. A **heading** (often called a *head*) is the title introducing a chapter or subdivision of the text. Typically, there is a hierarchy of different size headings throughout the book, which you will need to designate as Head 1, Head 2, or Head A, B, and C. Your author guidelines will specify how heads are handled at your publisher.

Those days (and the typesetters) are gone at many, if not most, publishing houses. In the age of computerized publishing, the rules have changed considerably, for both the publisher and the writer. Now, formatting requirements are designed to facilitate the production process.

Standard Formatting

As you've learned, most writers are asked to submit computer disks as well as hard copy (a printed manuscript). How the writer is asked to format the text on those disks varies somewhat from publisher to publisher. It depends entirely on the publisher's computer sophistication and editorial conventions. However, there are some fairly standard formatting requirements:

- One-inch margins around the page

- Standard 12-point type in a typewriter font, such as Courier or Times Roman

- Single-line spaces between paragraphs, rather than indents

- Double-spaced copy

- Unjustified text

- No double hard returns

- One computer file per chapter, named according to the house's naming convention

- Hard copy printed on a desk jet or laser-quality printer, on good 8½ by 11-inch white paper

- No double spaces after periods

Slush Pile

Don't use one of those old daisy-wheel printers for your final manuscript (the kind where you had to tear the pages apart). If you don't have a good printer, take the disk with your manuscript to a computer service center like a Kinko's and print it out there.

CAUTION **Slush Pile** _____

Don't make the mistake of turning in a disk with one enormous file on it (unless it has been pre-approved). Your editor will not be happy. At one unnamed publishing company, faced with a 340-page manuscript all written in one file (instead of saved one chapter per file), the editor had to hire a freelancer to electronically break up the file chapter by chapter. If you try submitting your manuscript this way, your editor could send it back to you and make _you_ redo it.

Most publishing houses have prepared very detailed formatting guidelines for writers under contract. These guidelines often specify particular coding for various design elements such as headings.

Many publishers send these guidelines out when they return the signed contract. Don't wait for that—as you know from Chapter 16, you might have finished the book before the signed contract comes!

CAUTION **Slush Pile** _____

Don't forget to number the pages on your manuscript before sending it in. There are horror stories of large manuscripts accidentally dropped on the floor, with pages flying every-where, only to find that—yikes!—the pages weren't numbered. Don't let this happen to your editor!

Don't assume that these guidelines are just suggestions and that you really don't have to follow the page setup guidelines or formatting instructions. Also, don't assume that your publisher will just fix the problems themselves and not bother you with it. You might get lucky, and you might not. It's terrible to have worked so hard to meet a deadline only to have your editor send your entire manuscript back to you to be put into the proper format. It could also jeopardize the schedule for your entire project. The work has to be done—and if it's your responsibility, it's going to fall to you.

Why So Many Copies?

Most publishing contracts specify that you submit your book on disk, along with at least two hard copies of the entire manuscript. This might seem excessive to you (especially at five cents or more a page for copying), but it is still required. Having more than one copy of the manuscript is critical for the production process. Here's why …

As soon as your manuscript arrives at the publisher, your editor opens it with great expectations. Typically, she hands your computer disk right off to an editorial assistant. The editorial assistant makes an extra copy of the disk for the design and production departments.

The editor keeps one hard copy of your manuscript for herself to read; the other copy of the manuscript goes to the editorial assistant. It is this extra copy that is copied and copied and copied in-house. Copies of your manuscript might end up in the hands of any other editor in line to read your book—everyone from other acquisitions editors who are curious about it to developmental editors, production editors, publicists, and other folks you haven't heard of yet. (You'll learn who all these folks are in the next chapter.)

Without two copies, each ready to initiate the editorial and production processes, delays could occur. And you wouldn't want that. So cough up the five cents a page and be done with it.

Garbage In, Garbage Out

GIGO is tech-talk for the phrase "garbage in, garbage out," an expression as applicable to publishing as it is to computers. The cleaner the manuscript you send to your publisher, the cleaner the book that comes out from your publisher.

Writers often complain about the finished product, as if that product were completely out of their hands. Particularly loathsome to writers are unnecessary tinkering by copy editors, typos, and formatting bloopers.

Yet as the writer, you have more control over this process than you might think. If you turn in a manuscript riddled with grammatical errors, typos, and formatting inconsistencies, you're asking for trouble.

So polish your prose. Check your grammar and your spelling. Follow your publisher's formatting guidelines to the letter. You'll be glad you did (and you'll impress your editor, to boot!). If you've forgotten everything you learned in English class, take a look at *The Complete Idiot's Guide to Grammar and Style*, now in its second edition, for a refresher course.

File Management Matters

You'll turn in those chapters, each tucked neatly into an individual file, cleverly named. Sometimes too cleverly named … Choose clear file names like "Chap. 1" and so forth. Stay away from using the actual name of the chapter—Chapter One, How It All Began." Clearly named files are critical because once the developmental editing or copy editing phase begins, many versions of your files will be flying back and forth through cyberspace, and it is easy to become confused. We like to do it this way:

- ◆ Chap1

- ◆ Chap1-revise

- ◆ Chap1-revise2

- ◆ Chap1-final

You'll develop a system that works for you, or your publisher might have a system they want you to use. Just remember to keep it as simple and clear as possible so that you (or your editor) can tell at a glance which version of the chapter this is.

> **Experts Say**
>
> *The Chicago Manual of Style* is the book publishing bible and every writer's best friend. It's a veritable treasure of information that addresses all the spelling, grammar, and language usage issues you're likely to encounter in a lifetime of writing. "Using *The Chicago Manual of Style* as your guide marks you as a professional and impresses your editor," says book doctor John Waters. The book is available in the reference section of the bookstore.

What About the Pictures?

Many book projects include interior art, a term that in book publishing refers to the photographs, illustrations, maps, and cartoons that might appear on the pages of the book. If your book does have interior art, you will need to find out exactly what your responsibilities are concerning it.

Some publishers—particularly the larger ones—provide all the art, and they like it that way. If this is the case, you, as the author, might be encouraged to contribute ideas for possible art. Or you might well be discouraged from contributing art ideas. Check your book contract to see what your publisher expects from you.

What to Send

What if you're responsible for providing art? You'll have to provide it in the proper way. Here again, this varies from publisher to publisher. Most often, it depends on the production department's technical sophistication.

Here are a few possible scenarios:

- ◆ If you're providing black-and-white photographs, you might be asked to provide simple 8 by 10-inch black-and-white glossies. Or you might be asked to provide color slides or electronic versions that you've scanned and delivered electronically in GIF or JPEG files at the publisher's required resolution.

- If you're providing maps, you might be asked to provide simple sketches that the publisher's art department can use to render final art. Or you might be asked to deliver *camera-ready*, professional-quality maps.

Bookmarks _____

Camera-ready art refers to the finished artwork that is ready to be photographed or scanned, without alteration, for reproduction. Sometimes it's called *mechanicals*.

- If you're providing actual illustrations (this is unlikely), you might be asked to deliver the originals or the camera-ready versions of those originals.

Permissions

Regardless of the form, remember that you must also obtain written permission to reprint any art that's not your own or that's not in the *public domain*.

Art is not the only thing that requires permission or a signed release form from the copyright holder. Many new writers make the mistake of not paying enough attention to the fact they probably need permissions or releases when dealing with the following:

- Art work, photographs, or screen shots from websites

- Interview subjects whose comments and names you plan to include in the book

- Quotes taken from other published works like books, magazines, or websites

- Song lyrics

- Contributions from other writers, such as in a story collection or when you have asked a writer to make a substantial written contribution to your book

Bookmarks _____

Written works or artwork that is no longer protected by copyright law is in the **public domain** and can be used without permission or cost by anyone. Artwork that is free to be used by anyone without obtaining permission is called *clip art*.

Ask your editor early in the game if the publishing house has a standard release form you can use. If you aren't clear on how or when to seek permission, your editor might be able to hook you up for a conversation with someone in their legal department so you have a better understanding.

Identify early in your project what material you will need, including releases, permissions, and who you'll need to contact. Keep good records and organize your paperwork. Your editor will be expecting all this documentation with your final submission.

Plagiarism

Plagiarism is a very real issue for publishing houses today. There are many misconceptions about what kind of material is *fair use*, how much you can use before permission must be obtained, and how it must be cited.

Bookmarks

Fair use could be the most misunderstood concept in writing today. Many authors think two sentences is fine, while others think there's a 500-word rule. The truth is, fair use can vary greatly depending on the size, type, and content of the original work. The legal definition has more to do with *how* the content is used—not so much *how much* of it is used. If you're excerpting material from other sources, be sure to check with your editor and get the publisher's guidelines for use.

Publishers do spot checks on manuscripts and some even go through legal vetting. But contrary to popular believe, rewriting isn't enough. Make sure you talk with your editor in advance of using material from other sources. Publishers are often the most up-to-date sources of information on what's happening in copyright law, as their cases are often defining the standard.

Slush Pile

We've known several editors who have had projects fall through because authors submitted manuscript full of uncited or improperly used material "We don't think most of them deliberately set out to plagiarize work. We just think most of them don't truly understand what they are doing is wrong," one editor told us. "We had a fully written manuscript almost published when an editor did a routine check of material. The authors had done their research using websites and cut and pasted material from various sites into their book with no rewrites and no cites!" The author's answer to the plagiarized material? They said, "It was on the Internet. You can't copyright material on the Internet. It's free." Needless to say, their book wasn't published.

Show Them the Money

Few new writers understand that if a fee is required to include material (such as a poem or song lyric), it is your responsibility as the author to pay it. Check your contract, and you will find that in almost all cases the author is responsible. Keep this in mind when you are writing your manuscript so you don't have to go back and cut things you literally can't afford, like that great Rolling Stone's lyric you think sets the tone for your whole book. Once you find out how many hundreds of dollars just a few lines can cost, you might quickly change your mind.

Slush Pile

Including art or photographs in a book can increase its production cost—and, thus, its price—considerably. So despite your opinion, if the publisher decides not to include art in the book, try to understand and be gracious. This is a business decision, not an emotional one.

"I'd Like to Thank My First-Grade Teacher ..."

Ah, the acknowledgments section. Here is your chance to tell the world where you learned to write, who has influenced you in your life, and to whom you will feel eternally grateful.

Many writers turn in the acknowledgments section of their manuscript last. And because it's sometimes quite lengthy, it might seems to the editor that the author spent the most time writing this section of the book.

Again, we would like to impress upon you that the most businesslike and professional approach to the acknowledgments section is to keep it short, perhaps just a few paragraphs. Understand that if you turn in a long one, you just might be asked to cut it.

Bye, Bye Book!

Good job. You've prepared your manuscript in strict accordance with the publisher's guidelines. Your manuscript is now ready to begin the labyrinthine journey known as the editorial and production process. It's ready to become a book. Read on to learn exactly how this happens.

The Least You Need to Know

◆ Computer illiteracy is not acceptable in today's publishing world; you must learn how to use a computer if you don't already know how.

♦ Very few publishers still accept manuscripts on paper only; most require a disk or e-mail version as well.

♦ Save each chapter in an individual file, never write a book as one long file, and be sure to manage your files during the editing phase.

♦ Ask your publisher early on for manuscript guidelines.

♦ Remember that getting signed permissions and paying any required fees are the responsibility of the author.

♦ Number the pages, make several copies, hold your breath, and send your manuscript on its way!

Chapter 18

Welcome to the Home Team!

In This Chapter

- ◆ Book production, step by step
- ◆ Responding to editorial queries and changes
- ◆ Cover copy and design
- ◆ Interior design and paper
- ◆ Page proofs

Much is often made of the solitary nature of the writer's life. Some writers—loners and dreamers at heart—like it that way.

Well, writing a book may be a solo act, but making a book is a collaborative one. Making a book requires that the author put aside her artistic, sensitive, prideful self and join forces with the cast of folks needed to produce a bound book. Maybe for the first time since you started writing your book, you've joined a team.

The process of producing a book is by no means simple. You, the writer, have provided the text of the book. But a book is much more than simply text. It's a product that must be polished, designed, manufactured, marketed, promoted, sold and shipped into retail outlets all over the country, and, finally, sold to readers.

Production in a Nutshell

The steps to producing a book include the following:

♦ Developmental edit

♦ Copy edit

♦ Interior design

♦ Front, spine, and back cover copy and design

♦ Final page proofs and proofreading

♦ *Bluelines*

♦ *F&Gs*

Bookmarks

The term *bluelines,* sometimes called *blues,* refers to the cheap proof—the test run off the press that's usually blue (hence the name)—that the printer sends to the publisher before proceeding with the actual printing. The **F&Gs** are the sheets of a book that have been "folded and gathered" in preparation for printing. In the rush to market, many publishers do not bother to review F&Gs, having already reviewed the bluelines. A notable exception to this is heavily illustrated books.

Join the Team

You are now part of a team of talented and resourceful publishing professionals whose contribution—whether it's the copy edit or the cover illustration—is as important to them as your words are to you. Let's meet this team and learn how you can make yourself a welcome addition to it.

We'll introduce you to these publishing professionals in the order you are most likely to meet them—or hear of them, as the case may be.

The Acquisitions Editor

The first person to read your final manuscript is usually your old friend, the acquisitions editor. By definition, this person is already a big fan of yours, having had the wisdom and foresight to offer you a book contract in the first place.

The acquisitions editor will work for a publisher, an editor in chief or a publishing director who may oversee an entire imprint or topic of publishing for a house. The publisher also will approve any final financial decisions the acquisitions editor makes. While you won't work directly with a publisher, they will be aware of the decisions being made on your book.

But I Thought You Liked It!

At this point in the process, however, your biggest fan may become your worst critic, all in the name of making the best book possible. She'll take a big-picture look at your manuscript, performing what's called a content edit. She'll be reviewing your manuscript for the following:

- Content
- Style
- Voice
- Structure
- Pacing and more

Especially for Fiction

If the book is fiction or creative nonfiction, the acquisitions editor will also be looking to see how you've handled these elements:

- Setting
- Plot
- Characterization
- Dialogue
- Point(s) of view
- Narrative
- Theme and more

Once your editor has completed her review, typically she'll write up her comments, proposed changes, and questions and then forward them on to you. As we'll discuss in a later chapter, it will be your job to incorporate all your changes with grace, professionalism, and speed—especially if you want to get your hands on that acceptance check. (The acceptance check doesn't come until these changes are made to your acquisitions editor's satisfaction.)

The Developmental Editor

If your acquisitions editor believes that substantial changes must be made to your manuscript before approving it for publication, she may assign your project to a developmental editor. In some houses, the acquisitions editor and developmental editor are the same person. Developmental editors work on actual content, helping you rework and reorganize your manuscript to the publishing house's expectations.

If you are for any reason unable or unwilling to make the changes requested, the developmental editor may serve as a book doctor, rewriting your book as she and the acquisitions editor see fit. The fee for this developmental editing either will be paid by the publisher outright at no cost to you, or will be paid by the publisher and then charged back to you against your royalties.

The Production or Project Editor

When you and your acquisitions editor have ironed out all the big-picture issues, you and your manuscript will be handed off to the production editor, who'll run your manuscript through the next lap in this publishing relay.

Just as your acquisitions editor has seen you safely through the acquisitions process (from query letter to signed contract to acceptance of the final manuscript), your production editor will see you safely through the production process (from copy edit to final proofs to bluelines to printed book).

Note: In some publishing houses, the production editor also assumes responsibility for the content editing, either doing the edit herself or sending it out to a freelance developmental editor.

The Copy Editor

The way some writers rant and rave about copy editors, you'd think they were insensitive, intolerant, inflexible ... well, you get the picture.

Wrong! Copy editors can be a writer's best friend. Sure, they're a little picky, but then, they're paid to be picky. Who else will catch all your inadvertent misspellings, grammatical errors, questionable punctuation, and inconsistent capitalization? Not to mention all those other things you didn't even know that those meticulous copy editors check, including these elements:

- Pagination
- Illustrations
- Front and back matter
- Contradictions and ambiguities
- Parochialisms and anachronisms
- Abbreviations and contractions
- Accuracy of names, dates, and places
- Cross-references
- Coding for headings, illustrations, and the like

Who (and where) your copy editor will be varies according to the publishing house. At some houses, the production editor does the copy editing herself. At other houses, the production editor sends the manuscript to the copy editing department, where an in-house copy editor does the job. At still others, the production editor sends your manuscript out to a freelance copy editor.

No matter where she comes from, the copy editor deserves your respect, and maybe even your undying love.

The Art Director

The art director is the person responsible for the way your book will look, both inside and out. In large houses, the art director heads up a design department that creates the interior and cover designs for each title. In smaller houses, the art director may create the designs herself or send them out to freelance designers.

Interior Design

Interior design varies greatly in its complexity, depending on the type of book you have written. Novels, made up primarily of *text*, typically require very simple interior designs. Nonfiction books can run the gamut, from simple text to highly illustrated, to books like the one you hold in your hands. This nonfiction book, *The Complete Idiot's Guide to Getting Published*, *Third Edition*, incorporates a number

Bookmarks

Words on a page are called **text**. Text that is set aside in a box or that runs down the side in a smaller size type is a **sidebar**. Sidebars are like little asides in a conversation.

of design elements such as *sidebars*, bullets, and numbered lists. If the design of your book dictates that text be arranged in a certain way (like this one does), you may be asked to write the text accordingly (like we were).

Cover Design

You may not be able to tell a book by its cover, but you can sell a book by one! The cover is a book's major sales tool. As you've learned in other chapters, that is why the publisher usually states flatly in the contract that the cover text and design is its decision, not yours. Moreover, the cover is usually the most expensive piece of the production process—it typically costs thousands of dollars for even the most basic cover and can cost thousands more if the cover includes an illustration or photograph. For a how-to book, the art director may choose a straightforward type solution, with no illustration. For books such as novels, the illustration is paramount.

The art director will present his designs for your book's interior and front and back covers to a panel that includes your editor, the marketing director, and the publisher.

The Copywriter

The copywriter writes the copy that appears on the cover of your book (front and back) as well as the inside flaps on a hardcover book. The cover copy must work with the cover design to entice the bookstore browser to pick up your book and buy it, right then and there. In effect, this is sales copy.

At some houses, the acquisitions editors write the copy for the books they acquire; at other houses, the copy is written by in-house copywriters in the marketing department. No matter who writes it, this sort of copy is an art form.

Will this be the same copywriter who wrote the description of your book for the catalog? It might be. But it might also be someone who is new to the project, so be kind and patient if that person calls you for information.

The Proofreader

The proofreader is the last person to read the formatted book pages before they're shipped off to the printer for manufacturing. The proofreader's job is to catch glaring mistakes only, such as typos, pagination problems, and so forth. Think of proofreading as a last-ditch quality-control effort.

Here again, who does the proofreading depends on the house. At larger houses, in-house proofreaders in the proofreading department perform this function; in smaller houses, the proofreading may be done by editorial assistants or may be sent out to freelancers.

Indexer

Not every book has an indexer, and not every house had indexers in-house, but they do work here toward the end. Many today index electronically, while other do it standard way on index cards. Indexing is a fine and traditional old art in itself that adds greatly to the usefulness of a book.

The Manufacturing Manager

The manufacturing manager is your publishing house's liaison with the printers. He's typically in charge of buying the paper on which to print the books and decides which printing company to use. In this age of escalating paper prices, many manufacturing managers are buying cheaper paper to keep costs down. As an author, you should know that paper is the most expensive component of the book, something like 70 percent. Complain to your editor if you like, but there may be nothing your editor can do about it, to his frustration as much as to yours!

Over to You, Now

Okay, now you've met the major players in the editorial and production processes at most publishing houses. Let's take you step by step through the interactions you'll have with some of these people as your book is produced.

As we've tried to make clear in the last several pages, much of what goes on at your publishing house is out of your control and is in the hands of your team members. And the order as we've described it might vary slightly from house to house. But when the ball does bounce back into your court, you want to make sure you do your part to keep the process going smoothly.

Responding to Your Editor's Comments

Your part first comes into play when your acquisitions editor reads your final manuscript and delivers her content editing comments.

No matter how pristine your manuscript, you can expect revision suggestions that include the following:

- Cuts (where you run too long)

- Additions (where you leave too much unsaid)

- Clarifications (where you might confuse the reader)

- Rearrangements (where your structure falters)

- Rethinking of sections (where you veer off track)

Especially for Fiction

If you're writing fiction, you can also expect comments concerning these factors:

- Characters who work, characters who don't

- Holes in the plot, plot contradictions

- Milking certain scenes, eliminating others

- Building suspense, stepping up the pace

- Dramatizing your beginning

- Sustaining interest in your middle

- Nailing your ending

What's Best for the Book

Take these comments in the spirit in which they are given. Your editor's only interest is in making your good book even better. No one is trying to hurt your feelings. The book's success (for both you and your editor) depends on it being the best book it can possibly be.

Sometimes editors are better at seeing what is wrong than they are at seeing how to fix it. Take a hard look at the problems your editor has identified, and if you don't like her solutions, then come up with your own. Feel free to discuss these issues with your editor, but don't drive her crazy over every detail. (You'll learn more on maintaining this all-important relationship with your editor in the next chapter.)

Get the job done, make the changes your editor needs, and get the manuscript back to her within the deadline she's given you. If you are slow in this step, you will jeopardize the production schedule, and your book may not be published on time. This is not a good thing.

Hot Off the Press _____

The publishing industry is replete with writers who have sabotaged their own book projects—and ultimately their careers—by objecting too strenuously to editorial comments. A case in point: A writer sold a book proposal to a major publisher about marriage and the devastating effect of adultery on the bonds of matrimony. When the manuscript came in, however, the editor objected to large sections in which the writer examined the feelings of the third party (the other man or woman). The editor insisted that the section be cut; it was inappropriate in a book about marriage. The writer insisted that it remain. The impasse was never resolved, and the manuscript was declared unacceptable. Deal over.

Copy Editing Changes and Queries

When you've made the content changes as requested by your acquisitions editor, your manuscript is handed off to the production editor. He'll review the manuscript and choose a copy editor based upon that review. The copy editor will make her edits, which will most likely include *author queries*.

It's your job to answer these queries as completely and swiftly as possible. If the copy editor seems a little overzealous, keep in mind that, by definition, copy editors are suspicious of everybody's copy. Don't take it personally—they are merely doing their job.

Bookmarks _____

Author queries are questions the copy editor needs you, the writer, to answer before the text proceeds to the layout stage. These questions can relate to meaning, accuracy, and research, among other things.

Man Overboard!

Of course, there are times when copy editors really do go overboard. If you feel this is the case, first get the opinions of other publishing pros as a double-check. If they, too, agree that the edit is excessive, talk to your editor first. He may want to handle it himself. Be polite—no ranting and raving. If your editor agrees with you, he might tell the copy editor to tone it down, or he may reassign the job to someone else.

Slush Pile _____

"But I gave them a perfect book," co-author Jennifer once heard an unhappy author lament. Wrong. There is no such thing as a perfect book, and that attitude will not make you any friends at your publisher. There is always room for improvement, if only a buff and polish.

More Deadlines to Meet

After the copy editing process is completed, your manuscript is ready to go into layout. In the typesetting days of old (before computers), authors would receive galleys to review. Galleys were long proofs pulled off the machine before the copy was divided into pages. Ask your editor if you can see a sample design for the interior layout for your book. Many houses use standard designs, but some books will have custom designs created for them.

Bookmarks

Manuscripts are no longer sent off to typesetters, but rather to **compositors**. The compositor then formats the book on a computer and gets it ready to go to the printer.

But galleys are mostly history now. What you are more likely to receive are page proofs, straight from the layout person's (also called the *compositor*) laser printer. These page proofs are reviewed by a number of people: the proofreader, the acquisitions editor, the production editor, the art director, the manufacturing manager—and, last but not least, you, the writer.

Page Proofs

As the author, you'll usually review what's known as the first pass, the first set of page proofs from the layout person. Do not go overboard on corrections or additions here; your opportunity to make big changes was during the copy editing phase. This stage is really just to catch computer errors and typos.

Changes at this stage are very expensive. And if you make too many, you will have to pay for them. Check your contract for details; each publisher draws the line at a different place. Even if you don't get charged, you'll possibly delay publication.

Usually there are two more passes of page proofs, but the author seldom sees these. One ensures that the first-pass changes have been made, and then there's one more: the final pass just before the book is shipped to the printer.

Stop the Presses!

As the printer prepares to print your book (a process known as "make ready"), he first makes a proof. This proof, as we learned earlier, is called the bluelines. Publishing pros just call them "the blues."

Will you get to see the bluelines? Probably not. Blues are meant to be reviewed posthaste by the production editor only hours before the presses actually start to roll.

Although some writers may insist on reviewing the bluelines, very few are allowed to do so. Without the clout of a best-selling track record behind you, you won't see the bluelines.

Hot Off the Press

Desktop publishing has revolutionized the editorial and production processes for much of the industry. The managing editor of a computer game book publisher described how quickly their books appear. It's crucial for the game guides to appear in the stores when the games do. "We do everything electronically," he told us. "Our writers deliver their manuscript via e-mail, chapter by chapter as they write it. The project editor reviews them and sends them on to the copy editor, again by e-mail. The same goes for design and layout. We often even send the finished book to the printer electronically—all to save time and get our books out to the marketplace as quickly as possible."

Even if you could, who'd want to? Leave the last-minute quality control to the pros, and get started on your next book. There's no better feeling in the world for a writer than to have one book at the printers and another one in the computer.

The Least You Need to Know

♦ The editorial and production processes require teamwork; this means cooperation between the publishing staff and you, the author.

♦ Try not to take editorial criticism personally; the editor's goal is to help you write the best book possible.

♦ Make all requested changes, and answer all editorial queries promptly so that you don't delay production.

♦ The later it is in the production process, the less likely you will be allowed to make changes to your book.

Proper Care and Feeding of Your Editor

In This Chapter

- ◆ Your book's best advocate—and yours, too!
- ◆ A day in the editing life
- ◆ Getting through to your editor when you need to
- ◆ 'Fessing up when you're in trouble
- ◆ Keeping everybody on your side

Your manuscript has now left the safety of your nurturing arms and has headed off to the big city. Its fate will now be determined by strangers, many of whom will remain strangers.

The notable exception to this is your editor. She is your link to this strange new world, so it's in your best interest to make this person your new friend.

Make a Friend for Life

Writers and editors as friends? It works for John Grisham.

When Grisham signed with Doubleday for his second novel—and first big hit—*The Firm*, he made sure to befriend his new editor, David Gernert. It's an association that has gone well beyond the usual editor/writer relationship.

Gernert edited (heavily, according to Grisham) the next several Grisham best-sellers. They both profited from the arrangement. Grisham went to the top of the best-seller lists, and Gernert went to the top of Doubleday as editor-in-chief.

When Grisham's agent, Jay Garon, died in 1995, Grisham asked Gernert to become his agent. Gernert, who left his job at Doubleday, acts not only as Grisham's agent, but also as his personal editor. And the best-sellers just keep on coming.

Your Book's Best Advocate—and Yours, Too!

David Gernert is literally John Grisham's advocate. And your editor, having acquired your project for the publishing house, is your book's advocate. What you want is for the editor to become your advocate, too.

> **Hot Off the Press** _____
>
> The most celebrated editor of all time was the legendary Maxwell E. Perkins of Scribner's. Editor and friend to such luminaries as Thomas Wolfe, Perkins was renowned for his ability to draw the best work out of his authors. "Do not ever defer to my judgment," he admonished F. Scott Fitzgerald in one of his remarkable letters. It is worth noting that, despite Perkins's warning, Fitzgerald took his editor's comments and criticism seriously—to his and his work's great credit.

The trick is to fuel your editor's enthusiasm for you and your book as your manuscript makes its way through the editorial and production processes. Be sure to maintain your editor's enthusiasm after the book is published, too, all the way through the marketing and promotion. At every point, your editor is crucial to the success of your book.

However, while your editor's excitement was initially high when the book was signed, this may fade over time. This apparent loss of enthusiasm and/or interest in your project is more a function of workload than anything else.

Remember, at any given time, your editor is juggling three lists:

◆ The list of books currently being acquired

◆ The list of books currently being produced

◆ The list of books currently being promoted

Depending upon the house, this can add up to anywhere between 20 and 100 books. That's a lot of books to track. When it comes to your editor's interest, there is quite a bit of competition for your book.

Hot Off the Press

Most acquisitions editors toil in relative obscurity. But a handful have become industry superstars and have earned the biggest reward of all: their own imprint. When this happens, an editor's name is right up there with the publisher. And so you have Nan A. Talese Books/Doubleday and Regan Books/HarperCollins. Both editors have had multiple best-sellers from high-profile names, and Judith Regan even had her own television show for a while. So there you have another reason to be nice to your editor: She might have her own imprint some day.

It's your job to sustain this interest and to accomplish this with grace and professionalism. This means you'll need to learn as much as you can about editors and how they operate. Let's observe an editor in the field, so to speak, and find out how she spends her time.

Editor for a Day

Your editor's day typically begins early. Although the work day may officially begin at 9 A.M., many early bird editors are already at their desks by 8 A.M.—and many can be found at their desks long after 5 P.M.

As you have learned before, there is little time in the editor's day to do the "real" work of reading and evaluating manuscripts and proposals. You'll recall that most of this work is done on the editor's own time, either at home or on the train, subway, or carpool. Many an editor has fallen asleep at night next to a stack of manuscripts.

8 A.M.

At your editor's office, the early bird editors are getting as much done as they can before the daily meetings start up.

Reading and Responding to E-Mail

One editor we know gets 100 e-mails a day, from authors as well as agents, other editors, and all manner of in-house staffers. As more editors and publishing houses go online, the number of e-mails will only grow.

Going Through Snail Mail

With any luck, your editor has an editorial assistant who sorts through the mail first. Still, many editors prefer to perform this formidable task themselves. Jennifer sits in her office at Prima and reads every query or proposal that arrives addressed to her. Formidable? Yes. Each day the mail may bring a dozen queries, a dozen requested manuscripts and proposals, and just as many unrequested ones! That's not to mention contracts from agents, catalogs from other publishers, trade publications and newsletters, interoffice correspondence, faxes, and maybe even the occasional postcard from a long-time author.

Making Overseas and Transcontinental Phone Calls

Many editors conduct a great deal of business with foreign publishers. They evaluate projects, make deals for translations, and work together on other projects. The best time to call Europe is early in the day. Likewise, West Coast editors are calling back east as early as they can.

Writing Rejection Letters

Yes, some editors do write their own rejection letters. This is a time-consuming job, but many editors consider it a professional courtesy crucial to maintaining good writer-editor or agent-editor relations. Let it never be said that editors don't care about writer's feelings!

9 A.M.

By 9 A.M., the meetings start. Ask any editor how she spends her day, and she will likely say (with some irritation), "In meetings!"

The first meeting on the schedule is the production meeting. Here, your editor meets with the production editors to discuss the problems and issues regarding books currently in production. At today's meeting, your editor learns that a conflict concerning the copy edit of one title has arisen. The writer is unhappy with the copy edit and is dragging his heels on responding to the author queries. The production editor asks for your editor's help in resolving the issue. They agree to meet later in the day to call the writer together and work things out.

10 A.M.

By this time, the production meeting has ended and the cover meeting has begun. At a cover meeting, the art director, editors, marketing execs, and often the publisher get together to brainstorm ideas for new covers and to review covers already in the design process. At today's meeting, they discuss ideas for four new covers and review the art for front covers on four books in production.

One cover for a new cookbook gives them particular trouble. Cookbooks are expensive books to produce, especially when the front cover boasts a beautiful photograph of a savory dish. Cover photos featuring recipes from the cookbook require a photo shoot, a top photographer, a food stylist, the cooperation of the cookbook author, and, of course, the food. It's an expensive production from start to finish.

Even then, the results are not guaranteed. Maybe the final photos are not what anyone—including your editor—had hoped they would be. The art director is defensive, the marketing executive is fighting for another photo shoot, and the publisher is unhappy at the prospect of doubling the cover costs with another shoot. Your editor knows that the cookbook author (a best-selling author currently being wooed by other publishers) will not like the photo either. "If we run with this cover, we could be giving the agent the ammunition she needs to convince the author to switch houses," your editor argues. The publisher agrees and approves a new photo shoot.

Noon

By the time these and other issues are have been resolved, it's after 12 P.M. Your editor, late for a luncheon with a top agent, runs down the street to the appointed restaurant, cell phone in hand. Once there, she sits down for a quick bite (no three-martini lunch, this) with the agent. In between bites, the agent pitches a few of his clients' top projects.

As the editor pays for lunch, the agent tells her that he will be in touch with her on the projects that most piqued her interest.

1:30 P.M.

Your editor rushes into her office to check her messages before the next meeting begins. As quickly as possible, she returns the most urgent phone calls. One is to an agent about a final contract point, one to an author about a rewrite in progress, and one to a rights manager trying to close a deal with a book club.

By the time she hangs up the phone, 45 minutes have gone by. She has only 15 minutes to collect her thoughts (and her information) for the most trying meeting of the day: the acquisitions meeting with the pub board.

The meeting begins. As you already know, this is the meeting where editors try to sell their colleagues and bosses on projects they'd like to sign up for publication.

The degree of formality at these meetings may vary from house to house, but the pressure does not. Your editor, and the projects she pitches, fall under close scrutiny during these meetings. As you've read in Chapter 14, each editor at the meeting presents one or more titles. This round-robin approach continues until all the books have been discussed or the time is up. Not surprisingly, acquisitions meetings often run late.

At this meeting, your editor is able to present two projects. The first, a follow-up book by an author whose first book did very well, is an easy sell. The other, an offbeat project by a first-time author that the editor loves, is not. Despite her passion for the project, she fails to convince her peers and will have to turn the writer down.

5 P.M.

Your editor finally returns to her office. Again, she listens to her voicemail messages and returns the most urgent calls. She checks her e-mail and her snail mail for afternoon FedEx packages. She sorts through her in-box, pulling out the catalog copy for a couple of new books left there by the copywriter, which must be reviewed and returned before she goes home. Ditto for the proofs of two covers for books due to ship to the printer the next day.

Depending on how late she works, she may also make the less urgent calls on her list and write more rejection letters. She writes a very encouraging and complimentary rejection letter to the writer whose project she was unable to sell at her acquisitions meeting earlier in the day. She recommends another editor at another house to the writer.

6 P.M.

She packs up the manuscripts she hopes to review at home that evening and leaves the office.

11:30 P.M.

Your tired editor falls asleep, a stack of proposals in her lap.

Tomorrow will bring more of the same. It's a tough job, but your editor loves doing it. It's her love for her work that keeps her coming back, despite the relatively low pay and heavy workload.

Experts Say

"There's a fine line between too much contact and too little," one weary editor admits. "The first note to strike is one of professionalism. If you treat your editor like a pro, odds are she'll return the favor."

Why Doesn't My Editor Ever Call Me?

Unless you slept through the last couple pages, you now know why. She's busy—busier than you imagined. But don't panic that she hasn't called lately: Generally, no news is good news.

Still, you want to believe that your editor has not forgotten you and your book. If you need to discuss an issue, call and talk to her about it. Given the time she spends in meetings, you may often be reduced to leaving messages on her voicemail. Voicemail can be frustrating, but don't allow your frustrations to influence the message you leave. Be brief and succinct. Be sure to let her know the best time to return your call so that you two don't wind up playing phone tag. An even better way to get together on the phone is to schedule a time via an e-mail exchange or just use e-mail to send regular updates.

Getting Through When You Need To

If you do not hear back from your editor in a reasonable amount of time, there are a number of things you can do:

- If your editor has an assistant, try getting through to him. Often he may be able to resolve the situation himself. Befriend the assistant. He can not only help you now, but he may be able to help you later—when he is an acquisitions editor himself!

- Try contacting your editor via e-mail. Most all editors have e-mail now, and many are finding it an increasingly efficient way to communicate.

- If it's an issue that has come up during the editorial or production process, try to resolve it with the production editor first. Only as a last resort should you antagonize your production editor by running around him to your acquisitions editor.

CAUTION

Slush Pile _____

Have an attitude? Don't. One writer we know turned in a manuscript twice as long as the contract specified and then refused to speak to her editor about it by phone. The writer demanded that, from now on, the staff communicate with her only by e-mail. The book was eventually published, but by then she'd made enemies all over the building. Did she sell them another book? No.

♦ The same thing goes for going over your editor's head to her boss. Before you do anything like this, talk to your agent. Let your agent talk to your editor or her boss. This is one of the biggest advantages of having an agent: You get to stay pals with the editor while your agent looks like a meanie. If you don't have an agent, do the best you can to work it out with your editor. If you do go over her head (and we advise against it), proceed at your own peril.

Hot Off the Press _____

If you feel you need to go over your editor's head, find out who her boss is and politely raise the issue at that level. One busy editor we know at a large house was surprised when an unhappy author sent an e-mail to the CEO of the publishing company's parent corporation complaining that his book hadn't received enough marketing attention. "I got a call from the CEO's assistant in London asking about the e-mail she'd received and if I could shed some light on the situation," she said. "Of course, the CEO understood the situation from our perspective and the author didn't get what he'd hoped. If he'd actually gone to my real boss—my publisher—he might have had his concern heard with a more sympathetic ear."

When to Confess You're in Trouble

Tell your editor sooner, as opposed to later. If for any reason you find yourself unable to meet your deadline, complete your rewrites, or turn around your author queries, speak up. Let your editor know as soon as possible.

The sooner she knows, the sooner she'll be able to do damage control. Damage control? Yes, your lateness will cause damage. Your editor will need to rework production schedules and perhaps postpone the publication of your book.

Writers hate to deliver bad news to editors. But the longer you wait, the fewer your editor's damage control options. You have to tell her straight away, while she can still do something to save your book! As long as you speak up soon, odds are that your editor will understand. Remember that books are published in "seasons," and if your book misses the manuscript deadline it might need to be pushed out to another season. This is important info to have as early as possible, as it might mean that your book will have to be represented by the sales force. If there is a chance that a book will slip, your publisher needs to know sooner rather than later.

Play Nice

As you've seen, editors are hard-working, underpaid people who love books and writers. They are also often job-hoppers, jumping from one publishing house to another. In New York, where much of the book publishing industry operates, switching houses is as easy as crossing the street.

This revolving-door pattern is one many writers come to hate. It's what's known as the orphan syndrome: You develop a good relationship with one editor, only to lose that editor to another house. Your new editor—often a hastily promoted assistant—may lack the experience that your departed editor had. Worse, she may lack enthusiasm for your project. Then you find that you and your book are orphans, with no strong sponsor.

Turnover in the publishing business can come swiftly and unexpectedly, as the longtime Executive Editor of Random House, Ann Godoff, learned when she was abruptly shown the door in early 2003 despite her long string of best-sellers (she was the editor of *Midnight in the Garden of Good and Evil*, which you might recall holds the record for being on the NYT best-seller list longer than any other book). The National Writers Union surveyed their members to ask about their greatest areas of frustration, and found that the high turnover rate of editors ranked up there near the top of the list.

What to do? Befriend the new editor as you had the former editor. Take the time to educate her about your book. Don't assume that any knowledge has been passed on from your former editor. No matter who your editor is, you need her. As your primary advocate at the publishing house, your editor is your single most important contact there. It's a relationship you must both guard and nurture.

Writers who do manage to develop strong and happy working relationships with their editors are loath to let them go. Many follow them (contracts permitting) from house to house. Of course, if you become a best-selling author, you can always do what John Grisham did: Hire your favorite editor to be your editor/agent!

The Least You Need to Know

◆ Your editor is your primary advocate at the publishing house; befriend her ASAP.

◆ Your second most important contact is your editor's assistant; befriend him as well.

◆ Respect your editor's time; she's busier than you imagine.

◆ Give your editor time to read your manuscript; remember that she does most of her reading at home.

◆ When you have bad news, deliver it early so your editor can look for solutions.

◆ Editors come and go, so try to make as many friends as you can within the in-house staff.

Chapter 20

So How Does My Book Get into the Stores?

In This Chapter

- ◆ An overview of the sales process
- ◆ Death of a sales conference: Do I get to go?
- ◆ Why won't Barnes & Noble take a display?
- ◆ Printing and shipping your book
- ◆ Should I go to the BEA?

When your book comes off the printing press, where does it go? The finished books are sent directly to your publisher's warehouse and from there (many, you hope) go directly to bookstores around the country.

How did that happen? When did those bookstores learn about your book? How did they know to order it? And how did they decide how many to order?

Good questions, all. What follows is a brief lesson in the sales process as practiced by the book publishing industry. The more you know about it, the less frustrated you will be later. Writers have a vested interest in how the sales process works, so here is your chance to get educated.

A Short Course in the Sales Process

As you know, the book publishing business was once a quaint pursuit, and the sales process is still more than a little quaint. The two critical elements in this process are the publisher's catalog and the publisher's sales representatives.

The Dynamic Duo: Catalogs and Sales Reps

You've read about the sales catalog in earlier chapters, so you know how important it is that your book be well described in the catalog description. But you haven't heard much about sales representatives yet. Here's how the two critical elements—catalog and rep—come together.

Several times a year, the sales representatives make appointments with the bookstore accounts for which they're responsible. Some sales reps have large geographic territories (all the Pacific Northwest, say, or all the Midwestern states), and some sales reps have large-volume national accounts (for example, all the Barnes & Noble stores, or all the Borders bookstores).

Most large publishing houses have their own full-time sales force. Many medium and small publishing houses use commissioned reps, sales reps who handle the sales for many publishers at once and receive commissions on the sales they create.

Are You Free on Tuesday?

The sales rep makes an appointment with a book buyer. That's the person who's responsible for deciding which of all the new books published the bookstore will carry, and in what quantities. In small, independent bookstores, the book buyer is often also the owner or the manager who buys books for the store in every category. These folks not only make buying decisions, but they also work on the bookstore floor and are in close contact with their customers' needs. With the large national chains, however, the book buyer is a staff position based at headquarters, far from the selling floor. These national book buyers also may specialize by topic area like health and fitness or business and personal finance. Reps meet with individual buyers depending on what topics their books cover.

> **Experts Say**
>
> Sales reps are so important that when Lewis Buzbee was putting together his proposal for *Alone Among Others: The Pleasures of the Bookstore,* he gathered letters of support both from publishers reps as well as booksellers to include. How did he manage to do that? Well ... Lewis himself is the former sales rep for Chronicle Books.

The actual sales call might be either a leisurely affair over lunch or coffee (with smaller stores) or just a hurried appointment in the cubicle of a national buyer.

Let Me Show You ...

During the sales call, the publisher's sales rep presents the titles that will be published in the next few months (or in the next season). With the catalog between them, the sales rep and the buyer move through page by page. The rep gives a short (very short) presentation on each book using a tip sheet or sales sheet. The tip sheet includes the editor's vision, book contents, market statistics, and other data that isn't included in the catalog. The presentation includes these points:

- A description of the book and its contents
- The publisher's plans to promote, market, and publicize the book
- The author's credentials, other books he has written, and sales by the account

Sound familiar? Except for the publisher's publicity and marketing plans, these are essentially the same things you needed to give the publisher to show that the world needed your book. Now it is your publisher's turn (through the rep) to convince the bookstores that the world needs your book.

You can see how important the material you provided is. The sales rep has just a few minutes to convince the book buyer to buy your book, and he needs the best and most compelling information possible.

You can also see, we hope, once again how important it is not to exaggerate or lie in your proposal (particularly about your credentials or your past book sales), because that information gets used over and over and over again throughout the process. If you didn't tell the truth, it will eventually be discovered. Booksellers can instantly access their accounts previous sales on a book and more editors and booksellers have access to services like BookScan that reveal the overall sales numbers of books in the marketplace. It will kill your books chances for success if the rep discovers incorrect information in the middle of a sales call.

The Numbers Game

If the book buyer likes your book, how many will she order? Small stores buy in quantities ranging from just 1 copy, to 10 or 20 or more for a potential best-seller. Large chains follow pretty much this same formula per store, but the total order for the entire chain might be several thousand.

Just-in-Time Inventory

Bookstores used to order what they thought they could sell in the first 30 days. With the rise of "just-in-time" inventory management, most stores now order only what they think they can sell in the first 10 days. When those copies sell, bookstores either turn to wholesale distributors (rather than the publisher) for fast reorders or ask the publisher to begin sending them the amount they needed automatically each month. The theory is that less of the bookstore's money is tied up in inventory that way—and fewer copies of your book are sitting in either your publishers or the booksellers warehouse. This allows publishers to better control their print quantities, inventories and—better for you—their returns.

Comparative Sales Can Make or Break You

Now that computers grace every office, book buyers rely on them to help with buying decisions. Imagine that the rep has just presented a cookbook on vegetarian pasta. The book buyer will turn to his computer and bring up the sales figures for other cookbooks on vegetarian pasta. If the sales look good, the buyer might order this new title, too. But if the sales look slow, chances are that he might buy very few copies or—worse—completely pass on it.

Can that really be true? All the hard work that you and your publisher put into writing and publishing your book, and the book buyer won't even put it on the shelf because of the slow sales of a similar book? Sad, but all too true. This is a business, and the book buyer just made what he thinks is a sound business decision, based on his knowledge of his customers' needs.

Bookmarks

All published books have an **ISBN**, an **International Standard Book Number.** These numbers are assigned by an industry publisher, R. R. Bowker. The first series of numbers always identifies the publishing house.

Imagine another sales pitch, this one by an author who's been published before. "This is his second novel?" the buyer notes. "Let me see how well his first book sold for us." The book buyer punches in the *ISBN* from the first book the author wrote, and the buy for the author's second book will be based in large part on the success of the first. Also frightening, but also true.

Experts Say

Just a handful of accounts (Barnes & Noble, Borders, Ingram, Crown, and a few others) make up most of a book's advance orders. So if one of these passes on your title, it can affect the initial print run. If several of them pass, the publisher may reconsider publishing the book at all. On the other hand, if they really like your book, it can be an almost instant success.

Prepping the Rep

The amount of time that the book buyer listens to the sales rep talk about your book is frighteningly brief—sometimes less than a minute per title. Does the sales rep base this critical sales pitch only on what he learned from reading the catalog? Not exactly. The rep also heard about your book at the sales conference he attended.

Let's move back to that time and go to a sales conference.

Death of a Sales Conference

The traditional sales conference is a face-to-face meeting between the sales staff (who are based all around the country in their sales territory) and the editors, publicity, and marketing folk. The purpose of the sales conference is to introduce the new books for that publishing season and educate the sales reps on how to best sell them.

These meetings, sometimes held over the course of several days for the larger publishing houses, unfold like this:

- Each editor gives a three- to five-minute presentation on the books that he's acquired (with longer presentations for the major titles).

- A large color slide of the front cover for the book is shown, and maybe some inside art as well, if it's a heavily illustrated book.

- The sales reps ask questions during the presentation.

- The sales reps break up into smaller groups with the sales and marketing managers to work out how to best present each book.

- The editors are alerted to any potential problems with individual titles that the sales reps anticipate.

How They've Changed!

In past years, the larger sales conferences were more like big parties than business meetings, often in resort areas such as Florida or even Puerto Rico. It was seen as an opportunity to reward the tired sales staff with a little vacation treat before the next season began. But as the publishing industry changed, so have the sales conferences.

Some publishing companies have even cut the face-to-face aspect of these conferences. They use videotaped presentations of the books, with each editor talking about the titles as though sitting up at the dais in a conference room.

> **CAUTION**
>
> **Slush Pile**
>
> Sales reps are very nice people, but do not attempt to call them. They (and your editor) will not be amused if you track them down and chat them up about sales for your book. There have been many instances in which overzealous authors have soured the publisher's sales reps on pushing their book.

Some large publishers like Random House have even tested the idea of using the occasional huge conference call in place of a live sales conference to keep costs down. Hundreds of folks around the country, sales reps, editors, marketing folk, and so on, all sitting and listening in to the same phone call to hear the book presentations.

Random House also supplies their sales reps with audio recordings that the editors make describing their books. This way they can develop greater knowledge of each individual title and be able to craft their own fresh-sounding way to pitch it to their customers.

Do Authors Go?

Occasionally, authors are asked to attend the sales presentation. Celebrity books and other types of books driven by the author's personality are the likeliest candidates for this. When this happens and the author has charisma, it does make a difference. Having met the author, and having heard the author's own take on his book, the sales reps are often more enthusiastic about selling that title.

Should you offer to attend the sales conference? If you are a dynamite public speaker and are comfortable addressing large audiences, sure. It never hurts to ask. But don't take it personally if you're given a polite "No, thanks." Author presentations are rare these days.

Getting Reps Revved Up

Short of attending in person, is there anything you can do to try to jazz up the sales reps? Over the years, many authors have tried many things. Cookbook authors have endeared themselves by sending along sweet things based on recipes in their books. Natural health authors have sent along herbal supplements. T-shirts, CDs, and all sorts of little freebies are generally welcome, but they should tie in with your book somehow. Ask your editor how he feels about the idea before you rush out to the store to buy gifts.

Dumps and Other Promotional Ideas

While the sales rep is working to convince the book buyer to order your book, he is also trying to convince her to take a number of copies. One of the best ways to do this is to package several copies of the book together in a display pack and offer it at a higher discount: "Order 12, get an extra copy," or "Order 8 copies and get this attractive *counter display.*"

The days of *dumps* and displays are fading, however. The large chains seldom buy them because space in their stores is at a premium; the publishers don't get enough orders to justify producing them. But savvy publishers continue to offer multiple-copy *pre-packs* to encourage larger orders.

Charging for Store Exposure

Booksellers are just as anxious to make money as publishers are. One of the more ingenious ways for them to make money is to charge publishers for special placement or displays. Let's say that Valentine's Day is approaching, and bookstore chain X is planning to build special Valentine's Day themes displays in all 500 stores. But they won't just wander around the stores pulling romance novels, sex books, and books with red or pink covers to use in the display.

These stores sell positioning. For a fee, a publisher can buy a place in the holiday display. Sometimes the display is on the *endcap*, the small area on the end of each aisle; sometimes

Bookmarks _____

Several copies of the book placed in a cardboard holder can be called either a **counter display**, a **pre-pack**, or a **counter pack**. Larger displays that stand on the floor and display eight or more copies are called **dumps**.

Bookmarks _____

The **endcap** is the shelf at the end of an aisle, a prime place for your book to be seen by browsers. Publishers can sometimes pay booksellers for the chance to have a display of their books on the endcap.

it's on a table. Keep in mind that almost all the special display space you see in a bookstore is paid placement by the publisher. In many cases, publishers can't even purchase the space unless the bookstore has already decided they'd like an extra large order.

Remember those free bookstore gift catalogs we urged you to collect for research? The publishers of the books featured in those catalogs paid for them to be there. The cost to be included in these catalogs can run into several thousand dollars per title.

Can't Hurt to Ask

Ask your editor about all these things. You, as the author, have no control over whether your publisher decides to offer a counter display or pay for an endcap display for your book. Depending on the subject of your book, it might not be appropriate at all. But it never hurts to ask your editor if there are any special plans for displays or in-store promotions.

Printing and Shipping Your Baby

After leaving the account with orders in hand (or in the laptop computer, as the case may be), the sales rep transmits these orders to the main office. When all the accounts have been seen and all the advance orders for your book are in, these numbers are then used to set the size of your book's first print run, or *first printing*.

> **Bookmarks**
>
> Just before a book is shipped to the printers, the publisher takes a close look at the advance orders received from bookstores and uses this information to decide the book's **first printing,** the number of books to be printed.

When the printer has printed and bound all your books (this takes four to six weeks, on average), it is ready to begin filling orders. Large bookstore orders are sometimes shipped directly from the printer to the store's main warehouse, bypassing the publisher's warehouse and distribution system. Other orders may be filled from the publisher's warehouse.

Warehousing the Rest

When all advance orders have been shipped, the rest of your books will be stored in the publisher's warehouse. There they wait, hoping to be sent out to fill other orders and reorders. Depending on the size of your book's print run, the publisher may have anywhere from 500 to several thousand copies of your book in the warehouse.

Smaller, more frequent printings are now the rule. The publisher hopes that demand for your book will soon deplete the stock on hand and that the book will go into a second, a third, and a fourth printing, and beyond!

Why such small numbers of extra copies? Because the publisher's best chance to make money is by not overprinting. Many a profit has been squandered on an unnecessarily large second printing.

If any of your books are returned unsold by the bookseller, those copies probably will rejoin the others in the warehouse. Returns affect the inventory levels and are always taken into account when a new print run is under consideration.

Book Shows

No description of the book sales process would be complete without at least mentioning the annual booksellers shows and conventions. Many come in all sizes and shapes and may cover more than just books (such as the Christian Booksellers Association shows in winter and summer that include music and gifts). While the smaller shows can be of interest, the biggest of them all is Book Expo America or BEA. Held once a year in late May or early June, this is the trade show for the publishing industry. The location varies around the country from year to year, but it is such a bog show that it usually ends up in a big convention town like Chicago, New York, or LA. Publishers take large booths and display glossy blow-ups of the covers of their top titles. Their booths are stocked with catalogs for the fall list, and many publishers have freebies to pass out to booksellers: posters, advance reading copies, pins, jelly beans, T-shirts—you name it. Some of the larger publishers hold parties to fete their big clients and their big authors. Yearly, publishers debate the value versus the cost of this show, which was designed to cater directly to independent booksellers buying books for the year, but has increasingly become simply an industry gathering place. Agents actively sell rights for titles, editors set up meetings and publishers prowl the floor looking at the competition's offerings.

Do Authors Go?

Yes, some authors do go to the Book Expo. Should you go? It depends.

It depends on why you want to go. Unless you are a big celebrity author, no one will make a fuss over you. It can be quite a humbling experience to be an unknown author at this big event. Long lines form for free, autographed books from well-known authors. Not-so-long lines form for authors whose books are little known. Your publisher may not be willing to invest the money or the time in having you there as one of its authors.

One thing to ask about though, is whether your book will be featured at your publisher's booth. If your book is just a few months away from being published and if your book is a key title on the list, your publisher might decorate their booth with large posters of the cover, or pass out galley copies to book buyers and media folk in order to generate buzz. Understand that the books that are featured at BEA are from the Fall list, the books are scheduled to be published in the autumn after BEA is held. Many an author whose book has just been published prior to BEA has been crushed to learn that his book won't be featured or that his publishing house may not even have a booth. It's not the kiss of death by any means. In fact, for the last two years, the books with the biggest authors generating the biggest buzz at BEA were all but dead by the time they actually published. You can ask your editor what the presence will be, but don't be discouraged if your book isn't a key title. Being featured at BEA may help a few books, but the vast majority do just fine without it.

If you want to go to the Book Expo on your own as a visitor to learn more about the book business, go ahead. This is a great opportunity to pick up catalogs from many other publishers and to learn about new books coming out. (Your publisher may be able to get you a free convention badge; just ask.) You can check out the information for this year's show at www.bookexpoamerica.com, and it will fill you in on the cost to register as a guest.

Smaller regional booksellers conventions also are held around the country. Ask your editor if there is a regional show in your area. These shows are more likely to feature local authors.

The Least You Need to Know

- Bookstores order books up to six months before the book is actually available.

- The size of the order depends on the popularity of the topic, the popularity of the author, and the publisher's publicity plans.

- With computer sales information, the order process is now formulaic and takes into account the actual sales history of other books on the topic, as well as the author's previous book sales.

- Celebrity authors might be invited to a sales conference or a bookseller's convention, but most authors are not.

Chapter 21

Maximum Publicity for Maximum Sales

In This Chapter

- What's publicity, and what can it do for your book sales?
- What to expect from the publicity department
- How two big promoters became mega-best-selling authors
- Generating your own publicity
- The beauty of radio
- Honing your radio talk skills

"Publicity? But I landed a big-time publisher," you say. "Why should I have to learn about publicity?" Your publisher has a whole department that does publicity. So isn't that its job?

Yes, it is the publisher's job. But it is also your job. You should learn about publicity, and you should start learning the minute you sign the contract with the publisher. Publicity is a critical element in the success of your book. As the author, you should become publicity-savvy, just as knowledgeable about this part of publishing as you've become about all the other steps thus far.

Remember that study we mentioned that the National Writer's Union did? Although writers groused about the high turnover for editors at big houses, the number one gripe that aired was in the area of promotion. Many authors felt their publishers hadn't lived up to the promises made in the sales catalog, and that promotional efforts were quickly abandoned if the book didn't take off immediately. So learn what you can, because it will be important later. On the other hand, big publishers work hard to stretch already thin budgets across many books and authors. They have to balance expensive advertising, press tours and marketing materials doing less with more.

It is never too soon to begin thinking about publicity for your book. By starting early, you can make media contacts now that you can call on in the future. You can send out copies of your proposal or manuscript-in-progress to writers and celebrities in the hopes that they will give you an endorsement. You can even watch more television and listen to more radio so that you have a better sense of which shows would be best for your book. Get started acting and thinking like a book publicist right away.

Was It Always Like This?

The role of the author has changed dramatically over the years. In times past, we hear, an author could turn in a completed manuscript, dust off her writerly hands, and allow the publisher to take it from there. Authors didn't sully themselves with commerce. The in-house publicity staff would handle all the details about the book's publicity, sending sweet and gentle notes to the author to let her know the details on the many upcoming reviews, book signings, and publicity appearances.

The Reality

Today, the publisher expects the author to take a very active role in publicizing the book, possibly even taking the lead (depending on how large the publisher's publicity staff is). "Does this author have a *platform?*" is a question asked in most editorial meetings today. When evaluating the feasibility of your nonfiction project, the publisher places a great deal of weight on how hard you plan to work on the book's behalf, with speeches, newspaper editorials, local appearances, magazine columns, and the like. The publisher took all this into consideration on that fateful day in the editorial meeting when your book received the go-ahead.

If you don't have an obvious platform, talk to your editor or marketing manager anyway. You may have contacts that are useful. One publisher we know rarely pays for author tours or appearances but can work to schedule signings and media appearances if the author is traveling to a city for another event. If you speak at seminars or conferences, travel for business or are going to visit your great aunt in San Francisco, let your publisher know—they may be able to capitalize on your schedule.

> **Bookmarks**
>
> More publishers are looking for authors who have a **platform,** a ready-made existing audience for the book. Your platform might include lectures, a radio or television show, or a widely syndicated column. These aren't the planks that hold your platform up? Better start building a bigger platform now! Become an expert somewhere, if only in your local newspaper.

Just What Is Publicity, Anyway?

According to the dictionary, *publicity* is defined as "the process of drawing attention to a person or thing." You should know, however, that in the world of publishing, publicity refers more correctly to "the process of drawing attention to a person or thing for free." Publicity is not an ad in *People* magazine; publicity is an article in *USA Today*. Publicity is not a direct mail piece sent to a million homes; publicity is your voice on the radio station broadcast to a million homes.

> **Bookmarks**
>
> Books become known to the reading public through **publicity:** reviews, articles, and mentions of the book and its contents in the media.

Why No Ads?

Print and television advertising is seldom done in the book business. Why? It has to do with the economics of advertising, the huge cost of the ad compared to the retail price of what is being advertised. General Motors buys lots of ads to sell cars, but remember how much a car costs. If just 10 or 20 cars sell, that pays for the ad. But if a publisher bought the same ad for your book, imagine how many books he'd have to sell at $22.95 to come close to breaking even.

So don't tell your publisher that your book would be a best-seller if only the publishing house would advertise on the *Today Show*. The exception is targeted advertising (placing an ad for a massage book in a massage magazine) or paying for the book to be featured in the catalogs published and distributed by large bookstore chains.

Experts Say

"We write up a press release and send it along with a review copy to our sources at all the major media," explains a publicist at William Morrow. "To be quite frank, our efforts are often dictated by the size of the book's first printing. If a book's shipping in numbers of, say, 25,000 copies and above, it'll receive greater attention and a longer publicity effort than one with smaller numbers."

Better to Get Unpaid Praise

Publicity is the stronger way to sell a book. Articles and interviews make you appear to be an expert and give an independent endorsement to your book.

What the Publicity Department Can Do

As dazzling as the idea of glamorous television appearances and a late-night interview with Larry King might be, it seldom happens with most books. Here is a clear-eyed view of what you, as a first-time author, can reasonably expect from the publicity department.

The actual legwork to publicize your new book begins in the publicist's office some three or so months before your book is scheduled to be released. Publicists may send out bound galleys or *review copies* to reviewers, work on setting up book signings and local tours, and try to make sure that your book gets into the hands of the right magazine and newspaper people. The publicists also make follow-up calls to be sure that the information arrived, to gauge interest, and to arrange for book interviews. Publicist Arielle Ford calls this part of the publicity process "smiling and dialing."

Bookmarks

Free copies of books sent out from the publisher to anyone who might help promote the book are **review copies**. These include book reviewers, celebrities, television and radio producers, columnists, and the like—sometimes their mail is so heavy with free books that they need help lugging the sack inside.

Although all authors dream of a nationwide book tour, it is becoming a rare thing indeed. To avoid disappointment later, ask your editor several months before your pub date if there are plans for a tour. You might as well find out now. If there *are* plans for a tour, you will need the advance warning to rearrange your schedule.

Novel Approaches

Publicizing fiction is a challenge. With fiction (particularly first-time fiction), a publicist can't do too much beyond sending out review copies to well-known authors in the hope of creating a stir, targeting literary review sources such as *The Bloomsbury Review*, and trying to arrange for profile pieces in an author's local newspaper. "We also try to arrange readings at well-known literary bookstores such as Elliot Bay Booksellers in Seattle or Tattered Cover in Denver," a fiction publicist explains.

Novels also can be promoted through magazine excerpts or serialization. This is arranged not by the publicity department, but rather by the rights department. If you retained first serial rights in your contract, it is your responsibility (or your agent's) to sell these rights. No matter who is selling them, this has to happen many months before the book actually is published.

A recent trend has developed toward newspaper and magazine lifestyle articles about young novelists. These articles seem to talk more about the loft apartments they live in, where they hang out with friends, or an intriguing story behind the writing of their book, then about the work itself. If you think there might be a cool lifestyle (as opposed to literary) angle your publicist could use, by all means tell them about it.

Hold Your Fire

Feel the need to call the publicity department for daily check-ups on what's going on with your book? Don't. Frustrated by what you view as a lack of effort and interest? Be careful how you communicate those feelings. A cranky author can turn off the staff—and once you're viewed as a problem, people there may do even less for your book. Remember what your grandmother told you: You can catch more flies with honey ....

The Publicity Department's Full Plate

If you think that the publisher's publicity department is going to work 24 hours a day to drive your book onto the best-seller list, guess again. The folks in publicity are responsible for doing what they can for as many as 10 or 15 books at one time. Understand that there is nothing for you as an author to gain by complaining about this situation. Instead, you can use this opportunity to take your book's fate into your own hands. To avoid duplication of effort and some bad feelings all around, it's best to let the publicity department have a clear shot at your book for the first few months after it is released.

When the people in the publicity department have let you know that it's time for them to turn their attention to other books (and they will be honest with you, if you ask), that's the green light you need to roll up your sleeves and take it from there.

"We are thrilled to work with authors who have taken the time to learn the ropes about publicity and can take an active role in it," says a longtime industry publicist. Don't worry that the interest will have disappeared because the book has been out for a few months. If your book is well written, well researched, and well targeted, you can promote it for years to come. Read on to hear how two guys whose first book came out a couple years ago are still on the road flogging it.

Chicken Soup for Everyone!

Mark Victor Hansen and Jack Canfield are the well-known authors of the best-selling series *Chicken Soup for the Soul*, with a mind-boggling 80 million copies in print. But were they always best-selling authors? Did their publisher (Health Communications) have a superhuman publicity department that did all the work for them? Not by a long shot. Let's see how Mark and Jack did it.

The two friends decided that they wanted their first book, *Chicken Soup for the Soul*, to be a best-seller. But instead of sitting back and waiting for a publisher to make that happen, these two took active steps to achieve their goal.

Ask the Experts

Long before their book was even published, they set out on a mission. They interviewed best-selling authors, people like John Gray of *Men Are from Mars, Women Are from Venus*, and M. Scott Peck of *The Road Less Traveled*. Mark and Jack asked each of these best-selling authors a very simple question: "How did you become a best-selling author?" Makes sense, doesn't it?

The Secret Formula

So, what did they learn on their fact-finding mission? The key to a best-seller truly is publicity, and lots of it! M. Scott Peck told Hansen and Canfield that he gives one interview a day to any radio station, regardless of size. His approach seems to have worked in a big way: *The Road Less Traveled* was on *The New York Times* best-seller list for 12 years—not 12 weeks or even months, mind you, but 12 years!

Hansen and Canfield have taken Peck's advice to heart. They not only give an interview a day, but they also let producers around the country know that they are always available as last-minute guests to fill in for a cancellation (a little trick they learned from best-selling sex advice author Dr. Ruth).

It is worth noting that Hansen and Canfield pay for most of their publicity efforts themselves. They work well with their publisher's publicity department, of course, and keep the staff informed of everything that they do. But they firmly believe that it is the responsibility of the author to create demand for a book.

The Idiot's Publicity Starter Pack

So how can you put what the authors of *Chicken Soup for the Soul* learned into action? Here are ideas and suggestions to get you started planning your publicity campaign.

Press Kit Starters

Start now to gather things for your press kit. Make yourself a file in which you keep a bio, a professional picture of yourself, videotapes of your appearances or audio tapes of your speeches, and newspaper and magazine clippings of articles about you or about the topic of your book. The earlier you start to build this file, the more you will have to choose from when the time comes to assemble your press kit.

Press Release Basics

A press release is a one-page announcement sent to various members of the media. Like the query letters you now know how to write, a press release serves to catch the interest of the person reading it. We have included an example of this in Appendix F. Follow the style shown there to learn where to place your dates, phone numbers, and other basic contact information.

Press releases start out with a catchy headline. Often these same headlines will be used in the newspaper or magazine articles that result, so choose carefully! Here are a few sample press release headlines:

- Authors Reveal Stunning Reasons for Juvenile Crime
- Rock Musicians Share Their Vegetarian Recipes for *Food Without Faces*
- Secrets to Surviving Your Husband's Midlife Crisis

Each of these was crafted to convince a jaded press person to keep reading and to learn more about you and your book. A press release needs to deliver the basics of who, what, when, why, and where. It also needs to have a clear purpose: Are you trying to interest the media in writing a feature article? Are you announcing a press conference? Or are you just hoping for reviews? To learn more about writing an effective press release, we recommend Marcia Yudkin's book, *Six Steps to Free Publicity*.

Useful Contacts

Draw up a list of media contacts you have now (and ask your friends who they know); work hard to expand this list by joining organizations or attending events where you might meet members of the media. The cub reporter that you befriend today may be the editor of the business section by the time your book is published!

Bookstores

Talk to your local bookstores about the fact that you will have a book coming out, and ask for advice on how to promote your book in their stores. Make it a point to attend events in many bookstores to learn what kind of event draws a crowd and what draws only the author's family members. An event in a bookstore described as a "book signing" is a flat-sounding event, and only draws a crowd for a celeb who has many die-hard fans content to just stand in line for a chance to gaze upon them briefly while waiting for a signature. We know one author who is usually so worried that no one will show up that he sends e-mails and flyers to all his friends and family. His signings are usually well attended but he doesn't sell many books.

Newspapers and Magazines

Read papers and magazines, and take note of who writes articles on topics that relate to your book. Jot down not just the book reviewer, but also the names of reporters whom you can try to interest in writing a feature-length piece about you and your book. One author sent a note to a woman at *USA Today* years ago to let her know how much he enjoyed one of her articles; now she is in regular contact with him as an expert in that field.

Promotional Items

When your publisher has the finished artwork for your front cover, have a printed postcard made with the book's cover, publication, and ordering information. They make great thank you cards or note cards and will help keep the name of your book in front of everyone's eyes. (On a similar note, co-author Jennifer and her own co-authors on *Christmas Miracles* had ink stamps made that said "I Believe in Christmas Miracles" and then used them on the outside of all their correspondence.) Other great, inexpensive promotional items can include bookmarks, sticky notes and bookplates.

That way, you can circulate the image of your book long before it appears on bookstore shelves. Of course, be sure to send a whole bunch out when your book is published to remind people to buy it.

One tiny tip—many of these types of promotional items aren't that expensive, and so publishers can almost always be convinced to pay the tab for you as a small way to keep an author happy.

> ### Hot Off the Press
>
> Arielle Ford, the La Jolla–based book publicist for many best-selling authors such as Deepak Chopra and Brian Tracy, is happy to tell authors how to get on *Oprah* and other national television shows. She says, "All you have to do is call this number." The room falls silent as she recites the phone number: 213-385-0209. "That's the number for the Prayer Line." And she isn't just joking—she says that two of her clients did get booked after leaving prayers. The folks at the Prayer Line will pray every day for 30 days to help your request come true. Hey, it couldn't hurt!

"And Our Next Guest Is ..."

Among the best ways that authors can help to publicize their book once they are available in bookstores is to arrange radio interviews. Radio is a tremendous medium for books; of all the different types of media, it sparks the quickest response. How does it work?

Radio Sells

If you see an ad for something on television, you file that impression away in your mind and perhaps will act on it in the future. But countless advertising studies have shown that the information we hear on the radio sparks an immediate response. If you hear something on the radio about a book that interests you, you think to yourself, "Hey, I'm going to stop off at the bookstore on the way home tonight and pick that up!" It's a powerful way to sell books.

Experts Say

"Authors as authors and books as books concern us not at all. Authors as experts who can talk knowledgeably about topical issues, that is what we want on the radio," says Joel Roberts, morning talk show host-turned media trainer. No producer for radio or television is really booking you to talk about your book, about why you wrote it and what's inside. She's trying to put together a show that will interest her audience, a lively and topical show that will grab and hold its attention.

All those folks trapped in their cars on the roadways have nothing else to do but listen to you explain to them how much better their lives will be and how much more money (or love, or sex, or jobs) they will have if they will only rush out right now and buy a copy of your book. Make it your goal to become an expert radio talk show guest, and your book sales will shoot through the roof. But how can you get yourself booked as a guest on the radio?

Selling Yourself to Radio

There are two ways to become a guest on radio shows. The first is to call up and try to get someone interested in you. The second is to let someone get interested and call you!

All the information you need to research radio stations across the country (from the size of the station to the phone numbers and addresses of the hosts and producers) is available in a really big and heavy book called *Bacon's Media*. Try to find this reference book at your library—keep in mind, though, that the cost to buy one is well over $100. Check out their website at www.bacons.com to see if there is any less costly way to get the info, and also take a look at Burrelles.com, which offers a similar service. These companies run occasional "free trials" and you might be able to get the information you need without paying the professional price tag. Using the information in *Bacon's*, you can draw up a list of stations you would like to target and can begin your campaign to sell yourself as a guest.

Bookmarks

Radio shows that play on more than one station are **syndicated** across the country. Giving one interview to a syndicated host helps you to reach several media markets and millions of people at once.

Which Stations, Which Shows?

How will you decide which stations in which markets? Ask friends and relatives across the country for advice about which radio stations in their area are the most popular and which ones have live talk shows. Make it a point when you travel to listen to the local radio stations, station-hopping along the band until you have identified a few that seem appropriate. Ask other authors you might know which stations have worked for them.

Be on the lookout for the largest stations in the area, those with the greatest broadcast area. Radio shows with *syndicated* programs (programs that play on more than one station) are gems that you that should always dig for.

Smiling and Dialing

When you have identified the likely stations, you are ready to begin your campaign. Call the station first to confirm that the information listed in *Bacon's* is still current; stations can change their format at any time. It is very important that you have the correct name for the producer, as it is the producer's responsibility to put together an interesting show.

Spend time and effort in creating your "pitch," your 30-second speech about why this particular producer should book you as a guest. Don't start your pitch off by saying, "I wrote a book on …" but instead say confidently "I'm an expert on … and your listeners will be inter-ested in the topic." If you don't come across well in those 30 seconds on the phone, the producer will not have high hopes for how you will handle yourself once you get on the air. When you are confident that your pitch is compelling, pick up the phone and call! Follow up a successful pitch with a copy of your book and that press kit you've put together.

> **Experts Say**
>
> "With the web, radio listeners can now just fire up their computers and order the book they just heard about," one author told us. "Which means that after every big radio interview nowadays, I check my sales figures on Amazon.com and can literally see the books selling from the earlier interview. It's a secret thrill!"

> **Slush Pile**
>
> On most radio programs, the producer is responsible for coming up with a lively show that sounds good on the air. Producers are always on the lookout for good guests. If you can present yourself and your topic in a way that sounds like it will make a good show, it won't be long before you hear the words, "You're on the air."

Get Them to Come to You

So is there an easier way to get booked? Do the producers ever call authors, instead of authors calling them? Yes. A magazine is sent each month to radio and television producers around the country to alert them to possible guests: *Radio-TV Interview Report*. Instead of calling producers around the country, you can simply buy yourself an ad in this magazine and let producers know about you and your expertise.

Not sure how to advertise yourself in a jazzy way to make producers call? Don't worry, the magazine staff folks can help you position yourself and your topic to appeal to producers. For more information on rates and scheduling, call Bradley Communications to find out about *Radio-TV Interview Report* at 610-259-1070, extension 408.

A Cross-Country Whirlwind Radio Tour

One way to hit a great many stations and markets in one short period of time is to arrange a satellite tour. Satellite radio tours are prearranged interviews with a large number of stations, all done in one single morning. You can sit at home in your bathrobe and give the same short interview over and over and over again to stations from coast to coast.

This type of interview is expensive (several thousand dollars) and needs to be professionally arranged; it is not something you can do on your own. Planned Television Arts in New York (212-593-5820) is the best-known firm for satellite tours.

Should You Be Media-Trained?

Not everyone makes a natural radio guest. But learning how to get your point across quickly, how to deal with questions, and how to work the title of your book into every other sentence are all skills that can be acquired. You can do it yourself by listening carefully to radio shows and analyzing what works, or you can have someone teach you. Practice talking in short sentences that will stick in people's minds. Media trainers specialize in helping you with your communications skills and your ability to field questions and think on your feet.

> **Experts Say**
>
> Media trainer Joel Roberts recommends the book *How to Get Your Point Across in Thirty Seconds or Less* to help you hone your message for radio. The host isn't asking you the right questions? Don't panic, Roberts says. "Just respond with 'That's an interesting question, but what I think is even more interesting is …' and cut straight to what you want to say."

If you're serious about being effective on the radio, media training can be money well spent. Training will increase your confidence and lessen your fears, and it will increase your ability to sell your book on the air. You can find the names of media trainers in the Yellow Pages, or even by asking radio producers for recommendations.

Three Key Points

To get your point across on the air, you must always have two or three key points at your fingertips. Write them down on index cards and have them handy while you're being interviewed. And don't forget that great politicians' trick: No matter what the question is, you can always turn it to your advantage by saying, "I'm so glad you asked that, it reminds me of something I point out in my book …." Then you're off and running with your own agenda!

Touring the Libraries

A quieter way to get the word out on your book is to arrange a tour of your regional library system. In the same way that you thought up an "event" for your local bookstore rather than a dull book signing, think of a lecture topic or presentation that would interest library patrons. Co-author Jennifer spent a Saturday morning not long ago driving between libraries in the Seattle are giving talks to writers gathered there. Libraries are happy to host novelists, sometimes more eager than bookstores, in fact. Call and ask for the head librarian and ask whether that location has author events. If they don't, ask which libraries do!

Reality Check

Editors love authors who see the reality of the situation and are willing to contribute to their own promotional platform—that is, bring in a publicist or PR firm to help promote them, or their speaking circuit, seminars, etc. and the book along the way. However, we've also had bad experiences with this approach. PR firms and publicists sell the author on what they can do (book them on big, big shows, pitch them to big, big magazines), and all too often, authors sign up to pay for the full PR treatment. In the meantime, though, your editor has seen the actual advance sales numbers from their accounts and knows that the industry isn't responding in an encouraging way.

Once the book comes out, the publicity folks pitch your book and … nothing happens, or perhaps just a few small hits that don't really get much of a sales response. The sad truth is that you can't make a best-seller happen by sheer force of will and money alone.

Maybe the lesson here is that as an author, you can do everything right and the publisher can do everything right and the book just doesn't pop. No one has a magic formula, but you can increase your chances of success by doing publicity on your own.

Publicity Pays Off

Now you know: Publicity can sell books, and lots of publicity can sometimes sell lots of books. You've learned that you may have to do much of the publicity for your book yourself, and that it really isn't such a hard thing to do after all. If you believe in your book and can craft a message that appeals to producers, you'll be on the air in no time. In the next chapter, we explore two other avenues for book publicity: television and the Internet.

The Least You Need to Know

- ◆ Publicity sells books better than anything else.

- ◆ Your publisher will do some publicity, but a more sustained effort is the author's responsibility.

- ◆ Publicity techniques can be learned, and persistence is the key.

- ◆ Radio producers decide which guests will be booked on a show. Your press kits should be targeted to them instead of the host.

- ◆ It is possible to advertise your availability as a radio and television guest.

- ◆ The longer you publicize your book, the longer it will sell.

Chapter 22

Television and Online Publicity

In This Chapter

- ◆ Getting on television
- ◆ Satellite TV tours
- ◆ The big shows
- ◆ Dress the part
- ◆ What really works online

You've learned all about radio interviews, but how do you get yourself on TV to talk about your book? The short answer is: you don't. You don't get yourself on television to talk about your book; you get yourself on television because you have something to say that is of interest to television viewers.

Bright Lights, Big City

Remember the advice from Joel Roberts, the radio guy in Chapter 21? He said, "We don't care about authors as authors and books as books." What he meant was that a producer's main concern (both on the radio and on television) is putting together an interesting show that viewers will enjoy. If viewers enjoy the show, more viewers will watch, so the channel can charge more for advertising, and the producer gets to keep his job. Got it?

"So," the interviewer begins, "why did you write this book?" And the viewer reaches for the remote control. An author sitting in a chair being interviewed about his book makes for flat TV. But someone sitting in a chair being interviewed about dramatic current events, or sharing information that viewers could use, or sharing a heartfelt story that will move the audience—that makes for good television. The fact that the person in the chair wrote a book is secondary.

So how do you get yourself booked on television to talk about your book? By convincing the television producer that what you have to say is of interest to her viewers and that it will make a lively show.

Gonna Make You a Star!

The process of getting booked on a television show is basically the same as for a radio show:

- ◆ Find the show you want
- ◆ Learn the producer's name
- ◆ Send information to the producer
- ◆ Follow up with a phone call to make your pitch

The standards for material for TV are quite a bit higher, however. Your press materials have to be more extensive. Instead of just the pitch letter and sample book that sufficed for a radio producer, your press kit for television should contain these items:

- ◆ A press release
- ◆ Suggested interview questions
- ◆ An author bio sheet
- ◆ A professional-quality author photo
- ◆ Suggestions for shows based on your book
- ◆ A copy of your book

Hot Off the Press _____

Family connections coach Beth Craig started getting booked on local television shows in her area even before she finished her book proposal. Seem premature? It wasn't. With the impressive tapes of Beth seated next to the TV hosts chatting about how women could be less stressed at holiday time and learn to give the gift of themselves to their families, Beth's publicist, Robin Lockwood, was able to approach national TV shows on Beth's behalf.

Please Ask Me

Send along a list of sample questions in your press kit. This is a great way for you to help the producer see how lively and thought-provoking your segment can be. If the producer ends up using those questions in the interview, you will be totally prepared and sound impressive.

And May I Suggest ...

Also send a list of sample show ideas. This is your chance to help the producer envision just how he could build a show around you. Help make his job easy: Describe as best you can a segment that features you and your book. But remember, your show ideas must be timely, informative, provocative, and/or amusing—not just you sitting around being interviewed about your book.

Perhaps you've written a book about dating. You can suggest to the producer that you will find several single people and counsel them on the air about the perils of being single, and then the cameras can follow them out on an actual date. That's much more interesting to watch than just you and an interviewer.

Pay attention to the news. Can you somehow tie a current event in to your book? Authors of relationship books can comment on celebrity couples, authors of health books can tie in to recent health studies, and authors of parenting books can comment on juvenile crime sprees. You get the idea. From now on, you must watch the news with an eye toward your own publicity.

Slush Pile _____

Don't go to the trouble of getting booked on television without also taking steps to be prepared once you step in front of the camera. Practice, practice, and then practice again. Write down your key points, and then memorize them. Develop short "sound bites," or talking points, with the information you want viewers to remember.

We've included a sample television pitch letter in Appendix I so that you can better learn how to craft these materials.

Show to Show

Sure, you know which local television shows you'd like to be on in your area, but how can you find the regional shows across the country? And is it worth your time to try to get booked on regional shows?

The very same reference books and websites like www.Bacons.com that list radio stations across the nation also list television shows. And don't forget to ask your friends and family across the country what they watch in their area.

Small Can Be Beautiful

Does regional television make a difference? "Regional TV is valuable," says Robin Lockwood, a California-based book publicist. "You reach a smaller market, but if you do enough regional TV, it can really add up. A great example of a strong regional show is *Good Day Atlanta*. They do lots of authors on that show." It also gives you a *video clip*, a professional-looking tape that you can use to pitch a larger show.

Bookmarks

A producer might ask you for a **video clip**, a tape of an appearance you've made on another television show.

Mail Call

When you have targeted the television show—and the producer—that you want to reach, pop your press kit in the mail. Then wait. A good rule of thumb is to give your press kit a one-week head start before you make a follow-up call. Call the show and ask for the producer. Tell him that you are following up on a press kit that you sent—did he receive it? And does he have any questions? Practice your 30-second phone pitch; the producer won't give you much time, so try to hook him quickly.

Satellite Television Tours

As with the satellite radio tours, it is also possible to sit in one place and do television interview after television interview. You are simply the talking head shown on the screen, while the host asks questions (the same questions the last host asked). These satellite television tours must be professionally arranged. Again, the best known firm is Planned Television Arts in New York.

With a satellite television tour, you spend a few hours in a studio doing television interviews across the country, one station at a time. "In 2½ hours, you can do 22 interviews," says Rick Frishman of Planned Television Arts. Most of the shows you're hitting are the local noon-hour broadcasts on affiliate stations for NBC, ABC, CBS, and Fox.

How much is a satellite television tour? To do the whole country costs in the $12,000 to $15,000 range. It's an expensive undertaking, but it can hit many markets all at once. And compared to the cost of actually going on tour ($1,500 to 2,000 per city in travel costs alone), it's reasonable.

Oprah and Friends

These small stations are all well and good, but what author isn't dazzled by the prospect of the big time: a nationally syndicated afternoon talk show like *The View* or *Live! With Regis and Kelly*. And all authors, regardless of what kind of book they've written, harbor hopes of appearing on *Oprah* before her show goes off the air for good.

There are two kinds of shows—live shows and taped shows. Live shows are really and truly shot in front of an audience and aired immediately. When you appear on a taped show, you will have to ask the producers when the episode will air.

> **Bookmarks**
>
> Shows that are aired as they are broadcast are **live.** Shows that are filmed and then shown some time later are **taped.** Barbara Walter's show on ABC, *The View,* is live. *Oprah* is taped.

Am I the Main Attraction?

Does an appearance on *Oprah* guarantee a best-seller? No. Although the show has certainly built many best-sellers, countless other authors have appeared on *Oprah* and have seen little effect on book sales. What makes the difference? On *Oprah*, as on any other television talk show, the theme of the show itself makes a difference.

Jennifer Openshaw was the only guest during an entire segment of *Oprah*, and her financial book *What's Your Net Worth?* was mentioned and shown on camera several times. Did it put

> **Experts Say**
>
> Satellite television tours didn't even exist until a few short years ago. "We started doing them in 1989," says Rick Frishman of Planned Television Arts. "To succeed in publicity, you've always got to think of new ways to reach people faster, cheaper, smarter. Think of a satellite television tour as the ultimate armchair publicity tour."

her on the best-seller list? There was certainly a spike in sales, but Jennifer's financial book didn't seem to grab the audience in the same way a more emotional self-help book might have. "An appearance on Oprah clearly credentials you as an expert in your field and gives you a bump in sales," Openshaw told us, "but one appearance on any show isn't going to make you an overnight best-seller."

Will It Sell Books?

Make sure to ask the producer if you and your book's topic are the sole focus of the show. If so, and if the host holds your book up in the air and says, "This book is incredible, everyone should buy a copy," that could make a dramatic difference in sales.

> **Bookmarks**
>
> On television, featured guests are those who are central to the show. **Panel** members are those who make up a roster of experts on a topic.

But if you are on the stage as a part of a *panel* of experts (each with a different viewpoint), there'll probably be little impact on book sales. But what the heck, you got a free trip to New York (or Chicago or Los Angeles). And all the producers from all the shows are watching, so you might get a call from another show. At the very least, you will have a tape of your appearance that you can now send to other television producers as proof of your knowledge and charisma.

Hands Off (for Now)

With the top national talk shows, let your publisher's publicity staff handle the bookings. If your book has been out for several months and nothing is forthcoming, ask as politely as you can if they mind if you take a crack at it. Remember, be diplomatic. Thank them for all the efforts the publicity department has made on behalf of your book. Then take it from there.

How do you pitch these big talk shows? The same way you pitch your local noon news: with a pitch letter, a press kit, and a follow-up phone call. As publicist Arielle Ford suggests (see Chapter 21), perhaps a prayer will help, too!

About That Plaid Jacket You Have ...

Going on television? Hey, great! Now, what are you going to wear? This seems like a silly question, but it really is not.

Here's your chance to watch a great deal of television and call it "work." Turn on the set and watch closely. Study what the news anchors wear, how reporters are dressed in the field, and what the characters on your favorite sitcom are walking around in. Take notes.

Does the woman on the 11 P.M. news wear a bright white sweater? No, she knows that it would create problems with the camera. And her co-anchor, is he wearing a loud plaid jacket and a paisley tie? Nope. He is decked out in a dark navy jacket and a light shirt, with a tie that has a medium-sized print on it.

Dress for (TV) Success

There is a real science to dressing for television. You need to consider not only the way your clothes look on screen—especially the colors and patterns—but also what your clothes say about you. Are you trying to position yourself as an expert on a scientific topic? Better dress like a scientific expert. Are you a romance novelist? Go ahead and let your outfit show it.

One great way to check how your clothes (and you, too) look on camera is to do a practice run with a video camera. Have a friend or family member tape you in a few different outfits, and then look at them all with a critical eye. Choose the outfit that both looks the best and presents you in the proper mode.

Different Looks for Different Books

Once during a two-week period, co-author Jennifer was featured on several different television shows, for several different books. So she had several different looks.

She appeared on the national show *American Journal* as a small-business expert with her book *101 Best Extra Income Opportunities for Women*. She wasn't there as a big-business expert in a dark blue suit, but as a small-business expert in a light turtleneck sweater and a camel-hair jacket. The effect was very friendly and approachable.

The next week, she appeared on a local television show for the *Christmas Miracles* book. Same outfit? No. She needed to look like the author of a Christmas book, not a business book. And although she does have an off-white suit embroidered with gold thread and decorated with sequins and bugle beads to wear to bookstore readings, she knew it wouldn't work for a minute on a television screen. So she appeared on camera in a bright blue, fuzzy sweater.

She made yet one more appearance that same month for the very book you hold in your hands, this time as a publishing expert on *C-Span's Book TV*. Was she in the fuzzy sweater? You guessed right, she wasn't. The dark blue suit was the appropriate choice for the topic and the show.

> **Hot Off the Press** _____
>
> Jan Tilmon of KVIE has produced many television shows featuring best-selling authors. Covert Bailey, of the *Fit or Fat* television series, and Leo Buscaglia, are among the successful folks featured on the PBS specials she's produced. From time to time, she's had to give wardrobe advice to her authors: "The first show we did with Covert, we didn't control the wardrobe," Tilmon recalls. "He showed up in an awful gray suit with cuffs. Here was this trim, energetic man wearing a stuffy-looking, poorly fitted suit. We put him in khakis, bright colored shirts, and fun ties that matched his wit and charm. He came to life on camera. It made all the difference in the world."

What Really Works Online?

A nice thing about the internet is that you don't have to worry about what you are wearing! Unlike other types of media such as newspapers, radio, and television, the idea behind web marketing is to "fish where the fish are." You can find highly specialized user groups that are most interested in your book. These are not mass audiences made up of people who may or may not be interested in you and your book; they're highly targeted groups of people.

Here are the steps to promoting yourself online:

♦ To properly promote your book on the web, you must first get a domain name that features your book's title, such as www.mybooktitle.com.

You should be able to get this from your local Internet provider at a cost of around $75.

> **Experts Say** _____
>
> Joining newsgroup discussions related to your topic can be a great way to promote your book. But don't be a jerk about it. "The most subtle way is to make sure that your book's title is embedded in your own online signature," says author and agent Bill Adler Jr.

♦ Register your domain name with all the major search engines, such as Yahoo!, Excite, and others. As of this writing, this is a free service. There are also companies such as Exploit that will register you with all the obscure search engines as well. This way, you will be listed in all of them.

♦ Join lists and participate in newsgroups related to your book's topic. Don't overdo it, but try to mention your book where you can. You want to create positive word of mouth about the fact your book exists, not annoy other members by talking endlessly about your book.

Should I Create a Website?

Creating a website can also promote—as well as sell—your book. As a matter of fact, websites can serve as a sort of 1-800 number for you. When you are promoting your book in an interview, you can tell folks that it is available from your website at www.mybooktitle.com. To actually sell books to the people who visit your website, both Barnes & Noble online and Amazon.com will partner with you as an affiliate. You can register with them to have them handle the sales from your site. Creating a website can be free—many e-mail services let their customers create free websites— or quite costly (if you hire an expert to do it for you).

But if your website is just a vanity site about your book, don't expect to be flooded with visitors. People who surf the web visit a new website and ask themselves, "What's in it for me?" If there isn't anything in it for them, in the form of excerpts, quizzes, interactive functions, links to related sites, or other jazzy tools, why would they stay? Ask yourself that question as you are planning your site. Try to achieve what web marketers call "stickiness."

Link Up

In addition to creating a website for your book, make every effort to link your website to other, similar topics. Contact other websites that would complement yours. With a health title, for instance, ask to be linked with the major websites for diseases and afflictions covered in your book. That will make it even easier for folks to find you online, even when they aren't looking for you!

Read All About Me!

Another great aspect of the web is that more journalists are poking around there. Why? They're looking for story ideas, for experts, and for ways to legitimize trends. Curtis Hougland, director of new media for Middleberg and Associates in New York, shared this success story with us:

> We had a client, AncientSites.com, who wanted more than anything to be featured in *The Wall Street Journal*. That was their number-one goal, and a daunting one at that! Their site was for history buffs, and we concentrated on getting them the best online PR we could. One of the stories we got was on Wired

News. And just one week after the Wired News story appeared, a writer from *The Wall Street Journal* called us. She'd seen the story, and in no time at all, there was a two-column story on AncientSites in *The Journal!*

So keep trying online; you never know who is out there.

Don't overlook another great way to get folks to read about you and your book online—by creating your own e-mail newsletter! Try to capture the names and e-mail addresses of friends, fans, and visitors to your website and send out a regular e-mail newsletter in which you can tastefully promote both yourself and your books to your readers. E-mail newsletters can generate tremendous book sales almost instantly. Best-selling financial author David Bach has successfully increased sales this way, as did Mark Victor Hansen not long after *The One Minute Millionaire* was published. Hansen sent e-mail messages to his thousands of fans on his newsletter list asking them to help him become the number-one book on Amazon.com that day. By including a link to Amazon.com so that readers could respond instantly, his book shot up quickly to that very spot!

Future Shock

Don't be frightened or intimidated by the online world. It can be an affordable way to publicize your book on your own. If you don't have the knowledge or the skills, seek out a web expert who does. Why ignore a great publicity venue?

The Least You Need to Know

- TV publicity can be booked directly with the show's producer by sending a press kit and a pitch letter, and then following up with a phone call.

- TV shows aren't looking for authors, per se, but rather for timely, topical, and interesting guests. So, send them a list of great show ideas based on you.

- An appearance on *Oprah* does not an automatic best-seller make.

- You can hit many TV markets in one day with a satellite television tour. It's an expensive option, but it's cheaper than touring many cities one at a time.

- Many publicity opportunities exist online; it can be a powerful way to create word of mouth for your book.

- Get a domain name that includes the title of your book, such as www. mybooktitle.com.

- Create an e-mail newsletter to build a following for your book and its topic.

Chapter 23

Real-Life Publicity and Marketing Ideas

In This Chapter

◆ Creating media interest in your book

◆ Secrets of the great book promoters

◆ How to make your bookstore event a success

◆ Can you really afford a best-seller?

Radio publicity, television publicity, online promotion—what does this all really mean for you and your book? It seems so unreal. Could you and your book really end up on national television?

Sure. From major *media markets* like New York to small markets like Lubbock, Texas, the media need programming 24 hours a day. Hundreds of newspapers are published around the country every single day of the week. Just think of how many stories need to be generated to fill up that space. And they can't all be about Bill Gates and Madonna. Many of those stories could be about you and the book you wrote. Your book could be getting *placement* in the news every day of the week!

Bookmarks _____

A **media market** is a geographic area covered by a particular station or newspaper. Some markets, such as New York, are large media markets; others, such as Omaha, are small. A **placement** is a story or a mention of the author or the book that has been placed in the media due to the PR efforts.

Yes, P. T. Barnum would be proud. No, not because of his famous quote, "There's a sucker born every minute." Barnum was the original publicity hound, creating media events out of thin air to draw attention to his circus. You also need to learn to create events. You need to learn how to get the media to come looking for you!

Creating Media Events

Bookmarks _____

A **press conference** is a meeting to share something newsworthy with members of the media.

Some of what you read in the newspaper or hear about on radio and television is the result of publicity efforts. It's either a staged media event, a press release, a _press conference_, or a story idea suggested by a public relations professional on behalf of a client.

Instead of moaning about the shallowness of this situation, though, why not jump in and learn to make it work for you?

Just What Is a Media Event?

A media event is an artificially created event staged solely for the benefit of the radio microphones, television cameras, and reporters' notepads. Once the media event is over, these members of the press return to the studio or newsroom and write about what just happened.

You can learn to create media events to promote yourself and your book. A successful media event is one that draws a great deal of press attendance. Events that create a draw usually have one (or more) of the following characteristics:

- Timeliness
- Visually interesting activities or backgrounds
- Controversial content
- Humorous subjects or backgrounds

The Timely Event

Is there a way to tie your book and its topic into what is happening in the news right this minute? You learned to think about how to do this when crafting a press release in Chapter 21. Let's imagine that you have written a book on sexual addiction and that a major political figure has just been caught in the act. This is a perfect moment for you to create a media event by calling a press conference. Alert the media (via a press release) to the fact that, at the press conference, you will reveal the number-one reason that politicians are likely to cheat on their spouses. A topic radio producers will think is just perfect for *drive-time* talk radio!

> **Bookmarks**
>
> Radio shows that play between 6 A.M. and 9 A.M. are morning **drive-time** shows. They're ideal for book promotions. Listenership is high during these hours, and many stations feature live hosts who do interviews.

Will anyone show up to your press conference? You betcha!

A Visually Interesting Event

We live in a visual world, and the press will come if you can supply a good visual image. You know the type—those large newspaper pictures of a cute child frolicking on the banks of a lake on a sunny day.

While managing a bookstore many years ago, co-author Jennifer created a media event on a sunny day by alerting TV stations to the fact that employees would be standing on a street corner blowing giant bubbles with wands. She was promoting a bubble book that came packaged with a plastic bubble wand. She was also promoting the bookstore. Did the television crews come? Yes. Those giant bubbles floating through the air made a wonderful visual image to show on the evening news.

Can you dress in a funny suit to promote your book? Can you ride a bicycle in public with a billboard attached to it? Can you have a large poster or photo on a tripod next to you as you speak? Anything that will make a cute picture stands a chance of drawing media coverage. Keep this in mind when you are creating an event. Always include a visual element to ensure that photos will run.

A Controversial Event

Is the topic of your book controversial? Can you create an event in which hundreds of angry people waving signs appear in front of a courthouse or a state capitol building?

Then do it, because controversy sells. So does a surprise announcement or an amazing revelation. But if you plan to stage this kind of event, make sure that you are prepared to verbally defend yourself and your beliefs.

> **CAUTION Slush Pile**
>
> You've heard it before: Practice before you go on the air! Practice before you stand at the podium facing a sea of television cameras. Practice before you call a newspaper reporter on the phone to discuss a story idea. If you don't practice and get it right the first time, there may not be a second time.

A Humorous Event

Can you create an amusing event around your book? Perhaps design a silly contest or create an attention-getting award that you will bestow on some public figure. These kinds of events are ideal for radio, particularly the kind of silliness that goes on during the morning radio shows. Producers of these shows are always on the lookout for something funny (or someone they can make fun of) and something that's outrageous. Be warned, though: Wear a thick skin because this sort of event could backfire.

What Good Did That Do?

You staged an event, and the media came. But when you turned on the TV that night, you heard the newsman say everything but the name of your book. And the lengthy newspaper article didn't even mention your book. So what good did that do?

> **" " Experts Say**
>
> Is there any kind of book that can't be promoted? Probably not. Even something as wacky as books about duct tape have received press coverage. Witness the story that appeared a few years ago in *The Wall Street Journal* about *The Duct Tape Book* and *Duct Tape—Real Stories*. According to the story, these two books have sold a combined 400,000 copies!

Quite a bit. Even if your book did not get any exposure, you did. You now have more experience in dealing with the media. You now have a newspaper article that you can send out, or a video or audio tape of you on the air. Keep trying. You will soon learn how to make sure that your book gets as much coverage as you do.

Let's take a look at two real-life examples from authors just like you. One is an author you've probably never heard of, and one is someone who started small and became prominent. How the heck did they get the media to pay attention to their books?

Secrets of Great Book Promoters

Many years ago, literary agent Bill Adler Jr. wrote a book called *Outwitting Squirrels: 101 Cunning Stratagems to Reduce Dramatically the Egregious Misappropriation of Seed from Your Birdfeeder by Squirrels*. It was rejected by 20 publishers (yep, even agents get rejected). Finally, Chicago Review Press agreed to publish it in 1988. Adler's book has been the focus of countless newspaper, magazine, and television stories and now has more than 175,000 copies in print. How did he do it?

Persistence Pays Off

He never gave up. He sent press releases to every newspaper he could think of—and some of them wrote about *Outwitting Squirrels*. He pitched television stories over and over again—and sometimes *Outwitting Squirrels* was on TV. He sent ideas again and again to the national talk shows, and one day, Rosie called. Well, not exactly; one of producers of the now-defunct *Rosie O'Donnell* show called.

Like millions of people who feed birds, Rosie had problems with squirrels. And Adler's book had answers (he suggests that, as a last resort, you can throw the book at them). Rosie liked *Outwitting Squirrels*, but doing a major talk show is more involved than simply showing up the day they want you. To get the most mileage out of his appearance, Adler brought along props: stuffed squirrels and sample birdfeeders, to be exact.

Do the Producer's Work for Him

"I've learned from other talk show appearances that producers love it when their guests can help put a show together," Adler says. "Anything you can do to make it easier for the show will make it easier for you to get on the show. Producers are typically juggling a dozen or more shows at a time, and they appreciate the help."

Was Adler's spot on Rosie successful? The week after the show aired, his book shot up to the number-one position on book distributor Ingram's nature best-seller list.

> **Experts Say**
>
> "Being on *The Rosie O'Donnell Show* was a hoot; it was one of the most enjoyable afternoons I had," says author and agent Bill Adler Jr. "When I suggested to Rosie that the best way to outwit squirrels is to get down on your hands and knees, crawl around your backyard, and look at birdfeeders from a squirrel's perspective, Rosie did just that on stage. The audience howled." And Adler's book sales soared!

The Christmas Cash Box

In the past few years, one young man has come to dominate the best-seller list at Christmastime: Richard Paul Evans, with his book *The Christmas Box*. With many millions of copies of *The Christmas Box* and his follow-up books in print, Evans is a master at publicity and promotion.

Was he always this way? No. Evans's story is now the stuff of publishing legend. He self-published the book and then sold it to Simon & Schuster for $4.2 million. But his background was not in writing and publishing; it was in advertising and campaigns. He took the same skills he'd honed while engineering political campaigns and applied the principles to book publicity. And it worked.

Experts Say

Even *The New York Times* Business section thinks that Richard Paul Evans is good at what he does. In a lengthy article, the paper noted, "Like any savvy pol [politician], he maintains a computer database with the names and addresses of 4,000 fans who have corresponded with him. His address is published in *The Christmas Box* and all of his other best-selling novels, and postcards are sent to his fans, alerting them to new titles." Good idea—an inexpensive way to stay in touch.

Radio-Free Utah

For the Christmas 1997 season, Evans created an unusual campaign. Drawing on his background, he produced a free two-hour radio program on the story behind *The Christmas Box*. This tape was sent, along with a copy of the book, to 896 radio stations around the country. Many of the stations ran the broadcast around Thanksgiving. In essence, it was a two-hour long commercial for Evans's books, a brilliant publicity campaign.

Could you do something like that for your book? Not right away. Evans's free programming was used because the stations were already aware of who he was and what his book was about. They'd seen his name on the best-seller list year after year after year ...

But take heed of what both Adler and Evans did: They made a producer's job easy. Whether it meant showing up with a stuffed squirrel or sending along a free two-hour radio program, both authors succeeded because they smoothed the process, making it easy for producers to create a show around them.

Effective Bookstore Events

Okay, so maybe you're not quite ready for prime time TV. But what about an appearance at your local bookstore? That sounds easy enough. It's simpler than getting on TV, but to have an effective in-store event still takes quite a bit of planning.

Many bookstores—particularly the large national chains—have a staff member whose primary function is to coordinate in-store activities. These folks are called *community relations coordinators*, or *events coordinators*. The book business is quite competitive nowadays, and every bookstore tries hard to become a community center of sorts, the type of place where you head on a Friday night just to see what's happening. Music, poetry readings, author signings, appearances by children's book characters—all kinds of activities go on at bookstores.

There are few experiences in life as disappointing as an author appearance that flops. To sit at a desk surrounded by a stack of books, looking hopefully at people as they walk past without stopping … it's pretty awful. Many authors have been there. Read on to learn how to create a successful bookstore appearance.

> **Bookmarks**
>
> Many bookstores have an **events coordinator** on staff. This person's primary function is to arrange author appearances and other kinds of bookstore events. Sometimes he or she is called a **community relations coordinator**.

An Event Is Better Than a Signing

An author book-signing is a pretty dull event, especially if the author is unknown. So anything you can do to turn a bookstore appearance into an event will help create excitement and a crowd. Steve Allen (or a Steve Allen lookalike) telling jokes and playing the piano before signing books is an event. Giving an informative talk on your topic is an event. Don't sit behind a table and expect strangers to approach you. They won't. Give them a reason to come over and see what's happening for themselves.

Invite Everyone You Know

Really, do invite everyone you know. A crowd builds a crowd. If a bookstore customer sees a crowd of people in a corner, curiosity will draw them over, too. For the author, it is always better to look out and see friendly and familiar faces. Just to play it safe, ask everyone you invite to bring a friend.

Don't Rely on the Bookstore for Publicity

Ask the bookstore what its standard procedure is for publicity, and then do more. Don't make the retailer angry, but don't assume that the bookstore will do it all for you. This is a perfect time to approach a reporter for a feature article on you and your book. Bookstore appearances that are preceded by a newspaper story (and that are mentioned in the story) are always more successful than those that haven't received any coverage. Be creative about where you try to get publicity; try to get the message out to whatever group you believe will be interested in your book. Appearing on local television shows a few days before the event is also a way to build attendance. Ask the producer to flash the information about your event on the screen while you are talking.

Ask for a Display

Even if your appearance is a disappointment, you might make some gains if your book is on display. Many stores have a special area where they display the books whose authors are coming. Many stores will also make large posters for your book or will display a poster that you make. If your book is on display for a week or two, that is a victory in itself.

> **Hot Off the Press**
>
> Every author has a tale of a disastrous bookstore signing. If no one comes, use this as an opportunity to learn how to do the next one better. While giving in-store readings from her book, *Christmas Miracles,* Jennifer spent several hours one weekend afternoon at two different San Francisco bookstores sitting alone on a chair reading Christmas stories into a microphone. Embarrassing, but true. Even an ex-boyfriend who happened by unexpectedly wouldn't stay and listen! So if it happens to you, don't feel alone. You are now a bonafide member of a very, very large club.

Bring Food

Yes, a plate of cookies can sometimes make a difference. Anyone who comes by for a bite will feel obligated to stop and listen to you for a moment, anyway.

Can You Really Afford a Best-Seller?

After all the information we've shared about publicity and how to get it, why would we ask you if you really can afford a best-seller? It may seem like an odd question, but it's worth thinking about.

Many of the authors that we have mentioned in this book—everyone from the authors of the *Chicken Soup for the Soul* series, to Richard Paul Evans and *The Christmas Box*, from David Chilton of *The Wealthy Barber* and M. Scott Peck of *The Road Less Traveled*—have one thing in common. They are driven to succeed. Becoming a best-selling author is a job that requires work 24 hours a day, 7 days a week.

Do you have that drive? Can you afford it emotionally, physically, or even financially?

♦ Are you willing to spend less time with your family? Many best-selling authors tour constantly, living in hotel rooms across the country and sleeping on overnight flights. More than one marriage has been strained as a result of this lifestyle.

♦ Do you have the stamina to be on the go all day long, from early morning interviews through to late-night talk shows? It can be a physically demanding job.

♦ Some authors pay for constant promotion of their books. Richard Paul Evans runs (and pays for) an elaborate publicity network that employs four people. Jack Canfield and Mark Victor Hansen pay for much of their own publicity. It is a costly undertaking, one that few publishers are willing to fund forever. (Of course, if your book makes it big and makes big bucks, then you'll recoup your investment.)

Before you take the plunge and dedicate yourself to building a best-seller, stop and consider the effect your decision will have on others in your life. This is a major lifestyle change, and once undertaken, it's hard to turn back.

Hot Off the Press _____

"I heard that Steve Allen was coming to town for a special Valentine's Day piano performance," says Terry Foley, former community relations coordinator for a Borders bookstore in northern California. "And I got on the phone and pleaded with his publisher to let him come for a book signing." To make certain there was a crowd, Foley alerted the retirement communities near his store. There was a standing-room-only crowd of 350 rapt fans who listened to Allen's snappy banter and piano playing for several hours. It was one of Allen's last appearances before he died. The moral of this story? Think about who your audience is, and then make every effort to let them know about your event.

The Least You Need to Know

◆ There is a constant need on the part of the media for new and interesting stories; learn how to exploit this for your book's benefit.

◆ Creating media events that receive coverage can be a powerful way to spread the word about your book.

◆ To catch the media's eye, your event should be timely, controversial, visual, or humorous.

◆ Anything you can do to make a producer's job easier will increase your chances of getting a good spot on TV.

◆ Bookstore events need much promotion and publicity to really work.

◆ Having a best-selling book can extract a heavy toll emotionally, physically, and financially.

Part  **5**

My Brilliant Career: Continuing Your Career as an Author

Your book is on the bookstore shelves, but for how long? The more you understand about what happens in the stores and what it means to you, the better you can make decisions about your future.

And is the life of an author really for you? How do you decide if your book is a success? Do you want to do it again? We'll help you make the decision on where to go from here, and we'll give you ideas on other ways you can make money with your writing talents.

Chapter 24

After the Party Is Over

In This Chapter

- The shelf life of a book
- Returns to sender
- Another chance as a paperback, new edition, or sequel
- Evaluating your success
- Getting better all the time
- Moving on to the next phase

Meanwhile, back at the bookstore .... What is happening with your book? Both you and your publisher are working as hard as you can to let the world know that your book exists. What happens to books once the box is unpacked and the book is placed on the shelf?

There was a time when books sat on bookstore shelves for years, growing ever dustier. Once or twice a year, a bespectacled bookseller would comb the shelves for the oldest-looking books and return them to the publisher. The average life span of a published book was long. But today, it is a different story.

You may remember from the beginning of this book that the retail book business is 100 percent returnable. Books that are ordered from the publisher, are placed on the bookstore shelf, and then remain unsold may be returned to the publisher for full credit.

Sold Once, and Then Again

One of the more peculiar aspects of publishing is that books essentially have to be sold twice. The first time, the sales rep sells it to the bookstore. Then the bookstore has to sell it to the customer. Until that second step occurs, you haven't really sold a single book.

Will a customer be able to find your book once she goes into a bookstore looking for it? If your publicity creates demand, will there be supply to meet that demand?

Experts Say

The publishing industry was rocked by massive returns in 1996 and 1997, and many smaller publishers were pushed to the brink by the unexpectedly large returns of unsold books. Much of this had to do with the buying habits of the superstores. With large initial orders, there is always the chance of large returns.

Bookmarks

In the long run, how many books were shipped out to bookstores doesn't matter. What matters is the number of books that **sell through**. Books that sell through are books that bookstore customers bought.

If someone goes into a bookstore looking for your title, both you and your publisher hope that she can easily find a copy on the shelf. And if she can't find the book (and a bookstore employee can't find it, either), she can order it.

And remember when we learned about how bookstores buy and reorder books? In today's bookstore, you hope your book is moving off the shelf. That is, if the bookstore has ordered multiple copies and week after week those multiple copies remain on the shelf, that means excess inventory is stacking up in their distribution center as a result of automatic ordering from the publisher. This inventory will eventually come back—as returns. If one day there are three copies of the book on the shelf and four days later there are none, don't despair! That means the book is "*selling through*" or moving from the publisher through to the customer. The book store will restock and books will be on the shelf again in a few days.

Online book buying habits have changed this somewhat. Whereas publishers have always feared that a lost sale due to a book not being in stock at the bookstore at the moment a customer wants it can never be regained, more book customers are becoming accustomed to the idea that hey, if it isn't on the shelf, why not order it at the bookstore? It would take the same amount of time as buying it online anyway …

Your Book's Inventory: It's Gotta Move

In this fast-paced world in which we all now dwell, the shelf life of a new book has shortened considerably. Some industry experts believe that the window of opportunity for a new book is as short as six weeks. The clock begins ticking the minute that a book is placed on the store shelf. You as the author hope it is placed on the shelf faced out with the cover showing, but all too often books are put on the shelf sideways with only the *spine out*.

With a heavy reliance on computers, many bookstores know exactly when an individual book arrived in its warehouse and when (and where) it was placed on the bookstore shelf. Unless the computer notes that it has sold, that book will someday be hunted down for returns.

Why? As far as the bookstores are concerned, that's money sitting there on the shelf. And money tied up in a book that isn't moving could be freed up and then spent on buying another book—one that might sell quicker!

Bookmarks

Books that are placed on the shelf with the cover facing out catch a customer's eye better than books that are **spine out,** placed sideways on the shelf so that only the slim back end of the book shows. But don't worry if your book can only be displayed spine out. Publishers and design teams spend a great deal of time designing the spine to make it as eye-catching as possible.

Extending Shelf Life

What keeps your book on the shelf? Steady sales. Publicity. Customer requests. Bookstore appearances. It has happened before (and will happen again) that an expensive publicity and marketing campaign has gone for naught because the book had already been returned by bookstores.

Do you, the author, have any control or input in this process? Not really. With bookstores in your area, you might be able to convince them that you are an aggressive marketer who will

Experts Say

Small, independent bookstores seldom return unsold books as aggressively as their larger cousins. "It is a dying habit, but we will give a new hardcover book six months or more before pulling it," says Ann Magruder of Beers Books in Sacramento. "We'd much rather sell it than return it."

send an endless stream of customers in looking for your book. But with the rest of the country, you will just have to cross your fingers.

Returns to Sender

Returns not only make your book disappear from the shelf, but they also make dollars disappear from your royalty account. When books are returned to the publisher, that is noted in the publisher's inventory system. When the publisher's royalty department factors in that information, your account could sink slowly into the west.

Remember, if you have received an advance, you are already in the hole. Your book must sell enough to earn back the advance and move into the black before you will make any more money. Books returned unsold can easily drag you back into the red ink, delaying the long-awaited day you earn back your advance and begin to accrue more royalties. That's another reason to cross your fingers and say your prayers (and send out another press release or two).

For many years, publishers have accused bookstores, both large and small, of returning books in lieu of paying bills. That may have been the case. Streamlined ordering practices can lessen that problem, but this has also lessened the size of publisher's print runs.

Bookmarks _____

A book that's currently available from a publisher is **in print**. A book that's no longer available from a publisher is **out of print**.

End of the Line

One day you get a letter in the mail from your publisher. Your book is being taken *out of print* (or "OP"). What does it all mean? And what will happen to the rest of your books?

Coming Out Again?

If your book was published first in hardcover, you might have something else to look forward to: a paperback edition, either in a trade paperback size or as a mass market paperback. The decision to publish in paperback will be based on sales.

The path from hardcover to paperback used to be quite routine but is now reconsidered with every book. Do the sales figures justify bringing it out again? They might, if the total figure is somewhere north of 10,000 copies and the information in your book is still current. A book on a topic that was timely in hardcover might not be a candidate for a paperback, though, if interest in that topic has flagged. But if your book meets these criteria, get ready for another round of cover design, copywriting, and publicity. If not, let's consider what else might lie ahead.

A Rose by Any Other Name ...

As Peggy Lee would sing, "Is that all there is?" If your book dies a slow death on the shelf, or even if it succeeds and sells for many years, is that all there is? You worked so hard for many months (and, in some cases, many years) to produce this book! Is it time to move on to the next thing?

Not necessarily. With a novel, yes, you'll have to take what you've learned from this first experience and get busy with another book.

But with nonfiction books, a few other options are left:

♦ A revised and expanded second edition

♦ A renamed and repackaged book

♦ Electronic publishing

♦ Series and sequels

Revised and Expanded!

If your nonfiction book sold in respectable numbers the first time around—respectable being solely determined by your publisher, you can certainly discuss with your publisher the opportunity to revise, update, and expand the material for a new edition— provided, of course, that it is a topic that still has an audience. Almost any nonfiction book can go through this phase—health books, travel books, reference books, and even cookbooks can be revised and expanded. If the second edition succeeds, you can look forward to a third, fourth, fifth, or sixth edition, and so on.

It never hurts to go into a book project with an eye on developing long-term income, and an annual edition or frequently revised book is a great way to go.

> **Experts Say**
>
> Sometimes a publisher will change the name of a book in between the hardcover and paperback editions. This is done to give the paperback book a fresh start and a better, more tightly focused title. A good example is a book on women in the corporate world called *New Success Secrets for Women* in hardcover that was changed to *What Women Don't Learn in Business School* in paperback. The second title gives browsers a better idea of what the book is about.

Renamed and Repackaged

So your book didn't sell well. The book has gone out of print. Check your contract to see what the publisher's process is for reverting the rights back to you. You might also be able to buy the remaining copies of the book for a fraction of the original price. If you do want a supply of your books, you'll have to buy them quickly. The publisher will offer any unsold stock to a remaindering company, who will, in turn, sell it to booksellers for a small price for their bargain tables.

Is it over? Again, if the topic is still timely, it doesn't have to be. But unlike a revised second edition, you will need to completely change your book. To dust it off and make it salable to another publisher, your book will need to undergo quite a face lift as well as a name change. Your book could be reborn with a better title, a tighter editorial focus, or a different format.

If you do decide to work to improve your book and resell it, you will need to be up front about it. Tell your agent, and tell any publisher that expresses an interest, that you once published a similar book under a different title. They'll probably find out later, anyway, and that could spell trouble.

Taking It to the Superhighway

We've discussed electronic publishing in several different parts of this book, and we bring it up yet again because it is something to consider for the future of your book. If the rights to the book have reverted to you, you can take what you have written and do several things with it:

- ◆ Turn it into an e-book, or break it up into a series of "special reports" that you market through your own website.

- ◆ Sign up with one of the print-on-demand services such as xlibris.com so that your book is always available somewhere, somehow.

Although electronic publishing possibilities are thrilling, that still leaves you, the author, with a basic problem: how to create sales for your book. It is up to you to create demand, a critical part of the print-on-demand equation. Here's how author Joe Vitale thinks it can work: "After 10 years of being published by mainstream publishers and never making enough to pay the rent, I came out with my first e-book and tasted blood. In 24 hours I sold 600 e-books of *Hypnotic Writing* for $29 each. The secret is a dedicated website with powerhouse sales copy on it, a strong guarantee, bonuses to encourage action now, a tested price, secure ordering, and oh yea, a good book focused on a specific theme for a specific audience helps." You can learn more about what Joe does and how he did it at his website, www.mrfire.com.

Series and Sequels

Are the sales of your book strong enough to warrant more of the same? Has your editor hinted that she would like to see you do another similar book? Welcome to the world of *series* and *sequels*, where, if one book sells, then another just like it should do fine, too!

Deciding whether to pursue either a sequel to a book or to build it into a series is strictly the publisher's call. A revised, expanded second edition can be developed by the author and perhaps sold to another publisher, but an author generally would not approach another publisher unless the publisher of the original book is not interested. If you aren't sure whether your publisher is interested in a series or a sequel, ask your editor. She will be honest about the chance that this might happen.

Bookmarks

A second book that features many of the same characters as the first is a **sequel**. Several books that are related either in theme, purpose, or content comprise a **series**.

Evaluating Your Success

How do you know if your book is a success? How many books sold are enough? Or worse yet, how many are too few? Evaluating your book's success strictly by the numbers is relatively easy. Evaluating your book's success in other ways is a little harder.

Show Me the Money

How many books need to sell to make it a success? That question needs to be considered in relationship to the size of your book's first print run.

- If your book had a modest first printing of 7,500 and sold at least 5,000 copies, you did fine.

- If your book had a first printing of 10,000 and sold 5,000, you didn't do as well.

- If the publisher printed aggressively (more than 25,000 for a first-time author) and you didn't sell through more than 50 percent, you didn't do as well either.

Remember, the size of the print run was determined by the advance orders. The advance orders were determined by how well the bookstores thought your book would sell. So if a book with a small print run (a book with modest sales expectations) sold well, that is a heck of a victory. But if a book with a large print run (big sales expectations) didn't do well, that is a disappointment. Does that make sense?

Personal Best

But was the book a personal success for you, the author? You wrote a book, you published a book. That sets you apart from most other people on the planet. Instead of just talking about how someday you plan to write a book, you did it.

Let's return to the reasons to write. In Chapter 1, you looked at a list of reasons:

- I'm compelled to write.
- I want the personal satisfaction of being published.
- I hope to advance my cause.
- I want to share my knowledge.
- I'd like to advance my career.
- I'd like to achieve fame.
- I'd like to earn a fortune.
- All of the above.

Which reason (or reasons) was yours? Did your book help you achieve it? Even a book with modest sales can easily achieve many of the reasons on the list.

Are you compelled to write? You wrote. Did you seek the personal satisfaction of being published? You have it. Did you want to advance your cause or share your knowledge? Everyone who bought a copy of your book, read about you in the newspaper, or heard you talk on the radio is now aware of both your cause and your knowledge.

Hot Off the Press

Many folks on the professional speaking circuit make money with "back of the room" sales. If a roomful of people already has paid to come and hear you speak on a topic, those people are primed to buy what you've got to sell. These people won't look to see which New York publisher is behind it; they just want to take a little of you home with them. A speaking career is a great way to promote and prolong the life of your book. Buy copies in bulk from your publisher; when those run out and the rights have reverted, publish it yourself. This can make a big difference in your bottom line.

Has your career been advanced? You now have the prestige and distinction of being published. And regardless of how well your book has done in bookstores, you have the opportunity to speak around the country and sell books to clients and your professional audience. If you want, you could keep your book in print forever in a self-published edition.

But Really, Show Me the Money!

Did you achieve fame or fortune? Ah, here is the tricky one. As you learned in the first chapter, it *is* possible to achieve fame without fortune, and vice versa.

Fame may still be achieved. If you continue to promote and sell your book on your own long enough, you can achieve a measure of fame.

Fortune is not always elusive, either. The mere fact that you published a book may someday spawn other opportunities. Other opportunities may have occurred to you during this long, long ride as well. Or, maybe fortune will come with the next book.

> **CAUTION**
>
> **Slush Pile**
>
> When trying to sell another book, don't ever point the finger of failure for your previous book on your publisher—at least, not when talking to an agent or an editor. Your complaints will fall on deaf ears, and your listeners will consider you a whiner.

But This Book Was Perfect!

"The publisher screwed up." Ask most authors why their books didn't sell, and that is the reason you will hear: The publisher screwed up, not me.

The book didn't get to the stores in time, the cover (or the title) was awful, they didn't do any publicity, they never cared about my book. The staff was incompetent, my editor left, the sales reps didn't sell it, the stores returned it too soon.

Perhaps. But indulging in that sort of thinking will not further your career as a writer. A better way to spend your time post-book is to do some follow-up work:

- ◆ Continue to work on your writing.

- ◆ Sharpen your ability to create a book that large numbers of people will buy.

And remember, if you feel this way about your first publishing experience, keep it to yourself. Grouse to your friends and family all you want, but button your lip when talking to industry folks. Agents and editors know full well from years of experience that someone who complains about their first publisher will sooner or later complain about their second publisher. They take it as a sure sign to steer clear.

Work on My Writing?

Yes, work on your writing. Continue to take classes, attend conferences, and seek out other writers. Build your own community of writers around you. No book is ever really perfect, and every writer needs to continue to practice and polish his craft.

You have been published. Now take that accolade and build on it. Write more. Get better.

What Book Will Large Numbers of People Buy?

Hopefully, they'll buy your next one. Again, take what you have learned with this first book and build on it. If that is your goal, work on developing novels and nonfiction books that have the potential to affect large numbers of readers.

Chapter 3 might not have interested you when you began reading this book. After all, you already knew what you wanted to write. Is it time to go back and reread that chapter? This gives you a clear-eyed view of how book professionals try to develop book ideas with big potential. Read this chapter, and try out a few of the exercises. It will help you begin to think like a publisher.

Co-author Jennifer's favorite writing success story holds great encouragement for anyone whose first published book didn't quite set the world on fire. Some seven or eight years ago she discovered a wonderful food writer named Marlena de Blasi.

> **Experts Say**
>
> Why continue to go to writers' conferences after you've already been published? Other unpublished writers will look at you with awe. It can be a nice little ego boost. You also will make new contacts with agents and editors, sharpen your skills, and come away reinvigorated.

Marlena wrote a delightful cookbook called *Regional Foods of Northern Italy*, which Jennifer published at Prima. Despite it's beauty and charm, the book was not a terrific success. Marlena did find terrific writing success though, but it wasn't as a cookbook writer, which was how she originally perceived herself. She wrote the lyrical story of her romance in midlife with an Italian man who swept her off her feet and convinced her to move on a whim to Venice, leaving her familiar American world behind. Marlena's book *A Thousand Days in Venice* became a literary travel best-seller in the vein of *A Year in Provence* and *Under the Tuscan Sun*.

Moving On to the Next Phase

What is your next move, anyway? Will you try to write another book, or will you try to return to your life as it was before you embarked on all of this?

If you are returning to your previous life, be proud of what you have achieved. You now have a lasting symbol of great and unusual accomplishment: a published book.

If you are committed to continuing your career as a writer, the next two chapters will share more information about how to earn a living with your pen—or, more correctly (as you've now learned), how to earn a living with your computer—your creativity, and an endless ability to keep going in the face of possible defeat.

The Least You Need to Know

- ◆ The life span of a new book on a bookstore shelf can be short, but steady sales, constant publicity, and customer demand combine to keep a book on the shelves for a long time.

- ◆ Between special orders placed with distributors and the rise of online book-selling, while your book is in print it is almost always in stock and available somewhere.

- ◆ If the sales were satisfactory, a hardcover book will come out in paperback, and a paperback might someday come out again as a revised and updated second edition.

- ◆ Sometimes a book is renamed during the transition from hardcover to paper-back to give it a better chance for better sales.

- ◆ To be considered a sales success, a book must sell through a majority of its print run.

- ◆ Even if your book has not been a sales success, you might have achieved your reasons for writing.

How to Sell a Book a Year for the Rest of Your Career

In This Chapter

- ◆ Changing your mind about writing
- ◆ What it really takes to succeed
- ◆ The number-one success trait
- ◆ Letting go of your writer's ego
- ◆ Other ways to sell your writing skills

Now that you know what happens to your book after the party, what happens to your career after the book? Some writers only write one book in their whole careers. Others write an endless series of books that seem to flow from their pens. And others try to sell more books, only to be stymied in the attempt. How is it that some folks can keep selling books and some folks seem to stall out so quickly? Fate? Luck? Or is it something else?

We think it is something else. We have crisscrossed the country and spoken at dozens of writers conferences since the first edition of this book came out in 1998. Since that time, we've been asked this basic question in many different states and holding many different glasses of wine during the get-to-know-you section of the weekend: Why are some writers more successful than others? We think the answer can be found in what we call the "key characteristics of successful writers." Check the front of this book for the handy tear-out card and you'll see that these key characteristics can easily be ripped out and posted on the wall next to your computer.

Open for Business

If you are going to reinvent yourself as a writer with several books to his name you will need to make one important shift in your thinking right now. You will need to think of yourself not as a writer, but as a key member of the book publishing business. How do you sell a book a year for the rest of your career? By deciding to be in the book business.

When someone asks you "What do you do?" we want you to smile broadly and confidently and say, "I'm in the book business." Then when they ask what you do in the book business, you can say "I'm a writer." Being a writer is indeed being in the book business. Give up your romantic notions of the life of a writer (sorry, no garret in Paris and lazy wine-soaked afternoons) and think of yourself in a different, more businesslike way. Trust us, best-selling authors are *in the book business*. James Patterson is in the book business. Suze Orman is in the book business. Nicholas Evans is in the book business. And once you make this mental shift, you will be, too.

The Six Habits Revealed

Drum roll, please, while we give you the major reasons some folks keep writing (and selling!) and some folks never do again.

- ◆ Persistence
- ◆ A keen sense of the marketplace
- ◆ A professional attitude toward your writing
- ◆ The ability to meet deadlines
- ◆ A good understanding of the book business
- ◆ The willingness to promote your books on your own

Sharp-eyed readers will note that these six habits are built on the very themes we have been sounding again and again from the moment you first began reading. That publishing is a business, that the more you learn about how it works the better you will succeed, and that the folks who try the hardest and longest usually succeed.

Where'd the Talent Go?

You'd think that on a list of what it takes, that talent would be the number-one reason. But no, talent doesn't even make the list. You need talent, you need creativity, those are givens. The number-one reason successful writers keep selling their projects is because they are *persistent*.

To sell book projects, you have to try. And try. And keep trying in the face of rejection. In 2003 alone, Jennifer had six different books published where she was listed as author or co-author. Sounds like a lot of work, eh? But how many projects did she *try* to sell in order to get six accepted? Quite a few more. Her list of failed book projects is a long one indeed.

Here are some famous examples of how persistence paid off:

◆ Richard Carlson had published several books with modest success and just keep trying with new ideas until one day his *Don't Sweat the Small Stuff* book took off and launched a million dollar series.

◆ John Grisham's first novel was rejected by major publishers and came out from a small press, but he kept on plugging and his second novel—*The Firm*—was bought by a big New York house.

A Question of Timing

One of the reasons it is so important to be persistent is that the reason your nonfiction proposal or fiction manuscript has been rejected might have very little to do with your actual project, but rather with the people who were in the room at the time it was presented, or the business conditions that existed at that moment. Sometimes half the success is just being in the right place at the right time. Remember the glimpse we gave you in Chapter 14? The hardworking editor was presenting a proposal and fielding questions from the various departments represented. The kinds of questions we left off were things like this:

◆ "Can we speed this meeting up, I've got a train to catch!"

◆ "The market for high level business books is too soft right now, we can't acquire in that category."

◆ "That is a Christmas book, and it is too late to consider anything for our Fall list."

Sometimes it is all a matter of timing, and the kinds of books that aren't selling one year might be selling the next. If an idea you are trying to shop is meeting with resistance why not try putting it aside for six months and then trying again? Perhaps the best time for you to send your diet book idea to an editor is in early January, when they themselves are sitting there feeling like perhaps they overdid it during the holidays!

Additionally, authors who are trying to catch a wave should think about what's going to be happening a year from now. It's one thing to pitch on a book on tidal waves. But if you know that a big disaster movie about a tidal wave is scheduled for 18 months from now, it might be a good time to pitch a book! Some writers keep abreast of what Hollywood has planned by reading the trade magazine *Variety*.

Hot Off the Press

Jennifer worked long and hard on what she thought was a killer idea for a women's business book. Her best idea ever, she was convinced. It was an inspirational business book for women called *Everything I Really Need to Know About Business I Learned from Watching Martha*. You know what Martha she was talking about, and you how public opinion has wavered on her. What seemed like a slam dunk one minute was a project no one would touch the next. But Jennifer is hanging on to that proposal, knowing that the winds of fortune are fickle and the subject of her book just might one day be on top again! Hope springs eternal, for both Jennifer and Martha.

So if you are going to be persistent, to try to sell book project after book project, you are going to need quite a few ideas. So many ideas, in fact, that at this point you might want to lie down and take a much deserved nap at the very thought of all that brain work. Go ahead and take a power nap, we say, as long as when you are lying there in the dark you are trying to come up with your next hot idea.

But we believe you can be an idea generator. All the tools you need are in your hands, just go back and reread Chapter 3. There were several exercises that we recommend making daily habits—reading the morning paper and trying to come up with three new ideas for books as a result of what you read. Book packagers and editors come up with idea after idea after idea, most of which never go anywhere.

We think you need to be working with three different ideas at once, and have those three projects in different stages of readiness so that if one goes down in flames, you've got another idea half-figured out in your hip pocket that you can begin to pursue immediately instead of sinking into a funk from the rejection.

Ego Patrol

To handle the rejection that comes along with being in the book business you will have to work hard to separate your ego from your ideas. Well, from the ones that failed, anyway. The ones that work, keep your ego firmly attached to those!

Checking your writer ego will go a long way toward helping you have a professional attitude toward your writing. Publishing is no place for tantrums, and remember how often those editors move around from job to job. If you get a reputation for tiresome behavior you might find your opportunities drying up.

Here is a quick example of how detached you will have to be from some of these ideas. Jennifer had an idea for a book title—*Hot, Sweet & Sticky*. She liked the way it sounded, like a rock song from her seventies girlhood. Her idea for *Hot, Sweet & Sticky* was to do a dessert book filled with desserts that were, well, sticky. Cinnamon buns with creamy frosting, bread puddings dripping with dulce de leche. When she broached the idea to the sales folks at Crown though, they didn't jump up and down. In fact, they said this very thing—we love your title, we hate your idea. We want to be able to sell a book called *Hot, Sweet & Sticky* as a Valentine's Day book about romantic cooking. Jennifer experienced a sharp, fast pang of regret for her original idea, and then said, "Sure!"

Far from confident, most successful writers worry constantly that they will never sell another project again, ever. You can rest on your literary laurels once you've achieved the financial status of a Danille Steel or a Nora Roberts or a Robert Kiyosaki. Until then, keep generating ideas.

Show Me the Money, Again

Now here is the really depressing news about money: It doesn't always go up. In most careers, you can safely assume that the money you earn as your salary will increase year after year after year. Writers get no such guarantee, and in fact quickly become accustomed to the harsh realities of advances. The advance you are offered for any project might bear no relationship to what you've been given before. Jennifer has earned advances for her book ideas that range from $150,000 to $3,000. In one year the different advances she received for different projects were:

- $20,000 flat fee for a packaging project for a major publisher
- $15,000 for an inspirational story collection
- $5,000 for a quote book

◆ $18,000 for a business book

◆ $8,000 flat fee for a lifestyle book

Why such a nutty spread between sums? Because in each case, she was made an offer by an editor and no one else was bidding! If only one publishing company is interested in your project, then that is the only offer you can expect. The biggest sums of all develop during an auction, when several publishers are hot on the trail of the same project.

Additionally, money can vary by type of project, potential for sales, type and size of publisher, and more! There is no standard advance or fee when it comes to book publishing.

Authors differ on which is better—a big advance that you never earn out, or a small advance that ultimately puts you into a royalty earning situation. Jennifer's jaundiced attitude is that she never really expects to see anything beyond the advance, so any further royalties are gravy. So to evaluate whether a project is worthwhile, she only looks at the money on the table.

You can see that this isn't an easy business to earn a living in. And that in order to keep the cash flowing you need to hustle. Although writers love to read stories about the hefty sums that drop into the lives of some of their colleagues, the fact is that one big book deal isn't always a life changing experience. Because once that six figure advance is gone, what next? As any fulltime writer can tell you, this is not a pursuit for the weak.

Plan to Sell a Book a Year

Now that you've changed your mind about who you are—you aren't simply a writer, you're someone in the book business—how do you get on track to sell and sell? Here are Jennifer's own methods for making multiple sales:

◆ Always have at least four viable book ideas in development.

◆ Only try to sell or circulate one proposal at any given time.

◆ To speed up the pace, combine efforts and do co-authored books.

Four Ideas at Once?

Yes, you need to have four (or more) ideas that you are developing at any one time. You don't have to have four fully developed proposals at one time, but perhaps two full proposals and two ideas that you are developing and researching. That way, when it is clear that one book idea isn't selling, you can cut your loses and move on to the next one without delay.

Only Sell One at a Time?

You don't want to confuse editors about who you are and what you can do by hitting them with too many different ideas at once. If a proposal for a diet book and a proposal for a personal finance book land together, both with you as the author, the editor might think you are spreading yourself too thin.

Join Forces with Other Writers?

Yes, you should consider working with another author every so often. It might benefit you both by allowing you to work on double the projects, offer double the credentials and expertise, and allow you to sell twice as many books!

How can you get started today to sell a book a year? Start working on developing your four best ideas into proposals. Start networking to find other writers whose skills and interests mesh well with yours. And most of all, start being as businesslike in your approach as you would be with any other kind of business. Write out goals that you want to achieve in the coming year and stick to them!

How Else Can You Make a Living?

Now that we've outlined some of the grimmer realities of writing for a living, is there some other way you can make money with your literary skills? There are several:

- Working with book packagers
- Writing for magazines
- Ghostwriting
- Marketing and public relations writing

Book packagers are generally folks who've been in the book business for many years and now have the ability and the contacts to work independently to make books happen. Many former editors, art directors, and production people end up as book packagers, thinking of idea after idea and selling the idea to a publisher and then finding a writer to do the job.

> **Experts Say**
>
> There are folks in the industry known as book packagers. Packagers start with their own ideas, develop them, and are able to deliver to a publisher—or a museum, corporation, or organization—anything from rough manuscript to an edited manuscript, from books on disk to bound books. Packagers rarely do all the work themselves; they often hire people—including writers—to help them.

Why do publishers like to work with packagers? It enables them to publish more books with less hassle. Instead of employing a large staff to oversee complicated books, the publisher can pay attention to other books and know that on the delivery date, a packager will deliver.

The *Cosmo* Quiz

Writing for a packager is not for everyone. To help you decide whether it is right for you, Sheree has designed a quiz. For every "Yes" answer, give yourself a point.

- Are you willing to write something and not feel proprietary about it?

- Can you regard writing as "just a job" rather than an expression of your own ideas?

- Do you prefer to write from assignments as opposed to your own ideas?

- Would you prefer someone else write the book proposal?

- Are you as good at expressing other people's ideas as your own?

- Would you feel comfortable earning less than the packager, who didn't do any of the actual writing?

If you can regard your writing talent as a skill that can be used to earn money, then maybe working with a packager is for you.

How do you find packagers? Ask your editor, ask your agent, and check out the website at abpaonline.com. Offer up your services as a writer they can depend on, and you just might find steady work for years.

Writing for Magazines

While thinking of your book ideas you will undoubtedly stumble upon many, many ideas that aren't really books, but would make great article ideas. So why not try to sell them that way? Magazine articles are a great way to further your career as a writer and keep your name in the public eye. They can also be a powerful way to promote the book you already have out.

Fiction writers can also benefit from magazine work. Developing and polishing a short story for a literary magazine can further hone your skills in between novels. Lewis Buzbee believes that "the pay isn't much, the circulations are small, but fiction editors are reading those magazines all the time, looking for new talent."

If you'd like to write and sell magazine articles, we recommend *The Complete Idiot's Guide to Publishing Magazine Articles*, which we wrote with our friend Lynne Rominger.

The Friendly Ghost

With a book or two under your belt, could you be a ghostwriter for someone else?

The real talent a ghostwriter needs to possess is the talent for organization. Ghostwriting often involves organizing someone else's ideas, thoughts, speeches, and writings into a readable book. Mimicry isn't a bad skill to have, either, as you are literally trying to write in someone else's voice.

How do ghostwriters get jobs? This is largely a word-of-mouth business. When you establish a good relationship with your editor, you might find that she recommends ghosting or rewriting jobs to you. Once you begin to ghost books, your clients will also recommend you to their colleagues. You can also let your agent know (at the same time you ask her if she knows any packagers who might need help).

Ghostwriting can pay well. With large jobs, you will want to negotiate a fee in the range of several thousand dollars, perhaps a portion of the book royalties, too. For smaller jobs, you can tell your clients that you charge by the hour. A standard hourly charge would be between $40 and $50 and hour, depending on your expertise.

Publicity and Promotional Writing

You learned how to write press releases to promote your book. Now that you have that skill, can you sell it to anyone else? Yes.

Many small-business people lack the ability to write press releases and other kinds of publicity pieces. Spread the word among small businesses that you are ready and available to help. You might find that they could use your skills helping to create media events as well. What should you charge for a press release? For a one-page press release (and all good press releases are only one page), you should charge at least $75. That's not too shabby for an hour's worth of work.

So how do you sell a book a year for the rest of your career? By weaving together all these fine strands for success—persistence, a professional attitude, a knowledge of the market and of the

> **Experts Say**
>
> Women read books. Women buy books. So why not write books for women? Never overlook the tremendous size of the potential market for a book that appeals to women. Fiction or nonfiction, keep this in mind.

book business, an ability to meet deadlines, and a willingness to promote—you will create a sturdy rope by which you can start your climb up the ladder of publishing success.

We've tried to give you a glimpse into how things work, but we also encourage you to learn more. Learn as much as you can about the bookstore business and about the publishing business. Learn as much as you can about your readers and what they want to read. The more you know, the greater your chances for success.

We do hope that this book has given you a solid understanding of what goes on in the publishing industry and how you can find your spot in it. Whatever you do, don't give up. If you believe in yourself and your writing, you will find a way to see your work in print. Remember, writers write. So turn on your computer and get busy!

The Least You Need to Know

- ◆ Shift your image of yourself: Decide to be in the book business instead of thinking of yourself as a writer.

- ◆ Persistence is the number-one factor for long-term writing and publishing success.

- ◆ Hot ideas can fade very quickly due to market conditions, so always develop several ideas simultaneously.

- ◆ The size of advances can vary widely, and don't always go up and up.

- ◆ If you want to sell one book a year, you need to try to sell several in order to get that one sale.

- ◆ Writers can also earn money ghostwriting or helping small businesses with their promotional writing.

Appendix A

Great Books for Writers

Appelbaum, Judith. *How to Get Happily Published: A Complete and Candid Guide*. New York: HarperPerennial, 1998.

The Chicago Manual of Style: The Essential Guide for Writers, Editors, and Publishers. Chicago: University of Chicago Press, 1993.

Children's Writer's and Illustrator's Market. Cincinnati: Writer's Digest Books, updated annually.

Gross, Gerald. *Editors on Editing: What Writers Need to Know About What Editors Do*. New York: Grove/Atlantic Monthly Press, 1993.

Harrow, Susan. *Selling Yourself Without Selling Your Soul*. New York: HarperResource, 2002.

Herman, Jeff. *Writer's Guide to Book Editors, Publishers, and Literary Agents*. Rocklin, CA: Prima Publishing, updated every two years.

Kremer, John. *1,001 Ways to Market Your Books*. Fairfield, IA: Open Horizons, 1998.

Lamott, Anne. *Bird by Bird: Some Instructions on Writing and Life*. New York: Anchor/Doubleday, 1995.

Levine, Mark. *Negotiating a Book Contract: A Guide for Authors, Agents, and Lawyers*. Wakefield, RI: Moyer Bell, 1988.

Literary Marketplace. New York: R.R. Bowker, updated annually.

Lukeman, Noah. *The Plot Thickens: 8 Ways to Bring Fiction to Life*. New York: St. Martin's Press, 2002.

Poynter, Dan. *The Self-Publishing Manual: How to Write, Print, and Sell Your Own Book*. Santa Barbara, CA: Para Publishing, 1989.

Shoup, Barbara, and Margaret Love Denman. *Novel Ideas: Contemporary Authors Share the Creative Process*. Indianapolis: Alpha Books, 2001.

Strunk, William Jr., and E. B. White. *The Elements of Style*. New York: Macmillan, 1979.

Underdown, Harold, and Lynne Rominger. *The Complete Idiot's Guide to Publishing Children's Books*. Indianapolis: Alpha Books, 2001.

Writer's Market. Cincinnati: Writer's Digest Books, updated annually.

Yudkin, Marcia. *Six Steps to Free Publicity: And Dozens of Other Ways to Win Free Media Attention for You and Your Business*. New York: Plume, 1994.

Zinsser, William. *On Writing Well: The Classic Guide to Writing Nonfiction: 25th Anniversary Edition*. New York: HarperResource, 2001.

Zuckerman, Albert J. *Writing the Blockbuster Novel*. Cincinnati: Writer's Digest Books, 1993.

More Good Resources

Professional Associations

Agents' association:

Association of Author's Representatives
PO Box 237201, Ansonia Station
New York, NY 10003
www.aar-online.org

Book packagers' association:

American Book Producers Association
156 Fifth Avenue
New York, NY 10010-7000
212-645-2368
www.abpaonline.org

Freelance editors' association:

Editorial Freelance Association
71 West 23rd Street, Suite 1910
New York, NY 10010-4102
212-929-5400
www.the-efa.org

Self-publishers' group:

Publishers Marketing Association
310-372-2732
www.pma-online.org

Writers' organizations:

American Society of Journalists and Authors, Inc.
1501 Broadway, Suite 302
New York, NY 10036
212-997-0947
www.asja.org
staff@asja.org

Author's Guild
330 West 42nd Street
New York, NY 10036
212-563-5904

National Writer's Union
113 University Place, 6th Floor
New York, NY 10003
212-254-0279
www.nwu.com

Romance Writers of America
13700 Veterans Memorial Drive, #315
Houston, TX 77014
281-440-6885

Sisters in Crime
PO Box 442124
Lawrence, KS 66044-8933
sistersincrime.org

**Society of Children's Book Writers
and Illustrators**
8271 Beverly Boulevard
Los Angeles, CA 90048
323-782-1010
www.scbwi.org

Publicity Agencies

Book publicists:

Planned Television Arts
Rick Frishman
1110 Second Avenue
New York, NY 10022
212-593-5820

Susan Harrow
www.prsecrets.com
(filled with good information
and tips on promoting yourself)

Book publicity information:

You're On the Air
A 90-minute videotape about how to
get on and perform well on television
and radio. $69.95 for the video and
two books. For information, call
1-800-562-4357.

Media trainer:

Joel Roberts and Associates
310-286-0631

Seminars and Publications

Seminars:

The Secrets of Getting Published
Sheree Bykofsky
The Seminar Center
New York City
212-655-0077
Info@seminarcenter.com

Mega Book Marketing University
Mark Victor Hansen
949-759-9304
www.megabookmarketing.com

Short-run book printer:

Morris Publishing
3212 East Highway30
Kearney, NE 68847
1-800-650-7888
www.morrispublishing.com

Trade publications:

Publishers Weekly
245 West 17th Street
New York, NY 10011
1-800-278-2991
www.publishersweekly.com

Websites of Note

amazon.com
(online bookstore, good for competitive research)

barnesandnoble.com or **bn.com**
(online bookstore, good for competitive research)

www.bookpublishing.com
(general publishing information))

www.bookwire.com
(timely publishing news from Bookwire)

www.publishersmarketplace.com
(info about agents, packagers, industry news, subscription "Publishers Lunch" e-newsletter)

www.pw.org
(poets and writers, literary links, links to small presses, writers' conferences)

www.shawguides.com
(current info about writers conferences)

shereebee.com
(information for writers)

www.writing-world.com
("a world of writing tips … for writers around the world")

www.writersdigest.com
(contact information for book publishers, information on conferences, and discussion forums)

Sample Proposals: *Exit Strategy* and *A Room of One's Own*

Exit Strategy

How to Build a Financial Plan and Lifestyle to Get Away from the Workplace for a While—or Maybe for Good

A proposal by
Peter Sander

A Big City Books Idea
Big City Books Group
7047 Hidden Lane
Granite Bay, CA 95746
916-791-2101

Another Week Has Begun ...

Monday: three morning teleconferences, a meeting with a colleague, lunch with a client, and then better get ready for the Tuesday morning project review—before making the evening day care run and rushing home to cook dinner.

Tuesday: Project review goes OK, but voicemail check yields 6 "urgent" messages about some new problem in your department's software. Meanwhile, you've taken on 4 new action items from the project review, all to be delivered by Thursday. The afternoon is consumed by meetings. Get home at 7:30 and yell at your kids for leaving their toys on the floor and your spouse for not taking the garbage out.

Wednesday: early morning voicemail to attend an emergency teleconference with your manager. You find out that your pet project has been put on hold—once again. Weeks—months—heart-and-soul selling, detailed preparation, troubleshooting, negotiation, communication—all lost in a sea of shifting priorities. Meanwhile you've put off your whole life ….

Five teleconferences a day. Twenty or twenty-five voicemails. Hundreds of e-mails. Scheduled meetings, unscheduled meetings. People issues, organizational inertia, fickle clients, difficult employees, job uncertainty. A grind, a rat race, a treadmill. Vacations that hardly seem more than a different venue to retrieve your voicemail. Dreaded Sunday night returns to the grind from those "vacations," and the dreaded "catch up" with everything that went wrong while you were gone. Even if things were going well you wonder if it was all worthwhile.

Suddenly it dawns on you. You need to escape for a while. Maybe not forever—just for a while. To set it aside, to get that work-life balance thing back in order. To recharge batteries, to sharpen the saw, to try something new.

- ◆ To exercise some long-dormant part of your brain or body that hasn't been able to participate.

- ◆ To write a book, build a deck, to enjoy your kids' preschool years, to take a class or two, to learn Spanish, to make wine, to learn to play the mandolin.

- ◆ To build a skill, refresh your perspective, or to just plain rest. A self-made sabbatical. While we're all creatures of habit to some extent, it simply does a mind, spirit and body good to do something else for a while.

- ◆ To escape, to exit. We're not talking about early retirement here—just a well deserved, needed break from the ever-accelerating treadmill.

Just ask—what if? What if I was able to escape for a while? To do something else? What would happen? Would I go broke? Or would I profit immensely from the experience? Read on ….

The Idea

Exit Strategy: How to Build a Financial Plan and Lifestyle to Get Away from the Workplace for a While—or Maybe for Good is a guidebook toward just that end—to get away from it all for a while. Three months, six months, a year, maybe more. Just long enough to rest, reflect, recharge, and re-enter. The book explores different ways to get away from the workplace without jeopardizing your career or financial future.

A balanced approach to pulling off a successful exit entails personal finance, career management, and self-help and motivation. The book brings together all three topics:

♦ As a personal finance book, *Exit Strategy* is about preparation and money management—what needs to be done in advance and during the "hiatus" to avoid financial disaster and undue stress during the time off.

♦ As a career guide, *Exit Strategy* deals with how to get time off without wrecking your career. Included are such issues as how to work company policies (like leave of absence) to your favor, how to ask for time off, and if a job change is required, how to make that happen. The career guide aspect also covers re-entry—how best to painlessly transition back to the workplace. Like the personal finance section, we're not talking about major career development strategies—just how to get it done without making your future career more difficult.

♦ As a self-help and motivational book, *Exit Strategy* explores how to make effective use of the time off to achieve your goals—goal setting, time management, and turning all aspects of the change into a positive, beneficial experience.

The Title

Exit Strategy: How to Build a Financial Plan and Lifestyle to Get Away from the Workplace for a While—or Maybe for Good

The Market

Fifty million working professionals would probably *all* like to exit their careers for a while. Sure, there are those who love their work—but even *they* would probably like to do something else for a spell. And there are the rest of us …

… who worked 70 or 80 hours a week during the booming economy of the 1990s and continue to do so as their companies scale back the workforce—but not the work.

… who worked steady nine-to-five Monday-through-Friday schedules day in and day out since they were 15 and yearn for a different routine.

… who see the writing on the wall in the job market, and wonder if it's better to escape the uncertainty, do something different, build a new skill set, and wait for things to get better.

… who, as small business people, realize that their idea wasn't so great anyway, and it's a heck of a lot of work for the slim return realized.

… who would simply like to achieve some *work-life balance*—to raise children, to care for elders, to take care of some other life priority.

The Book

Divided up accordingly, this book is in part a personal finance book, a career guide, and a self-help book. Each section offers strategies, and ideas for how to manage finances, manage transitions, and manage career and personal growth through the process of "exiting." Beyond ideas and strategies, the rich experience of those who have "exited" successfully are shared, as are relevant insights from personal and career counselors, human resource managers, and financial planners.

The Competition

Two books have been published in this space:

◆ *Six Months Off: How to Plan, Negotiate, and Take the Break You Need Without Burning Bridges or Going Broke*, Hope Dlugozima and James Scott, Henry Holt, 1996.

◆ *Time Off From Work: Using Sabbaticals to Enhance Your Life While Keeping Your Career On Track*, Lisa Rogak, John Wiley & Sons, 1994.

Both books address the essence of the *Exit Strategy* theme. While they both investigate personal finance, career, and motivational issues, the balance is shifted more towards motivation and self-help. Both books are written by journalistic authors—not authors with personal experience doing an "exit," nor strong personal finance backgrounds. They use the experience of others through interviews and anecdotes—not first hand experience. Furthermore, both books were conceived and created before the Internet and the "free agent nation" became a big force. *Exit Strategy* wouldn't diverge far from the *intent* of these books, but would provide a fresher, more financially focused and practical approach.

The Outline

Introduction

PART I: Preparation

Chapter 1: The Way Out

The many escape routes—sabbatical, leave of absence, time off without pay, part-time work, job sharing, buyouts, voluntary severance, involuntary severance, quit and subcontract, just plain quit.

Chapter 2: It Takes At Least One Goal To Win

Deciding what to do beforehand—setting goals, building a plan, deciding how you will use the time. Helps to make more productive use of the time, furnishes a better story in case your chill out requires permission. "I want to take a year off to write a book" works better than "I want to take a year off to play golf."

Chapter 3: Provisioning the Financial Ship

How to batten down the hatches and get your financial house in order. Reducing debt, learning how much you need during your chill out, saving, figuring out where it will come from.

Chapter 4: Popping the Question

How to approach your boss, your organization, your family, your friends, your clients and customers.

PART II: Time Off

Chapter 5: It's a Wide World

What do you do with the time off? So many choices, but solid, rational choices must be made. Why? To use time effectively and to accomplish goals. Explores aspects of starting a business, doing free-agent work in career field, and/or "sharpening the saw" through education, training, and professional organizations.

Chapter 6: Keeping The Financial Course

Budgeting and spending your money. Unemployment compensation, taxes, health and other insurance, learning to live cheap, adopting a financial lifestyle commensurate with the new situation. It is important to have a game plan and a solid "operating" style. Otherwise, financial issues will get in the way, cause undue stress, and cause one to prematurely "pull the plug" on the career hiatus.

Chapter 7: Keeping the Right Attitude

Tips on how to keep the right attitude and mental framework. How to avoid depression and the "midlife" stuff. How to keep the energy positive and keep momentum toward stated goals, dealing with setbacks, self-rewards.

Chapter 8: Keeping In Touch

Keeping the network alive is also an important "exit strategy." That network nourishes many needs during the time off, and is an important set of pitons for climbing back into the workplace.

PART III: Re-entry

Chapter 9: Raising The Heat Shield—Preparing Yourself

How to prepare for—and feel good about—re-entry. Evaluating yourself—what did *you* change, what did you refresh, what did you accomplish? Setting re-entry goals, defining a re-entry strategy.

Chapter 10: Does Your Parachute Still Open?

Evaluating career change—the wide world of work options. Does it make sense to resume where you left off, or might there be some other way to pursue your career interests? What if, at 40 or 50 something, your parachute is a little tattered?

Chapter 11: Getting to Splashdown

Job search techniques, use of executive search consultants, and other job search resources. What to say—and not to say—about the "time off." How to position yourself and your accomplishments. Internet resources and the effective use of networking to get back in the way *you* want to get back in.

Chapter 12: Keeping the Experience Alive

How to carry your new freshness and attitude into your post-exit life. How an "exit" really makes you a more effective performer even after re-entry.

The Author

Peter Sander has experienced the exact scenario featured in this book. A veteran of 30 years of career "service" at the age of 45 (yes, that's working and/or going to college since age 15), Peter finally saw the writing on the wall with his Fortune 50 company and used a voluntary severance program to make his break. Was this an impulsive decision? Hardly. Peter had saved, paid off his house, eliminated debt, and experimented with book writing long before the opportunity arose. Peter was ready—and now he enjoys his freedom and self-determination—and still writes books. And takes college classes, builds his own deck, and wholly participates in the development and sheer enjoyment of his two small boys. And is he tired and stressed at the end of each day? No—unless his chicken enchiladas don't turn out right. Peter has an MBA from Indiana University and has authored or co-authored five books, including *The Pocket Idiot's Guide to Living on a Budget*, *Value Investing for Dummies*, and *Niche and Grow Rich*. He is currently under contract to produce an executive recruiting guide and a formula personal finance book. He is approaching completion of CFP (Certified Financial Planner) certification at the University of California at Davis. And yes, he spent 20 plus years in the corporate world as a business professional and marketeer. And yes, it was one of those jobs that, particularly in the end, one would want to escape from.

A Room of One's Own

In Celebration of a
Single Woman's Independent Life

A proposal by
Laura Boswell

A Big City Books Idea
Big City Books Group
7047 Hidden Lane
Granite Bay, CA 95746
916-791-2101

The Idea

The comment comes mid way through a large party—"Oh, you're not married yet?" An eyebrow is raised, a quick look of pity passes over the face of your questioner as once again your single status is under the spotlight. "Don't give up hope, dear," the curious stranger advises before moving away to the drinks table.

"Don't give up hope?" Goodness, is that the best thing a single woman can hear? Why doesn't anyone ever say, "Lucky you!"

A Room of One's Own: In Celebration of a Single Woman's Independent Life says "Lucky you!" on every page. Filled with quote after quote to buoy the spirits of the millions of single women of all ages and remind them of the freedom and independence they possess. Sayings and observations from famous wits and sages to remind single women that their lives are full right now, that they are not sitting on the sidelines waiting for their "real" life to begin the minute some man asks them to marry him.

Why wait for your "real" life to begin when Helen Keller said that "Life is either a daring adventure, or nothing."

Why feel odd and out of place in a crowd of married couples when John F. Kennedy said "Conformity is the jailer of freedom and the enemy of growth."

Why feel the need for a compliment from a man when Oscar Wilde said "To love oneself is the beginning of a life-long romance."

Why be jealous of married women when best-selling mystery writer Sue Grafton said "I love being single. It is almost like being rich."

Why feel empty in your own bed when Liv Ullmann reminds us that "Sometimes it is less lonely to wake up feeling lonely when you are alone than wake up feeling lonely when you are with someone."

Page after page of pithy quotes will remind single women of the joys of living alone, of making their own decisions, of being able to take pride in their own daring and accomplishment. *A Room of One's Own* will be the perfect gift for single women on any occasion.

The Market

Is there a big enough market for *A Room of One's Own*? Recent studies show that 21 percent of American women have never married. And according to the U.S. Census Bureau, 42 percent of all women over the age of 18 are not currently married, whether from divorce, widowhood, or because they just haven't gotten around to it.

Single women get a bad rap, and are frequently made to feel like outsiders because of their unmarried status. But in the new millennium there is a growing feeling among single women that being single is not an obstacle, but an opportunity. Being single gives these women a chance to travel, to discover themselves, and to learn to do things themselves that they might traditionally ask of men. Buying houses, cars, investing, and moving by themselves are all skills—both mentally and physically—that bring with them great benefit.

But where are the books that celebrate the single life? Most current books have more to do with "coping" with the situation, with learning to take care of the unpleasant tasks on your own than with outright crowing about the wonders and joys of being on your own. *A Room of One's Own* gives single women ample evidence and encouragement that the life they are leading—the unmarried life—is a valid, courageous, and rewarding one.

The Competition

There are many books on the market that focus on a woman's life, but little that celebrates the joys of singledom. The two best examples are relatively heavy tomes, not lighthearted and congratulatory in tone like *A Room of One's Own.*

An Improvised Woman: Single Women Reinventing the Single Life, Marcelle Clements, ISBN 0393319539, $14.00 (Norton, 1999).

Flying Solo: Single Women in Midlife, Carol Anderson, ISBN 0393313476, $13.95 (Norton, 1995).

The market seems to be wide open for a beautiful gift book that women would be delighted to receive as a gift.

The Editor

Laura E. Boswell is single and happy and lives with her dog Chester and her cat Angel in Arlington, Virginia. A former editor at USAToday.com and Careerbuilder.com, she has written extensively on sports, careers, small business, and women's issues. Her first book *The Quotable Businesswoman* was published in September 2001 by Andrews McMeel.

Like many women my age, I expected to be married by now. In fact, there was a time when even 25 seemed ancient to me, let alone my current Jurassic age of 29. According to my high school diary, I was supposed to be settled in my hometown of Bartlett, Tennessee with my high school boyfriend and our three beautiful children by now. Thankfully, that isn't the way it turned out. The high school boyfriend lost his hair and married someone else long ago.

I live in the U.S. mecca of singles—Washington, D.C. Surely I won't be single long here, I thought when I first arrived. It would be only a matter of time before I met the handsome son of a senator or a strapping Redskin. Well … no. Not yet, anyway …

So at 28, after waiting and wanting and kissing frog after frog I slowly began to realize that things weren't turning out as I'd expected. So why waste the time I have here on earth waiting for Mr. Right to turn up? Why should any single woman waste one single moment? Being happy with ourselves is the best gift we can give ourselves. Being happy is its own reward. And as for life, to paraphrase Louisa May Alcott, "I'm learning to sail my ship." And I'm enjoying the journey.

Sample Quotes

When I am alone, I can sleep crossways in the bed without an argument.
—Zsa Zsa Gabor

I love being single. It is almost like being rich.
—Sue Grafton

Being solitary is being alone well: being alone luxuriously immersed in doings of your own choice, aware of the fullness of your own presence rather than the absence of others.
—Alice Koller

Don't compromise yourself. You are all you've got.
—Janis Joplin

Let me listen to me and not to them.
—Gertrude Stein

Love yourself first and everything else falls into line. You really have to love yourself to get anything done in this world.
—Lucille Ball

I'm not afraid of storms, for I'm learning how to sail my ship.
—Louisa May Alcott

Note to readers: The actual proposal contained four pages of quotes.

Sample Author/Agent Agreement

As we noted in earlier chapters, contracts and forms will vary greatly from agent to agent. Below is a sample form to give you an idea of what to expect from an author/agent agreement. We've noted material that may vary from agreement to agreement in brackets and parentheses. Remember two things. First, if you have a question, ask it. Your agent should be able to answer it in a fair and understanding way. Secondly, everything is negotiable. Well, maybe not everything, but no one ever got a better deal that didn't ask for it. Feel free to at least ask if you can improve rates, or change terms. Your agent might hold fast or it might be a change they make often (and they'll think you are one smart cookie!) One thing to remember, though. Publishing can have lots of terms that are unfamiliar to the average person. If it's non-negotiable, don't press it. Some items can be deal-breakers.

[date]

Dear [name],

This letter confirms the Agreement between [name of agency], (the "Agency") and you (the "Author"). Our Agreement is as follows.

In consideration of services rendered and to be rendered, the Author has appointed the Agency as the Author's sole and exclusive agent and representative with respect to [title], hereafter known as "the Work."

The Author represents and warrants that the author is the author of the Work and that the Author has the right to enter into the Agreement, having obtained the necessary agreements from any other participants. The Agency agrees to counsel and advise the Author with respect to the further development and completion of the Work, and upon receipt of a manuscript or proposal acceptable to the Agent to use the Agency's best efforts to place it for publication with a publisher acceptable to the Author, and to exploit and turn to account such other publication and subsidiary rights in and to the Work as may be appropriate under the circumstances. The Agency shall have the right to use and/or employ subagents and corresponding agents for such purposes.

The Agency shall have the right to receive and/or retain as commission the following listed percentages of all gross proceeds, emoluments, and other things of value at any time received or derived by the Author from the publication of the Work, in whole or in part, in any and all languages, and from the sale, lease, license, disposition, or other exploitation throughout the world of any and all rights in and to the Work:

   a. [Fifteen (15) percent] of such gross proceeds from the exploitation of English language publication rights in the United States and Canada, and from the exercise of print and related subsidiary rights in such territories.

   b. [Twenty (20) percent] of such gross proceeds from the exploitation of British and so-called "foreign" publication rights, and from the exercise of any and all subsidiary rights (both print and nonprint) in any territory outside the United States and Canada. However, if British and/or "foreign" publication rights are controlled and sold by the American publisher, the Agency's commission with respect to such proceeds shall be [fifteen (15) percent] thereof in lieu of [twenty (20) percent] thereof.

   c. [Fifteen (15) percent] of such gross proceeds from the exploitation of motion picture, television, radio, dramatic, and all other nonprint subsidiary rights in the United States and Canada. The Agency and its right to receive commissions hereunder shall be co-extensive with the life of the copyright of the Work and any renewals thereof.

In the event the Agency uses a subagent to sell foreign rights, it is understood that the Agency will keep [ten (10) percent] of the Author's income relevant to the sale, and that an additional [ten (10) percent] of the Author's income will be paid to the subagent. These terms will also exist in other situations where both the Agency and the Author concur that retaining a subagent would be advantageous.

All publishers of the Work, as well as all purchasers and licensees of subsidiary rights therein, shall be directed and authorized by the Author to remit the Author's payments to the Agency, as the Author's agent. Receipt of such payments by the Agency shall be deemed receipt by the Author.

The Agency shall remit payments to the Author, after deducting the Agency's commission, not later than fourteen (14) days after monies have been received. The Agency will send copies to the Author of all royalty statements, checks, and contracts received from the Publisher concerning the Work.

[There will be a clause in the Author-Publisher contract stating these terms and conditions. The Author's heirs will respect and adhere to this Agreement's intentions.]

[In addition to the aforementioned commissions, the Agency shall be reimbursed for the expenses incurred on behalf of the Work (not to exceed a total of $150 without written permission), including photocopying, messengers, cables, and overseas postage in connection with submissions for sales both foreign and domestic, long-distance telephone calls, copies of the published book when purchased by the Agency for subsidiary rights submissions, and other similar and related charges.]

The Agency shall bill the Author periodically for such expenses, or deduct same from funds received by the Agency for the Author's account.

Prior to or upon signing this Agreement, the Author agrees to provide the Agency with a complete written list of editors and publishers, if any, who have seen the Work or a proposal for the Work in its current form or in a prior form or draft.

The Agency or the Author shall have the right to terminate this Agreement in the event that the Work has not been placed for publication with a publisher acceptable to the Author within twelve (12) months from the Author's submission to the Agency of the Author's final completed proposal or manuscript, termination to be effective upon the expiration of 30 days. Notwithstanding the right of termination provided in the preceding sentence, if within four months after the effective date of termination of this Agreement a publisher to whom the Work had been submitted by the Agency prior to the effective date of termination of this Agreement, notifies the Author or the Agency that it wants to publish the Work and a contract results, the Agency is entitled to all rights provided to it under this Agreement, including, but not limited to, its right to receive commissions, and, if requested by the Author, the Agency will negotiate the book contract on behalf of the Author. In the event this agreement is terminated in accordance with the terms of this paragraph, the Agency will have no rights, including the right to receive commissions, in and to the Work and any derivations thereof.

If any controversy, claim, or dispute arising out of, or in connection with, this Agreement, or the breach thereof between the Agency and the Author, cannot be resolved, then the Author and the Agency agree to arbitrate their differences in [agent's state] in accordance with the rules of the American Arbitration Association, and judgment confirming the Arbitrator's award may be entered in any court of competent jurisdiction. The Agency agrees not to sign any contract for the Author or to otherwise make any commitment on the Author's behalf without written or oral authorization from the Author.

Any written notice called for by this Agreement must be sent by registered U.S. mail, return receipt requested to the addresses set forth in this Agreement.

This Agreement represents the complete understanding between the Author and the Agency, supersedes any prior oral understandings, and may not be amended except in writing signed by the Author and the Agency.

If the foregoing is acceptable to you, please so indicate by signing your name below.

Sincerely,

[agent name]

ACCEPTED AND AGREED TO:

Name _____

Social Security or Federal I.D.# _____

Appendix E

Sample Publishing Contract

We walked you through a contract clause by clause in Chapter 15, but following is an actual sample contract. Please note that all publishing companies have their own contracts, but this should give you an idea of what to expect when you receive your very first one in the mail.

AGREEMENT MADE this _____ day of March 2003, between [name of publisher] (referred to as the "Publisher") and [name of author] (referred to as the "Author").

WHEREAS the parties wish respectively to publish and have published a book (referred to as the "Work") provisionally titled "[book title]";

NOW, THEREFORE, they mutually agree as follows:

1. Grants of Rights: The Author grants to the Publisher during the term of copyright, including renewals and extensions thereof:

    a) Exclusive right in the English language, throughout the world, to:

        i) Print, publish, and sell the Work as a soft-cover (mass-market and/or trade paperback) book; and

        ii) License publication of a reprint edition(s) by other publishers.

    b) Non-exclusive right in the English language, throughout the world, to print, publish, and sell the Work as a hard-cover book.

c) Subsidiary Rights and Licenses:

i) The Publisher shall have the exclusive right, throughout the world, to sell or license the rights in the Work indicated below upon such terms as the Publisher deems advisable. The proceeds received by the Publisher from the sale or license of such rights shall be divided between the Author and the Publisher as set forth in paragraph 11:

a) book club rights;

b) textbook rights;

c) anthology rights;

d) first serial rights (i.e., publication of condensations, excerpts, digests, serializations, and extracts in newspapers and periodicals before first publication in book form);

e) second serial rights (i.e., publication of condensations, excerpts, digests, serializations, and extracts in newspapers and periodicals after first publication in book form);

f) selection rights, (such as a catalogue that produces its own edition of the work);

g) abridgment/condensation rights;

h) large print rights;

i) mass-market paperback rights;

j) trade (quality) paperback rights;

k) foreign language rights;

l) British Commonwealth rights;

m) merchandising and commercial rights;

n) audio rights (i.e., the right to use or adapt the Work or any portion thereof as a basis for audio through any method of recording or transmission now known or hereafter devised, including, without limitation, copying or recording by phonographic, magnetic, laser, electronic, or any other means and whether on phonograph records, audio cassettes, audio discs, or any other human or machine-readable audio medium and the broadcast or transmission thereof, now known or which may be devised in the future);

o) online database (via time-sharing access equipment or direct downloading);

p) CD-ROM optical discs in all forms now or to be utilized;

q) all other forms, formats, platforms, and standards now in use or which may in the future be in use during the term of this agreement and its option terms; and

r) picture, dramatic, television, radio, and allied rights.

Any subsidiary rights not exploited within 18 months of publication shall become nonexclusive.

d) Exclusive right to license in all foreign languages and all countries, the rights granted in subparagraphs (a) and (b) above;

e) The right of first refusal as to any sequel, revision, or republication of the work. During the period of this agreement, and for five (5) years thereafter, except in the case of termination in accordance with paragraph 17 herein, the Author shall not submit any sequel, revision, or republication of the Work to other publishers, nor seek offers from nor negotiate with others, with respect thereto until first offering said work to the Publisher. After submission of said proposed sequel, revision, or republication, the Publisher shall have thirty (30) days to determine whether to publish the said next work; if so, the parties shall negotiate in good faith the terms of the publishing agreement. If the parties are unable to reach agreement before the thirty (30) days shall expire, then the Author shall be free to offer the said sequel, revision, or republication to others, but only on terms more favorable than those offered by the Publisher. The Author shall notify the Publisher in writing of such offer, and all particulars, within seven (7) days of the receipt of said offer, and the Publisher shall have the right for thirty (30) days to match said offer of any other publisher.

f) To use or license others to use the approved name, likeness, and biography of the Author, the work and the title of the work, in whole or in part, or any adaptation thereof as the basis for trademark or trade name for other products or for any other commercial use in connection with such other products.

2. Delivery of Satisfactory Copy: The Publisher acknowledges receipt of an acceptable manuscript OR the Author agrees to deliver two complete copies (original and clean copy) of the revised manuscript of the work in the English language, together with any necessary permissions and all photographs, illustrations, drawings, and indexes suitable for reproduction and necessary to the completion of the manuscript not later than [date].

If the Author fails to deliver the manuscript within thirty (30) days after the above date, or if any manuscript that is delivered is not, in the Publisher's judgment, satisfactory, the Publisher shall give the Author written notice describing such failure and permit the Author to cure this defect within thirty (30) days of that notice. If the Author fails to do so, the Publisher may have the option to remedy the defect.

The Publisher may deduct its reasonable expenses for curing such defect from any proceeds that come due to the Author, and no proceeds will be paid to the Author until said expenses are reimbursed to the Publisher. Alternatively, the Publisher may opt to terminate this agreement by giving written notice, whereupon the Author agrees to repay forthwith all amounts which may have been advanced hereunder.

3. Permission for Copyrighted Material: If the Author incorporates in the work copyrighted material, she shall procure, at her expense, written permission to reprint it.

4. Author's Warranties and Indemnities: The Author warrants that she is the sole author of the work; that she is the sole owner of all the rights granted to the Publisher; that she has not previously assigned, pledged, or otherwise encumbered the same; that she has full power to enter into this agreement; that except for the material obtained pursuant to Paragraph 3, the work is original, has not been published before in the form submitted by the Author, and is not in the public domain; that it does not violate any right of privacy; and that it does not infringe upon any statutory or common-law copyright.

In the event of any claim, action, or proceeding based upon an alleged violation of any of these warranties, (i) the Publisher shall have the right to defend the same through counsel of its own choosing, and (ii) no settlement shall be effected without the prior written consent of the Author, which consent shall not unreasonably be withheld, and (iii) the Author shall hold harmless the Publisher, any seller of the work, and any licensee of a subsidiary right in the work, against any damages finally sustained. If such claim, action, or proceeding is successfully defended or settled, the Author's indemnity hereunder shall be limited to fifty percent (50 percent) of the expense (including reasonable counsel fees) attributable to such defense or settlement; however, such limitation of liability shall not apply if the claim, action, or proceeding is based on copyright infringement.

If any such claim, action, or proceeding is instituted, the Publisher shall promptly notify the Author, who shall fully cooperate and shall have the right but not the obligation to participate in the defense thereof, and the Publisher may withhold payments of reasonable amounts due her under this or any other agreement between the parties.

Such payments shall be released within one year if there is no action pending. These warranties and indemnities shall survive the termination of this agreement.

5. Conflicting Publication: The Author agrees that until termination of this agrement, she will not, without the written permission of the Publisher, publish or permit to be published any book that is directly competitive with the work. The Author does have the right to publish and distribute training manuals that support her seminar.

6. Date, Style, and Price of Publication: The Publisher shall publish the work at its own expense, in such style and manner, under such imprint and at such price as it deems suitable by [date]. The Publisher shall not be responsible for delays caused by any circumstance beyond its control. In no event shall the Publisher be obligated to publish a work which, in its opinion, violates the common-law or statutory copyright or the right of privacy of any person or contains libelous or obscene matter. The Publisher shall consult with the Author on the design of the book and the cover. The Publisher shall have final approval.

7. Proofreading and Author's Corrections: The Author agrees to read, revise, correct, and return promptly all proofs of the work and to pay in cash or, at the option of the Publisher, to have charged against him the cost of alterations, in type or in plates, required by the Author, other than those due to the printer's or the Publisher's errors, in excess of ten percent (10 percent) of the cost of setting type, provided a statement of these charges is sent to the Author within thirty (30) days of the receipt of the printer's bills and the corrected proofs are presented upon request for his inspection.

8. Copyright: The Publisher shall copyright the work in the name of the Author, in the United States, in compliance with the Universal Copyright Convention, and apply for renewals of such copyright. If copyright in any country should be in the name of the Publisher, it shall assign such copyright upon request of the Author.

9. Advance Payments: The Publisher shall pay to the Author as an advance against and on account of all moneys accruing to her under this agreement, the sum of X dollars ($X), payable:

   $X upon signing;

   $X upon acceptance; and

   $X upon publication

10. Royalty Payments: The Publisher shall pay to the Author a royalty on every copy sold by the Publisher and paid for, less actual returns and a reasonable reserve [note: typical reserves can be up to 30 percent of monies owed] for returns (except as set forth below):

    i) Softcover: For the first 10,000 copies sold: seven and one-half percent (7 1/2 percent) of retail price; From 10,001 to 50,000 copies sold: eight percent (8 percent) of retail price; From 50,001 copies sold: ten percent (10 percent) of retail price.

    ii) Hardcover: For the first 5,000 copies sold: ten percent (10 percent) of retail price; From 5,001 to 10,000 copies sold: twelve and one-half percent (12 1/2 percent) of retail price; From 10,001 copies sold: fifteen percent (15 percent) of retail price.

b) No Royalty Copies: No royalty shall be paid on copies sold below or at cost including expenses incurred, or furnished gratis to the Author, or for review, advertising, sample or like purposes.

c) Proceeds from revenues derived from the sale of all nonexclusive and subsidiary rights under paragraph 1(b) and (c) shall be divided as follows:

   i) Book club rights [note: typically 50 percent to the Publisher, 50 percent to the Author]

   ii) Hardcover rights [note: typically 50 percent to the Publisher, 50 percent to the Author]

   iii) First serial rights [note: authors can often get 90 percent here]

   iv) All other subsidiary rights

11. Reports and Payments: The Publisher shall render semiannual statements of account to the last day of December and the last day of June, and shall mail such statements during the third month following, together with checks in payment of the amounts due thereon.

    Should the Author receive an overpayment of royalty arising from copies reported sold but subsequently returned, the Publisher may deduct such overpayment from any further sums due the Author.

    Upon written request, the Author may examine or cause to be examined through certified public accountants or other qualified representatives the books of account of the Publisher insofar as they relate to the sale or licensing of the work. If there is a discrepancy of more than eight percent (8 percent), the cost of the audit will be borne by the Publisher.

12. Payment to Author's Representative: All monies due to the Author under the terms of this agreement shall be paid to the Author's duly assigned representative, [agent's name and address], whose receipt thereof shall be a valid discharge of the Publisher's obligation. The Author shall irrevocably assign to the Agent a sum equal to [agent's percentage] of the income accruing to the Author's account under the terms of this agreement, and the said Agent is empowered by the Author to act on her behalf in all matters arising from and pertaining to this agreement. The term "Author" as used in this paragraph includes but is not limited to all author(s) named elsewhere in this agreement and their successors, assigns, licensees, heirs, legal representatives, administrators and executors, and anyone acting on their behalf or in their place and stead.

13. Copies to Author: On publication, the Publisher shall give X (X) free copies to the Author, and X (X) free copies to her agent, each of whom may purchase further copies for personal use at a discount of [note: typically 50 percent] from the retail

price. The Author may order full case quantities at a discount of [note: can be as much as 60 percent].

14. Discontinuance of Publication: If the Publisher fails to keep the work in print and the Author makes written demand to reprint it, the Publisher shall, within sixty (60) days after the receipt of such demand, notify the Author in writing if it intends to comply. Within six (6) months thereafter, the Publisher shall reprint the work unless prevented from doing so by circumstances beyond its control. If the Publisher fails to notify the Author within the sixty (60) days described above that it intends to comply, or, within six (6) months after such notification, the Publisher declines or neglects to reprint the work, then this agreement shall terminate and all rights granted hereunder shall revert to the Author, subject to licenses previously granted, provided the Author is not indebted to the Publisher for any sum owing to it under this agreement. After such reversion, the Publisher shall continue to participate to the extent set forth in this agreement in monies received from any license previously granted by it. Upon such termination, the Author shall have the right for sixty (60) days thereafter to purchase the plates, if any, at one fourth of the cost (including typesetting).

If the work is under contract for publication or on sale in any book edition in the United States in quantities sufficient for distribution in the trade, it shall be considered to be in print. A work shall not be deemed in print by reason of a license granted by the Publisher for the reproduction of single copies of the work. If the Publisher should determine that there is not sufficient sale for the work to enable it to continue its publication and sale profitably, the Publisher may dispose of the copies remaining on hand as it deems best, subject to the royalty provisions of paragraph 10. In such event, the Author shall have the right, within two (2) weeks of the forwarding of a written notice from the Publisher, to a single purchase of copies at the "remainder" price.

15. Author's Property: Except for loss or damage due to its own negligence, the Publisher shall not be responsible for loss or damage to any property of the Author.

16. Suits for Infringement of Copyright: If the copyright of the work is infringed, and if the parties proceed jointly, the expenses and recoveries, if any, shall be shared equally; and if they do not proceed jointly, either party shall have the right to prosecute such action, and such party shall bear the expenses thereof, and any recoveries shall belong to such party; and if such party shall not hold the record title of the copyright, the other party hereby consents that the action be brought in his or its name.

17. Bankruptcy and Liquidation: If (a) a petition in bankruptcy is filed by the Publisher, or (b) a petition in bankruptcy is filed against the Publisher and such petition is finally sustained, or (c) a petition for arrangement is filed by the Publisher or a

petition for reorganization is filed by or against the Publisher, and an order is entered directly the liquidation of the Publisher as in bankruptcy, or (d) the Publisher makes an assignment for the benefit of creditors, or (e) the Publisher liquidates its business for any cause whatever, the Author may, subject to any orders or rulings from a Court of competent jurisdiction, terminate this agreement by written notice and thereupon all rights granted by him hereunder shall revert to him. Upon such termination, the Author, at his option, may purchase the plates and the remaining copies at one fourth of the manufacturing cost, exclusive of the Publisher's overhead. If he fails to exercise such option within sixty (60) days after the happening of any one of the events referred to above, the Trustee, Receiver, or Assignee may destroy the plates and sell the copies remaining on hand, subject to the royalty provisions of Paragraph 10. Publisher shall notify author within thirty (30) days of the occurrence of any of the events described in this paragraph.

18. Sums Due and Owing: Any sums due and owing from the Author to the Publisher, whether or not arising out of this agreement, may be deducted from any sum due or to become due from the Publisher to the Author pursuant to this agreement.

19. Law Applicable: This agreement, including all rights and liability of the parties, shall be governed by the laws of the State of [wherever the publisher is located].

20. Copyright: It is a condition of the rights granted hereby that the Publisher agrees that all copies of the work that are distributed to the public shall bear the copyright notice prescribed by the applicable copyrights laws of the United States of America. The Author hereby appoints the Publisher as his attorney-in-fact in his name and in his stead to execute all documents for recording in the Copyright Office evidencing transfer of ownership in the exclusive rights granted to the Publisher hereunder.

21. Assignment: This agreement shall be binding upon the heirs, executors, administrators, and assigns of the Author, and upon the successors and assigns of the Publisher.

22. Complete Agreement and Modification: This agreement constitutes the complete understanding of the parties. No modification or waiver of any provision shall be valid unless in writing and signed by both parties.

23. Dispute Resolution: Any controversy or claim arising out of or relating to this agreement shall be submitted in [wherever publisher is located], to American Mediation Council, LLC, under its Mediation Rules, before the parties resort to arbitration, litigation, or some other dispute-resolution procedure.

IN WITNESS WHEREOF, the parties have duly executed this agreement:

PUBLISHER

By: _____

Dated: _____

AUTHOR

By: _____

Dated: _____

Sample Press Releases

You read in the publicity chapters about how critical it is to catch the eye of a newspaper editor or radio producer with a catchy press release. Here are two real releases for real books, both of which received a great deal of press coverage as a result.

FOR IMMEDIATE RELEASE
Contact: Matt Jarrette
www.primapublishing.com
(916) 787-6928
mattj@primapub.com

Revealing the Tyrannous Legacy of the Great Emancipator

Roseville, CA (August 2002)—Most Americans consider Abraham Lincoln to be one of the greatest presidents in history. His legend has grown to mythic proportions as hundreds of books, a national holiday, and a monument in Washington, D.C., extol his heroism and martyrdom. But what if most everything you knew about Lincoln were false? In *The Real Lincoln* (Prima Forum, 0-7615-3641-8, $24.95), readers will discover another side of Lincoln and gain a deeper understanding of the reasons behind the Civil War, a bloody, and perhaps, unnecessary war.

Long revered as the Great Emancipator, Abraham Lincoln is portrayed in this provocative book as a man not so much interested in ending slavery as in building an American empire. According to author **Thomas J. DiLorenzo**, Lincoln's dream of an empire not only clashed with the Constitution but may very well have led to the most devastating war the United States has ever fought. In *The Real Lincoln*, DiLorenzo shows the sixteenth president as a man who devoted his political life to transforming the federal government from its limited origins into a powerful, activist state. Standing in his way, however, was the South, with its independent states, its resistance to the national government, and its reliance on unfettered free trade. A peacefully negotiated secession was within reach, yet Lincoln opted instead for a course of war.

DiLorenzo's extensive research and meticulous documentation portray Lincoln as a leader who subverted the Constitution, trampled states' rights, and launched a brutal war. According to the author, 600,000 American soldiers did not die for the honorable cause of ending slavery but for the dubious agenda of sacrificing the independence of the states to the supremacy of the federal government. *The Real Lincoln* finally reveals Lincoln's true ambition and legacy that until now has remained untold.

Thomas J. DiLorenzo is professor of economics in the Sellinger School of Business and Management at Loyola College in Maryland. Specializing in economic history and political economy, he is the author of 11 books and over 70 articles in academic journals, and he is also widely published in such popular outlets as the *Wall Street Journal, Reader's Digest, USA Today, National Review, Barron's*, and numerous other national publications. He lives in Clarksville, Maryland.

For additional information or to speak with the author, please contact Matt Jarrette at (916) 787-6928 or mattj@primapub.com.

FOR IMMEDIATE RELEASE
Contact: Matt Jarrette
www.primapublishing.com
(916) 787-6928
mattj@primapub.com

The Inside Story of Microsoft's Big Gamble—the Xbox

Roseville, CA (June 2002)—One of Microsoft's most surprising moves was their decision to enter the video game console market—a decision that threatens to derail Microsoft and diffuse its concentration on software. Why would Microsoft take such a risk? Veteran journalist Dean Takahashi goes behind the scenes to reveal the creative thinking, dramatic infighting, cutthroat competition, and billion-dollar deals that went into the creation of the Xbox. In *Opening the Xbox: Inside Microsoft's Plan to Unleash an Entertainment Revolution* (Prima, $24.95, **07615-3708-2) Takahashi explores the genesis of the Xbox project and the implications of the machine that could dramatically alter the highly competitive video game landscape** or possibly trigger a devastating loss for the world's largest software company.

Takahashi digs deep into the amazing story of this much-hyped machine. Through exclusive interviews with many of the top Microsoft executives, careful research, and a penetrating investigation, he unveils the tumultuous story behind the development of the project and how it could change the entertainment industry forever. It's hard to believe that just a few agitated renegades inside Microsoft convinced the world's richest man to challenge Sony and Nintendo in the video game business. But it's true. What started out as Project Midway spearheaded by Jonathan "Seamus" Blackley and three of his cohorts turned into the Xbox, a multibillion-dollar enterprise that has become Microsoft's largest internal start-up ever.

Bill Gates approved the Xbox even though he was advised that Microsoft could lose $900 million over eight years and as much as $3.3 billion if Sony forced them to cut prices heavily. The stakes have never been higher. *Opening the Xbox* is sure to enthrall the millions of gamers, investors, and business experts who—until now—have had to watch the Xbox saga from the sidelines.

Dean Takahashi is a senior writer at *Red Herring* magazine, where he writes about video and computer games, semiconductors, and consumer electronics. He has been a business writer for 14 years, working previously at the *Wall Street Journal, San Jose Mercury News, Los Angeles Times, Orange County Register,* and *Dallas Times Herald.* He lives in the metropolitan area of San Jose, California.

For additional information or to speak with the author, please contact Matt Jarrette at (916) 787-6928 or mattj@primapub.com.

Sample Collaboration Agreement

From the American Society of Journalists and Authors

When two (or more) people plan to collaborate on a book, it is a very good idea to have a written agreement that spells out precisely how the responsibilities—and the potential rewards—are going to be divided.

Such an agreement is a very good idea even if the collaborators are long-time acquaintances; even if they have previously worked together; even if (perhaps especially if) they are fast friends. It assures that each of the parties has the same understanding of each party's obligations; in the absence of a written agreement, unwarranted assumptions can easily be made and misunderstandings can easily occur.

The agreement should be drawn up as soon as the parties decide that they will collaborate, and before any work is actually done. If a literary agent is involved in the initial discussion, the agreement should include the agent as well, and the sample agreement that follows assumes such involvement. (If the potential co-authors are, instead, planning to draw up a proposal and then seek an agent, the agreement should so specify.)

A collaboration agreement can be as long or as short, as simple or as complex, as the parties wish, so long as it leaves no doubt as to (1) who is to be responsible for the various tasks necessary to produce the manuscript, (2) how expenses are to be divided, and (3) how income is to be divided. It should also deal with any other concerns the individuals may have. These may, of course, vary considerably and may include such considerations as potential conflicts with other works or contemplated works by any party; commitments to travel if the parties are geographically distant from each other; a designated successor should one party become incapacitated or otherwise unavailable before completion of the project; et al.

Sample Agreement

THIS AGREEMENT is made on the ____ day of _____, 20___, by, between, and among: John M. Yatros, M.D. of New York, New York (hereinafter referred to as Yatros); Wanda Wordsmith of New York, New York (hereinafter referred to as Wordsmith); and the Lunch Associates Literary Agency of New York, New York (hereinafter referred to as Lunch). These parties agree as follows:

1. Subject to the terms and conditions herein, Yatros and Wordsmith agree to collaborate exclusively with each other in the preparation of a book-length manuscript dealing with the subject of _____.

2. It is understood and agreed that Wordsmith shall prepare a proposal and outline for the work, and that Yatros shall cooperate with, and assist, Wordsmith in that preparation by meeting with Wordsmith and furnishing all necessary information regarding the content of the work.[1] Yatros shall pay Wordsmith a total of _____ dollars ($_____) to prepare this material, payable half on signing of this agreement and half on approval of the proposal and outline by Yatros, which approval shall not be unreasonably withheld. Yatros agrees to approve the draft, or correct inaccuracies and suggest reasonable revisions, within ten (10) days of receipt of the draft.[2] Wordsmith agrees to correct any inaccuracies, and to make necessary revisions, promptly.

3. Upon approval of the proposal and outline by Yatros and payment by Yatros to Wordsmith of the full amount stated above, Wordsmith shall deliver to Lunch one (1) original copy of the proposal and outline.

4. Lunch shall offer the proposed work to publishers and diligently endeavor to obtain the best possible terms for publication of the work. No contract or other agreement for disposition of rights in the work shall be executed by Lunch without the approval of Yatros and Wordsmith; such approval shall not be arbitrarily or unreasonably withheld. It is understood that Yatros and Wordsmith are obligated to sign a contract to publish the work if Lunch obtains a contract calling for a minimum advance of _____ thousand dollars ($_____) and standard book royalties and

licensing splits between authors and publisher, and providing neither of the authors puts forth any other substantive objection to the publisher or contract terms.[3]

5. When a contract has been signed by Yatros and Wordsmith, it is understood and agreed that the actual writing of the manuscript shall be the responsibility of Wordsmith. Yatros agrees to furnish Wordsmith with all materials and information necessary for preparation of the manuscript, sufficiently in advance to permit Wordsmith to meet the manuscript delivery date stipulated in the agreement with the publisher. Wordsmith agrees to deliver the text of the work to Yatros for Yatros's approval, and Yatros shall promptly approve said text or detail reasonable revisions, if any, in writing. Wordsmith agrees to revise the text, if necessary, according to Yatros's reasonable recommendations.[4]

6. Yatros and Wordsmith agree to revise the text according to the publisher's reasonable requests, if any.

7. The title of the work in all and any English-language publications throughout the world shall be subject to the approval of Yatros and Wordsmith.

8. The names of both Yatros and Wordsmith shall appear on the work, in all forms and languages throughout the world, separated by the word "and" or the word "with" as the authors may decide between them is appropriate.[5] The name of Yatros shall precede the name of Wordsmith, but both names shall be identical in size and type style.[6]

9. Copyright in the work, in all forms and languages throughout the world, shall be held in the names of Yatros and Wordsmith.

10. Yatros agrees to indemnify Wordsmith and hold her harmless against any claim, demand, suit, action, proceeding, or expense of any kind arising from or based upon language, information, advice, citations, anecdotal matter, resource materials, or other content of the work that was provided by Yatros.

11. Costs of typing, photocopying, and other ordinary expenses in connection with preparation of the work shall be borne equally by Yatros and Wordsmith.[7]

12. Yatros and Wordsmith hereby retain Lunch to represent them in connection with the work on an exclusive basis, and Lunch shall retain for services rendered _____ percent (___ percent) of all monies received for disposition of any rights in the work, except that Lunch shall retain _____ percent (___ percent) of monies received for disposition of any rights in foreign countries; any commission payable to sub-agents with respect to the disposition of foreign rights shall be paid by Lunch.[8]

13. Upon receipt of statements from publishers, Lunch shall promptly dispatch copies to Yatros and Wordsmith. Upon receipt of any monies from publishers or others for any rights in the work, Lunch shall promptly disburse such monies, less only agency commissions, to Yatros and Wordsmith in the proportions hereinafter specified.

14. Yatros and Wordsmith, jointly or separately, or their authorized representative(s), shall have the right to examine the records of Lunch pertaining to the work, upon request during normal business hours.

15. All proceeds and revenues received from the sale, lease, license, or other disposition of any rights in the work, throughout the world, shall be divided between Yatros and Wordsmith as follows:[9]

    (a) Of the first installment of the advance stipulated in the original publishing contract, Wordsmith shall receive eighty percent (80 percent), less only agency commission, and Yatros shall receive twenty percent (20 percent), less only agency commission, except that _____ dollars ($_____) shall be subtracted from Wordsmith's share and added to Yatros's share.[10]

    (b) Of the remainder of the advance stipulated in the original publishing contract, Wordsmith shall receive eighty percent (80 percent), less only agency commission, and Yatros shall receive twenty percent (20 percent), less only agency commission.

    (c) Thereafter, Yatros and Wordsmith shall each receive fifty percent (50 percent), less only agency commission, of all revenues, from any source, received in connection with the work.

16. The term of this agreement shall be co-extensive with the life of the copyright in the work.

17. This agreement sets forth the entire understanding of the parties hereto and may not be changed except by written consent of all the parties.

18. It is expressly understood and agreed that this agreement shall be automatically considered a part of any and all contracts and agreements made by the authors with respect to rights in the work.

19. The terms and conditions of this agreement shall be binding upon, and the benefits thereof shall inure to, the respective heirs, executors, administrators, successors, and assigns of the parties hereto.

20. All parties to this agreement warrant that they have no other contractual commitment which will or might conflict with this agreement or interfere with the performance of any obligations hereunder.

21. This agreement shall be construed in accordance with the laws of the State of New York.

22. Should any controversy, claim, or dispute arise out of or in connection with this agreement, such controversy, claim, or dispute shall be submitted to arbitration before the American Arbitration Association in accordance with its rules, and judgment confirming the arbitrator's award may be entered in any court of competent jurisdiction.

IN WITNESS WHEREOF, the parties hereto have set their hands on the date first above specified.

Rev 4/97

Notes

1. The physician does not, of course, always provide all the information; it may, for example, be agreed that the physician will furnish clinical data while the writer will be responsible for statistical research.

2. The parties should be certain that any time periods stated are in fact feasible in the context of their own commitments and schedules.

3. Publisher contracts are not limited to monetary terms, and either co-author may wish to specify additional conditions, if there are any of particular concern.

4. The parties may wish to specify time limits, either for the physician's consideration of the manuscript, the writer's revision, or both. It may also be desirable, especially in the case of a work of some length, to handle it in parts or sections and to specify interim deadlines—e.g., to agree that half the work be delivered to the physician, discussed, and revised by a date midway between contract signing and the manuscript due date.

5. If the work treats of the physician's theories or opinions or refers to specific experiences not shared by the writer-author—i.e., if the first person is to be used ("I have found," "among my patients")—the connective should be "with."

6. Different terms may, of course, be specified—that the writer's name be, for example, no less than two thirds (or some other proportion) the size of the physician's. Or, if the matter is of no concern to the writer, reference to type size and style may be omitted entirely.

7. The division need not be equal; one party may agree to assume more than half of such expenses, or clerical services may under some circumstances be available without charge. If additional expenses—travel, database searches, research assistants, or other outlays—are contemplated, how they are to be divided should also be spelled out.

8. The usual commission is 10 or 15 percent, with a higher percentage payable in connection with disposition of foreign rights; the latter sum enables the agent, in turn, to pay a commission to an agent, based in the foreign country, who handles arrangements there. A higher percentage may also be applicable in connection with disposition of other rights—e.g., film—involving co-agenting.

9. The proportions used here are chosen arbitrarily. In practice, the writer's share of the advance may range from 50 percent (rare) to 100 percent (also rare). Special arrangements may also be made: The writer may, for example, agree to a lower percentage if a higher advance is obtained; or, it may be agreed that the writer will receive the full first half of the advance, with the second half to be divided between the co-authors.

10. This is the sum previously paid for creation of the proposal/outline.

Appendix

Selected Writers' Conferences

The following were generously provided by and selected from "The Guide to Writers Conferences and Workshops" at www.shawguides.com, which provides more than 600 detailed listings, including upcoming dates, faculty, and programs. Please visit their website to find more conferences in your state.

American Christian Writers' Workshops
Reg Forder, Director
1-800-21-WRITE
RegAForder@aol.com

ASJA Annual Writers' Conference
1501 Broadway, Suite 302
New York, NY 10036
212-997-0947
Fax: 212-768-7414
www.asja.org
staff@asja.org

Aspen Summer Words
PO Box 7726
Aspen, CO 81612
1-800-925-2526 or 970-925-3122
Fax: 970-920-5700
www.aspenwriters.org
info@aspenwriters.org

Book Passage Writers' Conferences
51 Tamal Vista
Corte Madera, CA 94925
415-927-0960
conferences@bookpassage.com

Bread Loaf Writers' Conference
Middlebury College
Middlebury, VT 05753
802-443-5286
Fax: 802-443-2087
www.middlebury.edu/~blwc
blwc@mail.middlebury.edu

Cape Cod Writers' Conference
Cape Cod Writers' Center
PO Box 186
Barnstable, MA 02630
508-375-0516
Fax: 508-362-2718
www.capecodwriterscenter.com
ccwc@capecod.net

Centrum's Port Townsend Writers' Conference
Ft. Worden State Park
PO Box 1158
Port Townsend, WA 98368
360-385-3102
Fax: 360-385-2470
www.centrum.org
info@centrum.org

Clarion West Science Fiction and Fantasy Writers' Workshop
340 15th Avenue E, #350
Seattle, WA 98112-5156
206-322-9083
www.sff.net/clarionwest
kfishler@fishler.com

Erotic Pen Workshops
www.theeroticpen.com
info@theeroticpen.com

Florida First Coast Writers' Festival
Florida Community College at Jacksonville
101 W. State Street
Jacksonville, FL 32202
904-633-8327
Fax: 904-633-8435
www.fccj.org/wf
kclower@fccj.org

Florida Suncoast Writers' Conference
University of South Florida
4200002 E. Fowler Avenue MHH-116
Tampa, FL 33620
813-974-1711
Fax: 813-974-2270
english.cas.usf.edu/fswc/
edubmoss@chwna.cas.usf.edu

Haystack Writing Program at Portland State University
Portland State University
School of Extended Studies
PO Box 1491
Portland, OR 97207-1491
1-800-547-8887 ext. 4186 or
503-725-4186
Fax: 503-725-4840
www.haystack.pdx.edu
snydere@pdx.edu

Indiana University Writers' Conference
464 Ballantine Hall
Bloomington, IN 47405
812-855-1877
Fax: 812-855-9535
www.indiana.edu/~writecon/
alocklin@indiana.edu

International Women's Writing Guild
PO Box 810 Gracie Station
New York, NY 10028
212-737-7536
Fax: 212-737-9469
www.iwwg.com
iwwg@iwwg.com

Iowa Summer Writing Festival
University of Iowa
100 Oakdale Campus W310
Iowa City, IA 52242
319-335-4160
Fax: 319-335-4039
www.uiowa.edu/~iswfest
jswfestival@uiowa.edu

Jackson Hole Writers' Conference
University of Wyoming
PO Box 3972
Laramie, WY 82071-3972
1-877-733-3618 ext. 1
www.jacksonholewriters.org
kgville@uwyo.edu

Kenyon Review Writers' Workshops
The Kenyon Review
Kenyon College
Gambier, OH 43022
740-427-5207
Fax: 740-427-5417
www.kenyonreview.org/
kenyonreview@kenyon.edu

Key West Writers' Workshop
Florida Keys Community College
5901 College Road
Key West, FL 33040
305-296-9081, ext. 302
Fax: 305-292-5155

Livingston Writers' Workshop
106 S. Main Street
Livingston, MT 59047
406-222-7766
library.ycsi.net/new/writers
mcuminins@ycsi.net

Los Angeles Writers' Conference
The Writers' Program,
UCLA Extension
310-825-9415
writers@unex.ucla.edu

Marymount Manhattan College Writers' Conference and Workshop
The Writing Center
221 East 71st Street
New York, NY 10021
212-734-3073 or 212-734-4419
Fax: 212-734-3140
marymount.mmm.edu/home.htm
lorimartin@hotmail.com

Maui Writers' Conference and Writers' Retreat
PO Box 1118
Kihei, HI 96753
808-879-0061
Fax: 808-879-6233
www.mauiwriters.com
writers@maui.net

Mendocino Coast Writers' Conference
College of the Redwoods
1211 Del Mar Drive
Fort Bragg, CA 95437
707-961-6248
Fax: 707-961-0943
www.mcwcwritewhale.com
mcwc@jps.net

Mid-Atlantic Creative Nonfiction Writers' Conference
Goucher College
Towson, MD 21204
1-800-697-4646
www.goucher.edu/conference/writers/
nmack@goucher.edu

Mississippi River Creative Writing Workshop in Poetry and Fiction
English Office
Street Cloud State University
Street Cloud, MN 56301-4498
320-255-4947
meissner@stcloudstate.edu

Napa Valley Writers' Conference
Napa Valley College
1088 College Avenue
Street Helena, CA 94558
707-967-2900, ext. 1611
Fax: 707-967-2909
www.napacommunityed.org/
writersconf
writecon@campus.nvc.cc.ca.us

National Writers' Association Summer
3140 S. Peoria, #295
Aurora, CO 80014
303-841-0246
Fax: 303-751-8593
www.nationalwriters.com
Conference@nationalwriters.com

National Writers' Workshops
The Poynter Institute
801 Third Street South
St. Petersburg, FL 33701
1-888-POYNTER or 727-821-9494
Fax: 727-821-0583
poynter.org/connect.htm
cperezwaulk@poynter.org

New York State Summer Writers' Institute
Skidmore College
Office of Special Programs
815 North Broadway
Saratoga Springs, NY 12866-1632
518-580-5590
Fax: 518-584-5548
www.skidmore.edu/summer
jphaneuf@skidmore.edu

North Carolina Writers' Network Conferences
PO Box 954
Carrboro, NC 27510
919-967-9540
Fax: 919-929-0535
www.ncwriters.org
mail@ncwriters.org

Pacific Northwest Writers Association Summer Writers' Conference
PNWA
PO Box 2016
Edmonds, WA 98020
425-673-2665
www.pnwa.org
pnwa@pnwa.org

Philadelphia Writers' Conference
PWC Registrar D.O. Haggerty
535 Fairview Road
Medford, NJ 08055
215-497-9446
Fax: 215-442-1987
www.pwcwriters.org
info@pwcwriters.org

Pikes Peak Writers' Conference
PO Box 6726
Colorado Springs, CO 80934
www.ppwc.net
info@ppwc.net

Robert McKee's Story Structure
Two Arts, Inc.
PO Box 452930
Los Angeles, CA 90045
888-676-2533
Fax: 310-348-9095
www.mckeestory.com
contact@McKeeStory.com

San Diego State University Writers' Conference
SDSU College of Extended Studies
5250 Campanile Drive
San Diego, CA 92182-1920
619-594-5152 or 619-594-2517
www.neverstoplearning.net
extended.std@sdsu.edu

Sandy Cove Christian Writers' Conference
1-800-234-COVE

Santa Barbara Writers' Conference
SBWC
PO Box 304
Carpinteria, CA 93014
805-684-2250
www.sbwc.org
sbsc@digital.org

Santa Fe Writers'
826 Camino del Monte Rey, #A-6
Santa Fe, NM 87501
505-577-1125
www.santafewritersconference.com
litcenter@recursos.org

Sewanee Writers' Conference
University of the South
310 Street Luke's Hall
735 University Avenue
Sewanee, TN 37383-1000
931-598-1141/1541
Fax: 931-598-1145
www.sewaneewriters.org
cpeters@sewanee.edu

Society of Children's Book Writers' and Illustrators—LA County, CA Chapter
SCBWI LA County, CA Chapter
PO Box 1728
Pacific Palisades, CA 90272
310-573-7318
www.scbwi.socal.org
claudiascbwi@earthlink.net

South Florida Writers' Conference
PO Box 570415
Miami, FL 33257-0415
305-275-8666
Fax: 305-233-8680
greenfie@hotmail.com

Southern California Writers' Conference—San Diego
4406 Park Boulevard, Suite E
San Diego, CA 92116
619-233-4651
Fax: 253-390-8577
www.writersconference.com
wewrite@writersconference.com

Southern Women Writers' Conference
Berry College
Department of English
PO Box 495010
Mount Berry, GA 30149
706-368-6995
www2.berry.edu/academics/
humanities/English/swwc1page.asp
cbaker@berry.edu

Southwest Writers' Workshop
8200 Mountain Road N.E., Suite 106
Albuquerque, NM 87110
505-265-9485
Fax: 505-265-9483
www.southwestwriters.org
contactus@southwestwriters.com

Spoleto Writers' Workshops
Spoleto Arts
760 West End Avenue, #3-A
New York, NY 10025
212-663-4440
www.spoletoarts.com
CLINTONEVE@aol.com

Squaw Valley Community of Writers
10626 Banner Lava Cap Road
Nevada City, CA 95959
530-470-8440
www.squawvalleywriters.org
svcw@oro.net

Sun Valley Writers' Conference and Workshop
PO Box 957
Ketchum, ID 83340
208-726-6670
Fax: 208-788-0106
www.svwc.com

Symposium for Professional Food Writers
The Greenbrier
300 West Main Street
White Sulphur Springs, WV 24986
1-800-624-6070, or 707-963-0777
Fax: 304-536-7893
www.greenbrier.com/foodwriters
antonia@fcs.net

Taos Summer Writers' Conference
University of New Mexico
Humanities Building, Room 255
Albuquerque, NM 87131
505-277-6248
Fax: 505-277-2950
www.unm.edu/~taosconf
taosconf@unm.edu

Vintage Hudson Valley Travel Writers' Conference
Vintage Hudson Valley
PO Box 288
Irvington, NY 10533
914-591-4503
Fax: 914-591-4510
www.vintagehudsonvalley.com
info@vintagehudsonvalley.com

Wesleyan Writers' Conference
Wesleyan University
Middletown, CT 06459
860-685-3604
Fax: 860-347-3996
www.wesleyan.edu/writing/
conferen.html
agreene@wesleyan.edu

Whidbey Island Writers' Conference
PO Box 1289
Langley, WA 98260
360-331-6714
www.whidbey.com/writers
writers@whidbey.com

Writer's Center at Chautauqua
The Writers' Center at Chautauqua
PO Box 408
Chautauqua, NY 14722
www.ciweb.org
Writer999@mindspring.com

Writers' Retreat: Career Oriented Writers/Screenwriters Workshops
The Writers Retreat
15 Canusa Street
Beebe Plain, QC JOB 3E5 Canada
819-876-2065
www.writersretreat.com/workshops.htm
info@writersretreat.com

Writers' Workshop in Science Fiction
Center for the Study of Science Fiction
University of Kansas/English
Department
Lawrence, KS 66045-2115
973-864-3380
Fax: 973-864-4298
www.ku.edu/~sfcenter/index.html
jgunn@ku.edu

Sample Television Pitch Memo

Giving the Gift of You

[You'll want to create a document that is pleasing to the eye and not too long.]

**How to Create Closer Connections
with Your Family This Holiday Season**

Introduction

What people remember most is how we make them feel—it is what we say and how we say it. Our tone of voice can fill a loved one's heart *or* just as quickly, crush their spirit. It is the gestures that we make and the way we tune in to others. So often during holiday stress we are quick to lose our tempers or tune out to the moments around us, when *those* are the very moments we could be connecting with friends and family and giving the gift of ourselves.

What people remember most is how we make them feel. Long after the gifts under the tree are unwrapped and forgotten, we will have the memory of what someone said or did that made us feel loved or unloved. During the holidays, we tend to focus on things like having the perfect party, or finding just the right gift for Dad. The better focus, if we are to create close connections with our family, is how to give the gift of ourselves in the everyday moments of the holiday season.

More than ever, in these unsettling times, we desire to be close with loved ones. And yet, we struggle with HOW to do that. We are better at knowing HOW to give the gift of a tie or perfume or a teddy bear than knowing how to give the gift of ourselves. In this encouraging, humorous and touching holiday show, Beth Craig will address the question of what it means to give the gift of you and how to create close, loving, and lasting connections with your loved ones.

Segment Concepts

What does it mean to Give the Gift of You? As each of the following topics suggests, it involves discovery and mindset. Several of these questions could be explored during the show, where viewers are sure to find humor and wisdom as they discover how to experience closer connections for the holidays.

- This holiday season do you want to bless or impress? Why not give the gift of you?
- How does striving for perfection keep us from connecting during the holidays?
- Why do women protect the men they love from holiday responsibilities, and then complain of no connection with them during the holidays?
- How do family traditions prevent us from giving the gift of ourselves?
- How can we learn to love the process of getting ready for the holidays?
- How can we tune in while we task?
- How can we avoid "holiday hooks" that pull us in year after year?

B-Roll Suggestions

To illustrate our point that connection is in the everyday moments of the holiday season (and is often missed!) we'd like to suggest B-roll (television footage that can be played while a voice is talking to illustrate the point) that would show some of the positive and negative interactions we traditionally have during the holidays. These could include a family meal, shopping with friends, decorating, baking, or wrapping gifts.

Another B-roll approach could be profiling various people who struggle with connection and those who exemplify it during the holidays. (Example: My friend Karen, whose quest for perfection finds her rewrapping presents her family receives from friends so that, come Christmas morning, all of the gift wrap will match under the tree.)

C.A.R.E. to Connect

Four Tips for Giving the Gift of You

C: Create Mini-Moments Instead of Waiting for Mega-Moments

A mini-moment is tuning in to what is happening *that moment* and creating a connection. Are you wrapping presents right now? Who is with you? How are you talking to them or including them in the moment? Mega-moments are *events* that we look forward to, such as special parties, Christmas morning, or "the big present."

A: Ask Questions as Though You Are an Interviewer

Connection in conversation happens by showing interest and not just asking the same old questions. Instead of "how are you?" (to which most people routinely answer "fine") ask questions that really show you care and want to listen … just like an interviewer!

R: Respond Instead of React to Holiday Stress and Tension

For every stressful situation, you choose how to make it a moment of your life. Those who respond versus react to all the holiday button-pushers absolutely connect better with others.

E: Express Expectations with Esteem

The holiday season is *filled* with expectations, and a little respect goes a long way when it comes to expressing our requests. Many, many families disconnect during the holidays because of hurt feelings from communication blunders.

Glossary

acquisitions editor   An editor responsible for bringing in new books to publish.

advance   The money that a publisher pays to an author to write a book. Usually one half is paid upon signing a contract, and the remainder is paid upon delivery of an acceptable manuscript. This is an advance against future royalties earned, and the book must sell enough to earn the advance back before more royalty money will be paid out. Advance can also mean the number of copies sold by the sales reps for the first two months of the books publication.

assistants   The young, unsung folks who answer the phones, sort the mail, and otherwise keep publishing offices going (also known as editorial assistants).

auction   A sale, usually conducted by an agent, that gives several publishers the opportunity to bid on the rights to publish a book. The book goes to the highest bidder.

audience   That part of the population that will be interested in buying a specific book (also "readers").

author   The writer of a book or books; the term usually implies a published writer.

author guidelines   The set of guidelines a publishing house usually provides an author that detail the way the submission should come in, formatting, and often the process and people involved.

author queries   A part of the editing process in which the editor and/or copy editor ask the author to further explain meaning, answer questions about accuracy or intent, or rewrite small sections.

backlist   The list of books the publisher has available for sale that are older than 12 months.

best-seller   A term used quite loosely in the publishing world. Strictly speaking, the term refers to a book that has appeared on a bestseller list somewhere. In reality, publishers and their publicity staffs attach the word to almost any book that they haven't lost money on.

bluelines   The cheap test proof, usually in blue ink, that the printer sends to the publisher for approval before printing the entire job.

boilerplate contract   A publisher's standard contract, before the author or agent requests modifications.

book doctor   An outside editor who can be hired (increasingly by the author or agent) to rewrite or suggest major edits on a manuscript. *See also* proposal doctor.

Book Expo   The annual publishing industry trade show. It used to be called the ABA, but now it is the BEA, short for Book Expo America.

book packager   Packagers (also called producers) create books for publishers, providing them with finished manuscripts to finished books—or anything in between.

book proposal   A packet of information about the writer's book idea. A proposal typically contains a solid description of the book's content, the potential market for the book, competition, and the author's credentials. It also contains a table of contents, an extensive book outline, and at least one sample chapter.

bound galley   Often a paperback version of the book (sometimes unproofread) that marketing may produce four months before the book's publication date to enable reviewers to read the work and review for publication.

buyer   The bookstore employee who meets with publisher's sales representative to decide how many copies of a book to order.

buzz   The word-of-mouth excitement created in the publishing community before a book is released.

camera-ready art   The finished artwork that is ready to be photographed, without alteration, for reproduction.

chain   The large chain stores that sell books, like Borders or Barnes & Noble.

chapter book   A category of children's books that have longer stories and are written for the intermediate reader.

clip art   Artwork specifically designed to be used by anyone without obtaining permission.

commission   The percentage of the advance and subsequent royalties that an agent receives as his fee after selling your work to a publisher. This can run anywhere from 10 to 25 percent (the larger percentages are for subrights).

community coordinator   *See* events coordinator.

compositor   A person who designs and typesets manuscripts and then prepares formatted disks that are sent to the printer, also called a layout tech.

counter display   Several copies of a book in a cardboard holder for display in the bookstore. It is also called a counter pack or dump.

deadline   The due date for the completed manuscript as specified in the publishing contract.

demographics   Population statistics, age groups, buying habits, personal income levels, and other categories that can be used to estimate a book's potential success.

dump   Publishing industry slang for a counter display. Dumps are usually the larger cardboard displays that stand on the floor.

e-book   A book which is not available in printed form, only in an electronic file.

easy readers   A category of children's books, with short, simple sentences designed for beginning readers.

editorial board   The group of people who collectively make the decision to publish. Acquisitions editors present book proposals to the editorial board for its approval. This is also sometimes called a pub board.

electronic editing (also called online editing)   The process where all editing for a manuscript including copy editing, rewrites and increasingly proofreading and indexing, is done on computer instead of on paper.

electronic publishing   Paperless publishing.

electronic rights   Refers to a variety of digital rights.

endcap   The shelves at the end of an aisle in the bookstore. Publishers pay booksellers for the chance to display their books on the endcap.

English cozy   A type of mystery book that is set in England and that often features a quaint English atmosphere.

events coordinator   A bookstore employee who is responsible for arranging author signings, author appearances, and in-store events. This position may also be called a community coordinator.

exclusive submission   When only one agent or editor is considering your proposal, it is an exclusive submission.

F&Gs   Sheets of paper that have been "folded and gathered" in preparation for printing. This is another test step that the publisher can review and approve before seeing finished, bound books.

face out   Books that are placed on the shelf with the cover facing out toward the customer.

featured guest   A guest who is central to a television show's segment. If a number of experts are used on the same show, the guest is a panel member rather than the focus of the show.

fiction   Works of the imagination.

first printing   The number of books printed in the initial print run.

first serial   An excerpt that appears in a newspaper or magazine before the book's publication and actual release.

floor   The minimum bid in an auction.

formatting   The way the printed words appear on the page, including things such as margins, indentations, type size, and type font.

front matter   The first several pages of a book that typically contain the half-title page, the title page, copyright information, the dedication, acknowledgments, and the table of contents. Front matter pages are numbered i, ii, iii, iv, and so forth.

frontlist   The publishers current list of books just published, typically any book fewer than 12 months old.

galley (or loose galleys)   *See* page proofs.

genre fiction   A term applied to Westerns, romance, sci-fi, horror, thrillers, and fantasy novels.

ghostwriter   A professional writer who writes a book under another person's name. Ghostwriters are most often hired by high-profile celebrities or businesspeople who don't have the time or the talent to actually write the book.

head   The title introducing a chapter or subdivision of the text.

illustrated books   A category of children's books with lots of pictures and few words.

in print   Books that are currently available from the publisher. If a publisher decides to discontinue publishing a title, the book goes out of print and rights are reverted to the author.

independent booksellers   Locally owned and operated bookstores, not affiliated with a large chain such as Borders or Barnes & Noble.

instant book   A book that appears on bookstore shelves just weeks after the event that is the focus of the book.

intellectual property   According to Random House Legal Dictionary, this consists of "copyrights, patents, and other rights in creations of the mind; also, the creations themselves, such as a literary work, painting, or computer program."

ISBN   International Standard Book Number; each book has a unique number that identifies it.

list   A publisher's list of forthcoming titles, the books it plans to publish in the coming season or year. *See also* frontlist.

live show   A television or radio show that is broadcast at the same moment it is happening.

manuscript guidelines   A publisher's rules regarding the proper way to prepare the manuscript for submission, also author guidelines.

mass market paperback   A 4 by 7-inch softcover book often found in book racks in airports, drugstores, and supermarkets as well as in bookstores. It is sometimes called a pocket book.

mechanicals   Finished pages ready to be sent to the printer.

media market   A geographic area covered by a particular radio station, TV channel, or newspaper. Some markets, such as New York, are large media markets; others are small.

memoir   An account of the events in the author's own life.

midlist   Books that are acquired for modest advances, that are given modest print runs, and that have a relatively short shelf life.

morning drive-time shows   Radio shows that broadcast between the hours of 6 A.M. and 9 A.M., while commuters are headed to work.

multiple queries   When more than one agent or editor is approached at once about a book idea, it is a multiple, rather than exclusive, query.

nonfiction   Works that contain true information or observations.

option clause   A clause typically found in publishing contracts that requires the author to give the publisher the first chance to buy his next book. Also called a next work clause.

out of print   *See* in print.

overview   A Hollywood term now leaking into the book world. The overview is a one-sentence description of a book and its audience.

P and L   A profit and loss statement prepared by an editor in advance of acquiring a book.

page count   The number of book pages. Sometimes the minimum (or maximum) number of pages in a completed manuscript is stipulated in the book contract.

panel member   *See* featured guest.

parody   A comic imitation of a well-known literary work.

payment on publication   A term meaning that the writer is not paid until the work actually appears in print. This is the policy of many magazine publishers and some book publishers.

pdf file   An electronic file that contains camera images of book pages that cannot be manipulated.

permission   The legal right to use someone else's material in a book. The writer must get a permission form signed by the copyright holder.

placements   Stories or mentions of the author or book in the media, resulting from the efforts of publicity; also placement, the location of a book in the bookstore and/or the placement of a book into a promotion or promotional position in the store.

platform   The author's proven ability to promote and sell her book through public speaking, a television or radio show, or a newspaper column.

prepack   Several copies of a book offered at a special discount and together in a cardboard display.

press conference   A meeting to which members of the press are invited to hear something newsworthy.

print on demand (p-o-d)   Short-run printing from an electronic file.

print run   The number of books printed each time a book goes to press.

promotion   Free publicity methods and/or paid advertising for a book or its author to create public awareness and stimulate sales; also promotion, any paid placement in a bookstore paid for by the publisher to showcase a book; also promotion, a marketing/sales discount program to give bookstores incentive to buy more product from publishers sometimes offering discounts back to the reader ("buy one get one free" or "buy one, get the second at 50 percent off").

proposal doctor   Experienced editors and writers who are available for hire to help others whip their proposals into shape.

public domain   Creative works, such as writings and artwork, that are no longer protected by copyright law. Works in the public domain may be used by anyone without asking permission or paying royalties or fees.

publicity   Attention directed to a book or its author. Publicity is usually free and includes book reviews, feature articles, television and radio appearances or interviews, and online mentions.

query letter   The initial contact between a writer and an agent or editor. This short letter is meant to spark interest in the writer's project.

readers   The method by which university presses evaluate projects. Readers, or "referees," who are experts in that field are paid to read and pass judgment on the scholarship of a proposed work.

reading fees   A fee requested by an agent to pay for the time he spends reading a writer's project to decide whether it is worth representing.

rejection letter   A formal "no, thanks" letter from an agent or an editor, passing on a project.

remaindered   Books that have been sold by the publisher to a discounter for a fraction of their worth. These books end up on the bargain tables at bookstores.

review copies   Free copies of a book sent out to media people in the hopes that they will review the book or mention it in an article.

royalty   The percentage that the publisher pays the author for each book sold.

SASE   Shorthand for a self-addressed, stamped envelope.

seasons   Publishers put together their lists of books and their catalogs according to two or three seasons: fall, winter, and spring/summer.

second serial   Excerpts from a book that are published after the book is published and available.

self-published   A book that the author has paid to have produced and printed.

sell-through   Books that have actually been purchased at the bookstore level and are not going to be returned unsold to the publisher.

sequel   A second book that features many of the same characters as the first book.

series   Books linked by a brand-name identity or linked in theme, purpose, or content.

sidebar   Text that is set apart in a box, margin, or shaded area, or set in smaller type to distinguish it from the rest of the text on the page.

slush pile   The to-be-read stack of unsolicited manuscripts. They're usually read by an assistant instead of an editor.

small publisher   A general term that is applied to publishing houses with revenues of less than $10 million a year. It is also sometimes called a small press.

spine out   A book that is placed on a bookstore shelf with only the spine showing.

submission   The process by which a writer or agent submits a book proposal or manuscript to a publisher. If the author is not using an agent, it is called an unagented submission.

syndicated   Used to refer to a column or show that is packaged and sold to more than one radio or television station, or published in more than one newspaper.

synopsis   A 10-page summary of a novel, written in third-person present tense. It spells out the plot of the novel in an effective and readable way.

taped show   A television or radio show that is not broadcast immediately but at a later date.

text   Words on a page are called text. This distinguishes them from artwork.

trade paperback   Any paperback book of any size other than the 4 by 7-inch mass market size books.

video clip   A tape of an author's television appearance.

word count   The number of words on a page or in a book. This is often used in a book contract to stipulate the minimum or maximum number of words that a manuscript should contain.

work for hire   An arrangement in which a writer is paid one time for her work. Under a work-for-hire agreement, the writer does not own the copyright and receives no royalties.

writers' conference   An organized gathering of writers, which editors and agents attend.

YA (short for Young Adult)   YA books are those targeted at the 10- to 16-year-old market. The YA market is dominated by mass market paperback series publishing.

Index

A Little Knowledge Goes a Long Way ...

Check Out These Best-Selling COMPLETE IDIOT'S GUIDES®

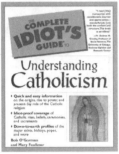

Understanding Catholicism

0-02-863639-2
$16.95

Learning Spanish on Your Own
SECOND EDITION

0-02-862743-1
$16.95

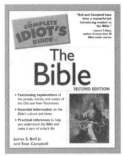

The Bible
SECOND EDITION

0-02-864382-8
$18.95

Feng Shui
SECOND EDITION

0-02-864339-9
$18.95

Playing the Guitar
SECOND EDITION

0-02-864244-9
$21.95 w/CD-ROM

Personal Finance in Your 20s & 30s
SECOND EDITION

0-02-864374-7
$19.95

Creating a Web Page
FIFTH EDITION

0-02-864316-X
$24.95 w/CD-ROM

Digital Photography
THIRD EDITION

0-02-864453-0
$19.95

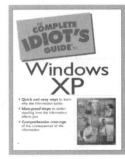

Windows XP

0-02-864232-5
$19.95

More than *400 titles* in *26 different categories*
Available at booksellers everywhere

ALPHA